# GLOBAL GIRLFRIENDS

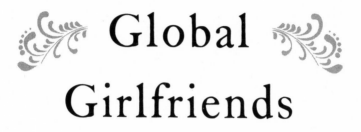

# Global Girlfriends

HOW ONE MOM MADE IT
HER BUSINESS TO HELP WOMEN
IN POVERTY WORLDWIDE

## STACEY EDGAR

FOUNDER AND PRESIDENT OF
GLOBAL GIRLFRIEND

ST. MARTIN'S PRESS    NEW YORK

www.stmartins.com

Library of Congress Cataloging-in-Publication Data

Edgar, Stacey.
  Global girlfriends : how one mom made it her business to help women in poverty worldwide / Stacey Edgar.—1st ed.
     p. cm.
  ISBN 978-0-312-62173-5
  1. Global Girlfriend (Firm)  2. Clothing trade—Developing countries.
3. Poor women—Developing countries.  4. Women in development—Developing countries.  I. Title.
  HD9940.D462E34 2011
  382'.45687091724—dc22           2010043556

First Edition: April 2011

10  9  8  7  6  5  4  3  2  1

*To my amazing family,*
*Brad, Dakota, Cali Ann, and Ellie.*
*Thank you for making my journey possible.*

# CONTENTS

# GLOBAL GIRLFRIENDS

# INTRODUCTION:
# NO PASSPORT REQUIRED

We are the ones we have been waiting for.
—JUNE JORDAN

Early one fall morning, I opened my e-mail in-box to find a message I wasn't expecting. It was from a woman named Josephine Karimi from Kenya, and the subject line read "Jorova Crafts still remembers Stacey." I remembered Josephine too. She had contacted me five years earlier through the mail with glossy photos of some rough handcrafted goods and a letter asking for support. Her brown envelope covered in Kenyan stamps still hangs on the magnet board next to my desk. Josephine first wrote to me one year after I started Global Girlfriend, with the mission of helping disadvantaged women artisans find a market in the United States for their handmade products. In 2003, at thirty-two years old, I launched my global import business from my dining room table, using a $2,000 tax refund to buy my first products from women around the world. I had three small children, I had never traveled outside the United States, I had no business plan, no passport, and virtually no start-up funds. What I did have was a dream to help women out of poverty.

As a social worker and a mom, I believed—and still believe—that economic opportunity for women holds the promise for real change in the world. When women have an income, they reinvest it in their children's health, nutrition, and education, creating stronger families and communities over time. I wanted to help women earn that income. Two powerful statistics fueled my idea: (1) Of the 1.3 billion people living in extreme poverty on less than $1 per day, 70 percent are women. That means 900 million women in the world struggle to meet basic needs for food, water, and shelter for themselves and their children. (2) Women in the United States control 80 percent of all consumer purchasing decisions (and consumer purchases make up two thirds of U.S. gross domestic product, or GDP). In other words, more than half of all the money put into purchases in the United States is controlled by women. We buy the family groceries, as always, but we also buy the clothes, the furniture, the health care, the vacations, the cars, and more. In October 2009 Kevin Voigt wrote an article for CNN titled "Women: Saviors of the World Economy?" He began by pointing out that "the largest growing economic force in the world isn't China or India—it's women." He was right. Collectively, we hold a very powerful purse. I am passionate about connecting women in need with their sisters holding those purse strings.

Women also need a gateway into the global economy. Having a great product is of little or no economic value unless the producer has an entrée to the marketplace. Global Girlfriend was created to be a conduit, connecting talented but poor women artisans with conscious and compassionate women customers in the United States. I based my company on three core values: the products would be women-made, fair trade, and eco-friendly. I applied fair trade to empower women in poverty through employment. Simply put, fair trade means disadvantaged artisans earn a fair living wage for their work and are equipped with business development strategies to foster prosperity and reduce poverty. I believed that Global Girlfriend should form long-term partnerships that provided women a fair and sustainable wage, equal employment opportunities, healthy and safe working conditions, and ongoing product-development and technical assistance. Global Girlfriend would not simply place orders and hope for the best; we made a commitment to work with our partners toward finding their market niche. We worked to create new economic opportunities where few existed, making certain that those opportunities for women in developing countries included fair working conditions, many times nontraditional ones like working from home so they could care for their families. And eco-friendly products only make sense. We share one earth, and it must be healthy for all of us to thrive. We support women in making products that protect their local environments, producing healthier children, rivers, and skies.

Why does it matter how women are doing globally? Because women's well-being around the world is an important barometer of human global well-being. Women are the caretakers and first educators of every new generation.

And women are the backbone of the global economy. According to the United Nations Development Fund for Women, women do 66 percent of the world's work but earn only 10 percent of the income and own only 1 percent of the property. Globally, women are largely denied access to business training and credit from traditional lenders. In rural Africa, over 70 percent of young girls are not allowed to complete primary school because their families cannot afford to send them. The United Nations World Food Programme reports that women in developing countries produce 80 percent of the food, but still account for over 60 percent of the world's hungry. And poor women's unpaid daily tasks are arduous. Collectively, women in South Africa walk a distance equal to sixteen trips back and forth to the moon (over 245,000 miles) every day just to supply their households with water. For too many women, these statistics mean a life of grinding poverty and few opportunities.

Furthering a woman's economic position directly affects her ability to purchase needed improvements in health, housing, and education; her bargaining position and power in the family; and her ability to act against violence in her home and in her world. Expanding economic opportunities for women decreases a woman's vulnerability to human trafficking, HIV/AIDS, and violence. By opening fair-trade market opportunities, providing design assistance, and helping build microenterprise for women, I wanted to create an opportunity for women to band together with simple acts—like buying fairly traded products made by women in poverty—that could change lives one Global Girlfriend at a time.

When Josephine first wrote to me, Global Girlfriend was a very young company functioning on a shoestring budget. I had to choose products wisely in order to stay in business and be able to help women at all. While my heart wanted to support every woman artisan who contacted me, my head knew that the products Global Girlfriend carried needed to appeal to U.S. consumers, or we would not stay in business. Products could not be considered "too ethnic," or of rough or inferior quality, and they had to be in colors and shapes that were on trend. Most of all, they had to appeal to women who might not care about the cause. I wanted products that could be sold on their own merit, even though their mission in the marketplace was to empower poor women. Desirable, quality products would allow Global Girlfriend to reach a broad consumer audience, giving women artisans the largest market possible, and making Global Girlfriend a more viable company in the long term.

I was careful about the items we invested in because every sale we made allowed me to turn around and buy something new to further support our women artisans. Josephine's original brown envelope of photos had revealed that her group's products were pretty rough. Bags had uneven straps, the jewelry was big and bulky, and the color schemes were not in line with American tastes. I struggled to find something that might work, but in the end, I couldn't see anything I felt confident buying. From the pile of photos, I picked out the least troublesome product, a hand-woven sisal basket with a rough leather handle and a bone button closure, and wrote to Josephine about the bag's merits. I replied honestly but encouragingly to Josephine with my feedback, advice, and best wishes for the group. I left the door open for her to contact me in the future—but I didn't buy their products. The order that I didn't place bothered me for a long time because Josephine and her friends were just the kind of women Global Girlfriend set out to support. This was always a line I had to straddle: the divide between applying good business practices and choosing products that were sellable, and my moral obligation and desire to support the women who need the most help.

I had not heard from Josephine since our exchange five years earlier until I opened the e-mail that morning and read:

*Hi Stacey,*

*Perhaps I should start by re-introducing ourselves. My name is Josephine and I run Jorova crafts a women handicraft artisan organization.*

*Actually the purpose of writing is to actually thank you and share with you the significant role you have played in our organization, we do feel we have to let you know! Though Jorova Craft has not done any business with Global Girlfriend we still consider you as a special friend in that you were the first person out of many whom we had approached who gave us the first positive response at a time of need when we were desperate and to the verge of closing up as there was no business. Were it not for your positive response and your liking of that particular sisal basket we could have closed and our dreams could have been shattered.*

*I remember sharing your email with my fellow women artisans and they were very happy and we prayed. Today we regard Global Girlfriend as the Genesis of our success and may God bless Global Girlfriend.*

*Currently we have two customers in the US and we are still praying God will provide us with more customers so as to achieve our objective of economically empowering our women in that we believe by empowering women you empower the whole society. We are currently thinking of developing a website if funds allow where we can display our products.*

*Attached please find some of new line of shopping bags, purses and jewelry we have made. I look forward to hearing from your end.*

*Kindest regards,*
*Josephine*

The letter brought tears to my eyes for all I had not done for Josephine and her friends. For all I had learned over the past five years and had not shared with her. But it made me smile to know that sometimes hope is what people need most. For every way I had failed to help, my few words of encouragement had meant much more to them than I could have ever known. After looking through the new product photos, I was impressed with their designs, and I saw that their products had improved dramatically. From a small market stall in Nairobi's Dandora slums, the group had developed simpler earring designs that were distinct, yet had universal appeal. They had begun crafting with recycled magazines and glass beads, creating fun and colorful bracelets and necklaces. Some of the women were hand-painting greeting cards with bold garden graphics, and others had started recycling the plastic bags that were littering the slums of Nairobi by crocheting the bags into sturdy, innovative totes. I replied immediately, thanking Josephine for her touching letter and placing a large order for the products the women had worked so hard to develop. The next morning she responded:

*Hi Stacey,*

*Thanks so much for your email! It is encouraging to learn that our products have progressed over time. Actually this is a result of hard work and sacrifice. I have this morning shared your email with my fellow artisans and they were very happy.*

*We are also happy to learn that Global Girlfriend too has grown and are able to accommodate more groups. This is great news and by this we know God has been hearing our prayers.*

And mine.

Josephine taught me a lesson that I hold dear: that the smallest seemingly insignificant act can change someone's life. Kind words and encouragement from others can impact how a person sees herself and her abilities. And if words can change a person's life, just think what small acts of kindness—and better yet, small investments of capital—can do for women in poverty.

Josephine's group was not market ready when we first corresponded, and both of our businesses were new and inexperienced. Looking back, I wish I had committed my time and energy to helping her develop their products. Luckily, she went ahead and did that on her own. But Josephine's story and the friendship we have forged have led me to make those investments with new groups of women, groups needing assistance in developing a product in order to bring it to market. In Haiti, in Guatemala, in India, and in Kenya, Global Girlfriend has since worked with women who were in Josephine's shoes and needed more than just words of encouragement—they needed patient and caring business mentors to help them unlock their potential.

Working with women on economic development does not solve all of their problems. It doesn't change their local resources, the violence of war, natural disasters, poor public transportation, local food security, corrupt government rulers, or unfair water rights—but it does give them money. Money is good for women. Good for kids, for schools, for farmers, for markets, for medicine, for irrigation, for digging a well, for cleaner latrines, for a cup of milk instead of a cup of dirty water with breakfast. Money is a tool for a better life. An opportunity to work and to make an income is one way for women to control their own lives. For some women in the developing world, the opportunity to decide how you spend your money, or what basic needs you meet for yourself and your family, is revolutionary.

Even more revolutionary is the fact that as consumers (especially women controlling 80 percent of America's purchasing power), we can change women's lives by simply changing the clothes we wear, the purse we carry, or the coffee we drink. We have an opportunity to shop according to our values. Choosing women-made, fair-trade goods means money in a woman's hand, an education for her children, bellies full of food, and a more just and peaceful world for us all.

I do not know what the future will look like. It depends on how we choose to apply our collective energy. What I know for sure is that if we apply it to extreme poverty, we can end it. We can engage people in their own futures—if we first engage in our own personal actions for a better tomorrow. Our small acts can come together to form the large shifts in beliefs and actions that can change the world. We each have a responsibility to our global community, but you don't have to have all the answers. You need only to be willing to work on behalf of others. It was a series of small choices, a small personal investment, and a leap of faith that led me to found Global Girlfriend. I took a risk and made promises to women half a world away that I personally would carve out new opportunities for them to make an income and prosper. I reinvested all of my profits for five years back into the business, until my $2,000 tax refund turned into over $1 million in sales annually of women-made, fair-trade goods. But while I set out to change the lives of women in poverty, they have been the ones who have inspired my life. I hope their stories will inspire you as well.

# 1

## PEACE CORPS REJECT

Remember that not getting what you want
is sometimes a wonderful stroke of luck.
—THE DALAI LAMA

As I watched my twelve-year-old son, Dakota, and his best friend, Robert, standing across from me in the back of an open pickup truck, I could hardly believe we were together in Guatemala. Dakota and Robert had accompanied their mothers, me and Mary-Mike, on a product development trip to work with women weavers and jewelry makers in the Lake Atitlán area. Mary-Mike, my longtime neighbor and dear friend, had been my right hand at Global Girlfriend since early on. Formerly a foreign currency trader at US Bank, she started helping me in my then fledgling basement business when she left corporate America to spend more time at home with her sons. After eighteen years in banking, she didn't mind the change of scenery and never complained about having to climb over my dirty laundry to get to the office. We had come a long way together over the last few years, and this latest journey was Mary-Mike's first to work directly with the women we support.

Global Girlfriend started on my dining room table in 2003

based on a big idea to help women in need, but on a very low budget. I convinced my husband, Brad, to let me use our 2002 tax refund of $2,000 to import products made by women living in poverty. I knew nothing at the time about importing and not much more about fair trade (a market-based approach to solving poverty that aims to help producers in developing countries obtain fair trading conditions and achieve sustainable incomes), a concept that would become the cornerstone of my company. What I did know was that women in need deserved other women to advocate for them. As a social worker, I had worked for ten years with women and children in the child welfare and social service system. I had come to learn that even in America, the land of opportunity, women are the hardest hit by poverty. Of the 37 million Americans living below the U.S. poverty line, over half are women. But women in the rest of the world fair far worse. Women make up 70 percent of the world's poor.

This statistic came to life for me in January 2000 when my mother-in-law, Brenda Edgar, traveled to Africa with the United Nations World Food Programme. Brenda returned from her journey with stories of hunger, thirst, illness, and lack. But I was more struck by her stories of tenacious women, women who walked miles each day to set out blankets or small tables of handmade goods and sat all day in the hot sun in hopes that just a few foreign aid workers or travelers might want to buy some souvenirs. The necklaces and scarves she brought me as gifts were more than just trinkets from Brenda's travels. These small treasures were proof of the true talent and entrepreneurship of the women she had met—women who needed a larger market and a broader opportunity than aid workers at the Addis Ababa Hilton could offer.

I didn't start Global Girlfriend immediately after Brenda came home. The idea for a business helping women rise out of poverty brewed slowly for a few years, and was always stifled by my own doubts about how to connect with women so far away. In early 2003 I decided to forget about what I didn't know and just jump in, starting a fair-trade business focused specifically on helping women, with all that my good intentions and $2,000 could buy. The investment went much further than I could have dreamed.

In the beginning, Global Girlfriend customers were my girlfriends, my neighbors, and the moms at my kids' schools. As my company grew from home parties to an e-commerce Web site, then added a mail-order catalog and a wholesale business, our customer base expanded to twenty thousand women around the country who eagerly used their purchasing power to help their girlfriends around the world gain economic security. In five years, our initial work with seven women's groups had grown into a bona fide women's fair-trade company supporting over fifty women's economic development projects globally.

I had wanted Dakota to come with me to Guatemala to see for himself why I am so passionate about working with women in poverty. He had watched me start and grow my business from our home in Colorado, and I wanted him to observe firsthand the impact we were making on people. I also needed his seven years of Spanish classes to help me communicate. Mary-Mike had the same goals for Robert, but when our transportation pulled up we started having second thoughts. She and I exchanged fretful glances when our guides directed us to hop up into the back of the truck. We never let our boys ride bicycles without helmets, and yet here we were letting them ride in the back of an open pickup, brimming with people, traversing a steep gravel road. As this was the only transportation to the government housing resettlement for victims of Hurricane Stan, we climbed in. Celestina was waiting for us.

We turned off the main road onto the drive of the resettlement housing. The resettlement was simple and sufficient, but it felt cold and impersonal when compared to the colorful people and places we'd seen in other parts of Guatemala. The cement-block rectangles of government-issued houses were evenly aligned into tidy rows resembling a military barracks. The gray houses stood in bold contrast to the natural setting that surrounded the development. Lush green expanses of palms and pines were dotted with fields cleared for subsistence farming. On the horizon were beautiful hills and valleys that seemed to stretch on forever. Million-dollar views and a survival instinct were the community's greatest assets.

I knew that each inhabitant had moved here because of the devastating mud slides brought on by Hurricane Stan in 2005. In the weeks preceding the hurricane, torrential rainstorms had soaked the area with over twenty inches of precipitation. When Stan blew in from the coast, the already saturated ground couldn't absorb the new rains, and flash flooding and mud slides resulted. Whole mountainsides collapsed and engulfed the villages below. An estimated two thousand people lost their lives. Others lost their homes, which three years later were still buried under immovable mounds of earth. Many survivors now lived in this community of cookie-cutter shelters, missing their gardens, their animals, their personal things, and the homes many had built with their own two hands. It made me sad thinking of all they had lost. I couldn't help considering how I would feel if my home was washed away and I was given a lesser space in a new, unfamiliar place. Ducking under a line of hanging laundry, Celestina greeted us warmly just outside the door to her home. She stood less than five feet tall, and was dressed in brilliantly colorful traditional Mayan wear, a *huipil* blouse and skirt she had woven herself. Her wide smile revealed a lifetime without dental work, and she looked much older than her thirty-six years. Celestina's home had been destroyed in the mud slides that followed Hurricane Stan, and she was trying to rebuild her family's life. Her village of Panabaj had been one of the hardest hit. There, she and her husband had proudly built the only two-story home on their street with their own hands. Their home had been brightly decorated with Celestina's weavings, and the backyard was a large garden, where she grew food for her family and at times had extra produce to sell for a profit in the local market. Her new government-issued house was a twelve-by-twenty-foot cement-block rectangle with a tin roof, a metal door, and no yard.

Celestina invited us in, and as we entered, I peered around, carefully trying to make room for our group of five adults and two preteenagers in the confined space. The stark home was separated into two rooms, a small living room and an even smaller bedroom with one tiny bed. There were no carpets, paint, or wall hangings and seemingly few possessions other than some mats under the bed, which were rolled out for the children to sleep on at night, and a few cement blocks stacked in one corner, which were offered to us as seats. But Celestina's prize possessions were clearly visible, taking up much of the minuscule living space: a long wooden thread separator that looked like a bench with spikes; a thread winder; long thin shuttles wrapped with weft strings; and a backstrap loom attached to the top of the doorjamb. These are the essential tools of a master Mayan weaver. The backstrap loom weaver literally becomes part of her loom. One end of the loom's warp strings are attached to a door frame or somewhere with a higher elevation. The weaver then sits on the floor and straps the loom around her back, causing the warp to become taught and firm, able to accept the crisscross of the weft strings that are woven in and out to make a pattern.

We each took a seat on our low cement blocks, forming a semicircle around the loom. Celestina settled in the center of the cement floor on a small woven mat she had made herself. Her hands began to weave together the once loose and meaningless threads that found structure woven into harmony on her loom. Stripes of sky blue and purple made up the warp that would become the base for the fabric, and Celestina combined a rainbow of blue, green, yellow, and purple in the weft, skillfully forming shapes that looked like small flowers. Each shuttle held a different color weft string that she passed through the warp with speed and accuracy until a pattern took shape before our eyes. Each thread was suddenly part of something much larger and lovelier than what it had been alone. Celestina's hands never stopped moving as she wove and at the same time recounted the events of the mud slides, which our interpreter, Maria, translated from their native Kathiquel language. The mud slides that had overwhelmed parts of the peaceful Lake Atitlán area had taken her home, her neighbors' homes, and many of her neighbors' lives. She and her children had escaped death only because her house had two levels and they were all upstairs when the thundering rush of earth and water overtook the homes all around her.

Watching the movement of Celestina's skillful hands on the loom, I thought about the threads of experience that make up the tapestry of each of our lives, and about the path in life that had led me to her home. I thought of how blessed I was to be here now, with my son, showing him why this work was so important to me. Working with women internationally is what I had always longed to do, but it had taken years to get here.

———

I went to college at Western Illinois University as a journalism major. I hoped to be a reporter who covered meaningful stories—stories about injustices or, better yet, good being accomplished in the world. I dreamed that maybe someday I would report internationally. The problem was that I didn't love the many required English classes. We were reading novels that didn't move me when I wanted real-life stories. (I also was, and still am, a horrid speller, which seemed the kiss of death in an English class before the age of computers and spell-check.) But everything changed second semester sophomore year when I took an introduction to social work class as an elective.

My instructor, Mike Finmen, was a short man with a goatee who almost always wore jeans to class. Mike was open, comfortable, and casual and treated us like smart colleagues he was mentoring rather than like students he was grading. Mike had a long history in the field of social work, doing direct practice even after he earned his PhD. He had worked in rural poverty in Arkansas and had strong opinions on building opportunities and social safety nets, but also on fostering personal responsibility. His favorite career advice was "Where you stand depends on where you sit," and he suggested we take the time to learn where each person in a situation sits before we judge from our personal throne. His other favorite pearl of wisdom was "CYA," or Cover Your Ass. He advised us to do so by keeping thorough and copious practice notes about our social work clients. I loved his candidness. I loved that he believed in doing; not just teaching or researching, but getting his hands dirty in human affairs. It was what I wanted to do—not just observe and report, but get messy in people's lives in order to help them. I switched majors immediately.

By my junior year in college, I had decided I would commit my short-term future to the Peace Corps. Something inside me drew me to the larger world. I wanted to understand what life was like in other lands. I wanted to learn about other cultures and traditions. Part of that curiosity came from hearing about both my grandfather's and my father's time at war. My paternal grandfather, G. Clark Nehring, had served in the army along the northern border of India during World War II. He spent over two years guarding bridges and roads in India and fixing tires at an army facility located in a tropical area north of Calcutta where rubber was plentiful. On the rare occasions when he talked about his time in India, I marveled as the details of the land and the people poured out from my mostly stoic grandfather. He had lived in a tent camp surrounded by tea fields, small villages, and wild animals. Once, he and some friends helped the local villagers kill a twenty-foot python that was pursuing the locals' goats. The villagers thanked the soldiers with traditional food and tea, and with friendship that reached past their language barrier. I could just picture how foreign Indian food and culture, and India itself, must have been to him as a young soldier.

My dad had followed my grandpa in service to our country as a naval officer in the Vietnam War. My father wasn't drafted like many young men from his generation but instead enlisted as a Seabee—a member of the navy construction unit that built the air force runways and other infrastructure the United States needed inside Vietnam. Like my grandfather, my father didn't talk much about his time in the military. Sometimes, out of the blue, he'd mention something random about the temperature in Vietnam or the bugs, or in the 1980s when the TV show *China Beach* aired, he'd say something like, "I helped build the real airstrip at China Beach." These casual comments over the years made me curious about other places. When my grandfather and father talked about India and Vietnam, they always talked about their love of the people. Even during war, people were friendly and eager to learn about them, to learn about America, and to share their own culture. I daydreamed about places I might go and friends I might meet. When I was a kid, it was hard to believe that Grandpa and Dad had both been halfway around the world and the farthest I had been from my small Illinois farm town was Florida—twice.

My family traveled rarely when I was a child. As part of our family business, Hinckley Concrete Products, we did go to the annual Midwestern Pre-Cast Concrete Convention in gripping locations like Peoria and Mark Twain's hometown of Hannibal, Missouri. My paternal grandparents, Clark and Irene, were much more worldly, traveling to Wisconsin and Florida every year and even journeying to Portugal when I was about six. It was my grandparents who took me on my first airline flight, when I was in the third grade. We went to Disney World in Orlando, Florida, and I remember how anxious I was about flying. (I still perspire, pray, and find myself unable to talk to my fellow passengers until I hear the ding of the bell that represents our arrival at ten thousand feet.) My mom cried as I left the gate to board the plane, which didn't help. But my first pair of airline wings and a thick blueberry compote on delicious pancakes quelled my nervousness.

Growing up in Hinckley, Illinois, a small town with a population of twelve hundred people, the only other person I knew who had traveled to other places in the world (besides my family war veterans) was my town's retired history teacher Charlie Hillman. He taught history to decades of Hinckley–Big Rock High school students, including both my grandma in the 1930s and my dad in the 1960s. One night when I was nine or ten, dozens of us poured into the community center's basement to watch Mr. Hillman's slides from his trip to China. The most vivid memory I have from his show is of two slides of toddlers with the back cut out of their pants. One child had just a slip of plastic covering his otherwise bare behind, and Mr. Hillman had captured the other child squatting to poop right in front of him on the sidewalk. We all gasped and giggled. We examined each slide as if it were a new moon rock or a specimen of bacteria from Mars. Mr. Hillman had gone far away; the people were different there, and he had come back to tell us just how wonderfully interesting and kind they were. Mr. Hillman might as well have been an astronaut.

But it was *Cry Freedom,* a movie my mom recorded from cable reruns, that made me want to help right injustices around the world. As I watched Denzel Washington play anti-apartheid activist Steven Biko, murdered by the police for his work to secure equal rights for black citizens of South Africa, I felt angry that this level of blatant discrimination could still exist in modern times. With his bold escape from South Africa to take the story of Biko's murder and apartheid's oppression to the larger world, Biko's friend Donald Woods (played by Kevin Kline) inspired me to think about how each of us is personally responsible to take action against injustice. If you are not directly affected, it is too easy to accept that bad things happen to other people in other places. It is easy to sit quietly by the sidelines, inactive. As a white journalist, Donald Woods did not have to risk his own life or endanger the lives of his family to stand up against apartheid, but he did stand up for his friend Steven Biko and for all black South Africans, and in acting, he became an agent for change. So a year later when a Peace Corps recruiter held an informational session on my college campus, I was there with bells on. I wanted, even if it was in a small way, to be an agent for change in the world. The Peace Corps seemed like a great place to start.

While typically supportive, my friends and family thought my Peace Corps bid was a bit harebrained. After all, who bases her career choice on her favorite movie? My best friend, Ann, was especially skeptical. No one is more loyal, funny, self-deprecating, and just plain fun than Ann. (She is also stunningly beautiful. Standing six feet tall, she made the rest of our group of friends somewhat easy to overlook when she was around.) Ann has always loved to plot her future in her head and had already reserved a place for me in the future of her mind. We would graduate college, move to Chicago, meet the men of our dreams, become wildly successful at whatever we attempted, and live happily ever after.

Naively, I assumed the Peace Corps would take me simply because I wanted to go. I dedicated my junior and senior years of college to the single-minded pursuit of getting accepted to the Peace Corps (okay, I was also a bartender and a sorority girl, so single-minded may be a bit of an overstatement). But after jumping through every hoop my Peace Corps recruiter held up for me—tutoring a chain-smoking Korean exchange student in English, meeting monthly with a returned Peace Corps volunteer bent on shocking me with his tales of bug-kabob dinners, and being grilled in interviews on what a social work undergrad had to offer in concrete skills—I never got the call.

It seemed that the Peace Corps considered my bachelor of social work degree a generic brand in the grocery store of degrees. While I knew that social work meant understanding people, seeing the world from other perspectives, and advocating for those with little voice in the system or in the world, after several conversations with my recruiter I felt like the Peace Corps saw social workers as people with big hearts and few skills. I wasn't a teacher, an engineer, a watershed management or public health expert. I couldn't speak a different language.

I was as generic a worker as existed. I was a Peace Corps reject. Devastated, and tailing my roommates in the race to jump on the career path, I took the first child welfare job offer that came along.

The job was at Edison Park Home in Park Ridge, Illinois. Edison Park was a child welfare treatment center for "juvenile delinquents" in the foster care system. Teenage boys and girls who had been abused or neglected and who were found to be too troubled for placement in a family foster care setting ended up living in the stark cement-block confines of Edison Park Home. I was assigned the 2:00 P.M. to 10:00 P.M. shift on the adolescent boys' unit, keeping the boys under control from the time they got off the school bus until bedtime. Some of the guys were charming and likable, some were sad, others, like James, were smart. James (not his real name) read Malcom X and lectured the staff about the importance of not allowing kids to become institutionalized, while sliding under the radar at school, doing just enough work to get by and staying out of trouble. The simple activities I brought in to pass our weekends, like making taffy apples and coloring Easter eggs, amazed the boys. I was shocked at the level of abuse they had suffered, and more shocked at the discrimination we all felt every time we ventured out into the community as a group. I remember the uncomfortable feeling of being closely watched by store clerks when we went school-supply shopping, as if the guys were there to steal instead of to shop. And I knew that the next time I shopped at the same store, by myself, the experience would be completely different. I hated when the staff at the community center where we swam gave our boys a lecture about appropriate behavior I had not seen given to any paying customer in line ahead of us. And even the school debated letting one of our boys play on the high school football team, fearing his gang background. But how could he or any of the other guys grow without opportunities, coaching, and new teammates for sports as well as for life?

The big problems of their childhoods—which included physical and sexual abuse, abandonment, neglect, poverty, and witnessing extreme violence—at times seemed too overwhelming to ever solve, so I learned to tackle the small stuff first. I worked with the kids to find simple, doable solutions to the problems they could control. They couldn't change their families, they couldn't change discriminatory attitudes toward young black men, but they could make new positive choices every day to create the lives they wanted. They could study for a spelling test, do their daily chores without debate, offer to help a friend, and take pride in their own small accomplishments. They could choose how they behaved in school, they could choose how they treated one another, they could take advantage of the education opportunities now available to them, and they could seek help from the adults around them who wanted them to grow into successful young men. Isolated from the abuse, gangs, drugs, and violence that many of them came from, the boys could have their daily needs met, leaving them time to choose who they wanted to become. Sometimes they found success with this approach, and other times, well, not so much.

On a Saturday afternoon four years after leaving Edison Park, while shopping at a Gap outlet store on Chicago's northwest side with my baby son in tow, I noticed the store's security guard watching me. There were several customers browsing the racks, but his eyes followed me everywhere I wandered. I was offended briefly at the thought of being suspected of shoplifting, until the stoic guard smiled and said, "Stacey, is that your baby?" It was James. He was not only gainfully employed but was weeks from graduating with an associate's degree from community college and had also recently enlisted in the army. He shared stories of other guys who were on similar successful paths. But he also told me that one of the guys had gone to prison and another was a drug dealer.

In the end, my job at Edison Park Home was the best thing that could have happened to me at the start of my career. I had thought understanding people meant I needed to leave the country and see the world, but in reality there was a lot of world I still needed to see just sixty or so miles from where I grew up. The boys had been good tour guides, teaching me about discrimination but also about resiliency.

I met my husband, Brad, the summer after I left Edison Park Home to go to grad school. If the Peace Corps had worked out, I'd have been somewhere in Africa digging clean latrines, instead of drinking beer with Brad at a famous Chicago church street festival (I usually just say we met at church, which is technically true).

Brad and I met at Old St. Pat's World's Largest Block Party in 1993. Old St. Patrick's Church is one of the oldest public buildings in Chicago, and one of the few downtown buildings to survive the Great Chicago Fire of 1871. When Father Jack Wall took over the parish in 1983, the church was in danger of closing, with only four registered members on its roster. Undaunted, Father Wall concocted an innovative marketing plan for Old St. Pat's to host an annual "World's Largest Block Party," fostering fellowship by bringing people together with beer and bands. Father Wall's block party drew over five thousand people in the first year, and as the allure of the block party grew, so did Old St. Patrick's membership. The church eventually boasted a family of over five thousand parishioners.

Neither Brad nor I knew at the time that Father Wall's block party was famous for much more than resurrecting an almost dead congregation. As of our meeting in 1993, over sixty couples had married after meeting at Old St. Pat's World's Largest Block Party. The magic certainly worked on us. Brad proposed to me six months after our block party introduction, and we were married the following summer. Our ceremony at Central Baptist Church in Springfield, Illinois, was followed by a grand reception at Brad's parents' home—the Illinois governor's mansion.

I married into a very dynamic family. My father-in-law, Jim Edgar, had served for ten years as Illinois secretary of state and four years as the state's governor when I entered the family. Our wedding happened in the middle of his 1994 reelection bid for the governor's office, which he won handily. But it was the work my mother-in-law was doing as First Lady of Illinois that impressed me most. Brenda Edgar had supported her husband's political career as a stay-at-home mother for the first twenty years of their marriage. Now, with her two children grown, Brenda had focused her energy on the women and children of Illinois. She pioneered several innovative statewide programs for families, including a statewide reading initiative; a women's health resource called "Friend to Friend"; CHAD tags, which were identification tags for child safety seats used to identify children in car accidents; and her most powerful and wide-reaching program, "Help Me Grow": a statewide partnership with the Ronald McDonald Foundation to provide childhood immunizations and health care to low-income children in Illinois. But Brenda's favorite project was the stuffed animal she designed named P.J. Hugabee. Brenda and her amazing assistant, Tom Faulkner, created a partnership with Marshall Field's (since merged with Macy's) to sell P.J. in the downtown Chicago flagship store. P.J. was more than your average teddy bear. For every P.J. Hugabee bear sold to the public, Marshall Field's donated one to a child entering the Illinois foster care system.

This was Brenda's way of sending a warm motherly hug to the state's loneliest children and giving them something of their own to hold on to.

When it was time for Jim to leave the governor's office in January 1999, he and Brenda were each asked to be on separate boards for the United Nations World Food Programme (WFP). Brenda's friend Catherine Bertini was the head of the WFP and had a clever idea to form a new women's auxiliary board with a group of like-minded, influential women in order to round up new interest and, of course, financial support for the work of the program. Brenda was quickly recruited.

Catherine Bertini was visionary in implementing strategies to help the World Food Programme achieve better results worldwide. Too often, poor infrastructure or government corruption impeded distribution in the developing countries the WFP was targeting. Corruption unfortunately goes hand in hand with power, and in places where food is scarce, controlling large quantities of consumable commodities is power. The WFP had ways of investigating and restricting government misuse of food aid, but the personal corruption of too many men who controlled the actual distribution seemed incomprehensible. Instead of distributing the food aid that was supposed to be free to people in need, those in power often sold the food at a profit. Catherine was good at analyzing all of the social motivators that could help food distribution enhance not only basic nutrition but also social goals like keeping kids in school, teaching better farming techniques for better crop yields that can help combat local hunger, and helping promote employment opportunities so families can afford the food they need. I admired her for her commonsense approaches. While she headed the WFP at the policy level, she seemed to be most committed to the simple actions that resulted in real changes for people's lives.

One example was a cooking oil program her staff implemented in Afghanistan. The World Food Programme found that, as in many places in the world, Afghan families often kept their daughters home to do household work instead of allowing them to attend school. Catherine's team had an idea to use weekly free cooking oil distributions to qualifying families as an incentive to get girls back into the classroom. If a girl attended school all week, she would be given her family's ration of cooking oil to take home with her at the end of the week. If the family did not send their daughters to school, they would not have access to the free cooking oil. Opportunities for the family were tied to opportunities for girls. Attendance for girls spiked in the areas where the Food Programme's cooking oil education incentive was introduced.

In January 2000 Brenda made her first trip with the World Food Programme, to Ethiopia. While Brenda felt prepared for her trip because she was well-traveled and had done so much work in Illinois with low-income women and families, she was stunned at the conditions in Ethiopia. A struggle for resources, food, water, and fuel was affecting every aspect of daily life. Brenda had always been impressed by the beauty of the handsome, statuesque Ethiopian men and women she had met in America. In Ethiopia, the lack of proper nutrition had stunted the growth of many children, leaving twelve- and thirteen-year-olds looking physically closer to five or six. Twins were very common, but the group was told that it was automatic to let one die because a mother could not feed two babies. The landscape looked barren because most of the trees had been cut down for firewood. Women seemed to do most of the wood gathering and hauling. It was common to see little women bent in half with enormous bundles of firewood on their backs. There was very little infrastructure throughout the country, even in the capital city of Addis Ababa. Brenda was shocked to see women rebuilding a main road by hand. The women did all of the heavy lifting, carrying, and setting heavy stones to form the pavement, while men stood around watching. It was damp, and the huge stones were slippery, as was the mud beneath the women's feet. The women were poorly clad, and their feet were bare or shod with shoes that offered no protection for carrying stones on slippery surfaces. But if the city seemed underdeveloped, the countryside was utterly primitive.

A UN Jeep jostled Brenda and her travel mates along a rustic dirt road for four hours deep into the vast countryside. As they approached the community they had come so far to visit, she saw very few huts or buildings, only a large hill where a group of women and men were working. The hillside was expansive and barren, but they were diligently attempting to terrace it into leveled fields for agricultural planning. Women carried and piled stones to make walls, while men with simple hoes broke away at the hardened ground. There was no water source to be seen. "Everyone was dressed in dirty rags," Brenda told me on the phone after her trip. "They had nothing. They weren't just poor like we think of poor in America; they had nothing, nothing, nothing."

She told me that seeing the people working so hard at what looked like such a futile effort made her want to cry. "I wished for a moment that they would have just shown me a photo or a film of this place," Brenda confessed, "but no picture would have communicated to me the scope and reality of these people's lives."

Brenda's experiences ignited an ongoing dialogue between the two of us that seemed to last a few years. Early on, I gave her a laundry list of my own ideas on how the auxiliary board might ignite new excitement around the World Food

Programme. How they might enlist women around the country who were just like me, not former First Ladies or high-powered corporate executive women, but stay-at-home moms, teachers, hairdressers, and the rest of us who care but don't know how to get involved or what to do to help. One auxiliary board member was a VP at Tiffany & Co. I thought she should arrange a special sale at a Tiffany store in New York or Chicago where the jewelry the women made in Ethiopia might sit on a Tiffany counter with honor—even if it was only for one night. I thought they should start an awareness program in schools to help involve kids to take action against hunger. I thought they should buy some of the products these women were making and sell them at events or home parties to raise awareness but also funds for the cause. They could at least organize a fund-raiser for the WFP. But none of these things happened.

I admired Brenda's deep concern for the fate of the women she had met. I respected her personal commitment to pray for them daily. But I also felt frustrated by this powerful group. So many important women with amazing connections that could be leveraged, and yet they seemed instead almost paralyzed by what they had seen. People were too poor. Governments too corrupt. Problems insurmountable. The group seemed to feel small steps might be too inconsequential, so, it seemed to me, they stood still.

Revisiting the topic on the phone one afternoon, Brenda confided, "The voice of the woman council member who came out to meet our Jeep still haunts me. I don't remember what all she said, as she was talking so fast and with such urgency I don't know if the translator was truly keeping up. But what I remember vividly is when she begged me, 'Please, please don't forget us!'" There was a long pause on the phone. "And I never have. I never will forget her, but what can I do?" Brenda and

Jim were people who made things happen. In their service to Illinois I saw time and again how they recognized the problems of the citizens in their state and promptly worked to try to find solutions. Still, the poverty Brenda had witnessed left even someone as capable and connected as she is feeling helpless to make a difference.

"We should do something," I stated boldly. "We could do something."

"We should," Brenda agreed.

Then a waking toddler shrieked from upstairs at my house. "Cali Ann is up from her nap," I said.

"I'll let you go, and we'll talk later," Brenda replied.

Like the spark of so many brilliant ideas, the flame of our vision for women in poverty was doused by everyday life. Brenda went back to racing around the country with my type A, semi-retired father-in-law, Jim, and I went back to tending to my young family. Dreams for the women Brenda had met took a backseat to the diapers and dinners of my daily life.

## 2

## 911

The world is round and the place which may
seem like the end may also be only the beginning.
—IVY BAKER PRIEST

Argentine is a tiny woman standing no more than four and a half feet, supported by two crutches and huge metal leg braces. But despite her size she has overcome towering obstacles, growing up with polio in a rural village at the heart of the ongoing fighting in eastern Congo. Argentine works as a seamstress at SHONA, a women's artisan cooperative in Goma, Congo, where she creates unique print tote bags and tops for Global Girlfriend. She learned to sew at the Center for Handicapped People, where she underwent operations and treatment for her physical disabilities and was given basic literacy and sewing classes. SHONA provided her a sisterhood of women artisans who also had physical challenges, and an opportunity to use the sewing skills she learned at the center to earn a living. Her income from sewing enables her to live independently, and even to pay the school fees of her younger siblings and to help support her mother. An incredible accomplishment for any young woman in Congo, but an even greater feat once you learn of Argentine's journey.

Argentine came from a very poor family, and when she became sick with polio as a young child they were unable to bring her to a hospital for treatment. She was confined to her rural home, quickly lost the use of her legs, and was never able to attend school or do so many of the things that children do. As the war in eastern Congo grew worse and worse, her mother was left with the weight of an incredible question. How could she protect her young disabled daughter from the armed men who would sometimes invade their town? Even very young children growing up in eastern Congo learn to flee. But what do you do with a daughter whose legs can't carry her across the room, much less out of danger? With five younger children to think about as well, and no money to move to a safer area, Argentine's mother came up with a plan. She would put Argentine on her back and carry her into the woods. She would dig a hole and cover it with brush, hiding Argentine inside. And Argentine would remain there for days or weeks, singing to herself and praying. Her mother, after taking care of her other children during the day, and scrounging for food, would return at night, to sleep with Argentine in the bush, bring her food, and keep her company. When she would leave again, to search for more food, and to try to earn a living, she would tell Argentine that if she didn't return in a few days God would take care of Argentine. Argentine marvels at the love of her mother, who carried her on her back, and at a God who she says has carried her the rest of the way.

God carried me to Argentine and other women like her unconventionally, by way of an ambulance ride. On a nice fall day in 2001 I found myself staring up at a round dome light above my head, trying to grasp what had just happened. The sirens that had just blared through my neighborhood were abruptly turned off. The ambulance slowed from a fretful clip to a laid-back Sunday drive. In that moment it became clear that the only thing I might die of on this day was embarrassment.

The young paramedic sitting beside me in the ambulance had hosted my son Dakota's kindergarten field trip to the firehouse. I prayed he didn't remember me as he called my vitals back to the dispatcher. Normal, normal, normal.

The pain in my chest had been crushing. The panic in my every nerve had left me light-headed. Standing in my house, with my three little kids plus a friend of my son's whom I was supposed to drive to Pee Wee soccer, I was sure I was about to die—a complete breach of my parental and carpooling duties. In a moment of terror, I called 911.

I was usually so confident, so together in my own messy way. Sought after by my friends and family for practical advice on everything from romance to dynamics in our family business, from breast-feeding to balancing motherhood and a part-time job. When we moved from our home state of Illinois, I had seamlessly made a life for my young family in Colorado, supported by a network of good girlfriends all surfing the waves of motherhood together. I had worked out a part-time job for the Denver Public Schools and had even become a doula, assisting teen mothers during births. So what on earth had landed me in an ambulance at thirty-one, mistaking a whopping anxiety attack for a heart attack?

Motherhood coupled with the catastrophic national events that had occurred within the first year of each of my children's lives had affected me deeply. To me, motherhood somehow felt like the weight of the world. I loved being a mom, caring for the sweet little people I had helped bring into the world. But the world was turning out different than I had planned. As an action-oriented social worker, I was used to looking objectively at a person's problem and coming up with plans to get my client to a better place. There was a decent solution to most problems, whether my clients chose to use them or not. There is great comfort in being a problem solver. While you can't make everything better for everyone, you can at least help people to take concrete steps in the right direction most of the time. So I was blindsided by the major national tragedies that happened during my children's baby years. I had no answers, and I felt as helpless to change the state of the world as Argentine's mother had been helpless to keep polio from taking the function from her daughter's legs.

My son was born at the time of the Oklahoma City bombing. I was doing my graduate internship as a school social worker at Glenbrook South High School in Glenview, Illinois, when I was pregnant with Dakota. As a social worker, I needed to set a date to leave; I couldn't just wait until the contractions started and then abruptly abandon my students. They needed time for termination of our therapeutic process. Of course, being an optimistic soon-to-be new mom, I thought I'd better take off the week before my due date to nest. My nest itself was a one-bedroom apartment on the top floor of a three-story walk-up across from Graceland Cemetery on Chicago's North Side. There wasn't much space, so I'm not sure what I thought I needed to do. I guess I was under some delusion that Dakota might come early, or at least on time. But after a few days of cleaning, washing onesies in Dreft in our shared basement coin-operated laundry room, freezing some dinners, and keeping a watchful eye on the toilet bowl for the mysterious mucus plug we'd learned about at Lamaze class, I reverted to some good old American TV watching. On April 19, 1995, I sat alone in front of our small screen in horror. It doesn't take much to get a pregnant woman crying, but I sobbed uncontrollably at the sight of tiny limp and bloody bodies being carried out of the remains of the Oklahoma City Federal Building day-care center. We welcomed Dakota to the world fifteen days later, and the only action I could take against the hatred I had witnessed was to love my new baby and hope to never see the heartless murder of children ever again.

Four years later, in April 1999, when Cali Ann was about ten months old, I was driving her and Dakota home from a morning playdate when a reporter on the radio interrupted the music broadcast to announce that there was a police standoff under way at Columbine High School—a school just ten miles from my new home. The next day I was called in by the Colorado chapter of the National Association of Social Workers to do trauma work in the aftermath of a mass shooting of children by children. I tried to comfort kids at Ken Caryl Middle School, assuring them that when they went to Columbine the next year they would be safe. I worked the community hotline and listened to fears about teens in trench coats and old traumas unearthed in people's psyches by the shootings. Every trained professional in the state who was recruited to volunteer did our best to reassure parents, kids, the community at large, and ourselves that eventually we would all be okay again.

When my youngest, Ellie, was two weeks from celebrating her first birthday, the planes flew into the World Trade Center towers. I watched like millions of Americans in disbelief as these gigantic buildings crumbled to the ground. The same towers where my husband, Brad, had spent three weeks training at the Morgan Stanley headquarters just one year earlier. I called Ann repeatedly at her midtown Manhattan office at *In Style* magazine, at her home, and on her cell, but I got the same busy signal every panicked American heard as we frantically called

New York City. I muted the volume on the TV so my kids wouldn't hear the repeated screams and continuous speculations about what in the world was happening. Wiping crumbs from my kitchen counters, refilling sippy cups, and doling out handfuls of Goldfish crackers, I cried without sound as I watched the demolition replay over and over and over. Ann finally called. "We're all just walking," she said flatly. "The whole city. We're all just walking home."

In the days following 9/11, news show pundits bantered about a new religious war of "jihad" nightly. People were openly promoting racial profiling and closing borders. The collective karma of the world felt pervasively negative, if not hateful. We learned of the oppression Afghan women lived under, as visions of full-body burkas imposed on them by the anti-women Taliban regime filled our television screens. As I drove to preschool in my minivan or stocked up on snacks at Costco, I couldn't help but wonder: What was this world I'd brought three children into? And what could I do to change it?

The morning after my embarrassing ambulance ride, I woke up and weighed my options. Maybe I could succumb to my embarrassment and become a self-proclaimed agoraphobic. I'd just never leave my house again. On the other hand, if I felt that overwhelmed by the state of the world, maybe I should do something about it. My panic attack was brought on by my fear for my children, as the world seemed to be in a downward spiral. But I knew, in my heart as well as from my experiences, that the only way to change the things we don't like in life is to take action. If I felt helpless to keep my kids safe in my suburban Colorado neighborhood, which is essentially Mayberry, how could other mothers around the world make it through the day? What would become of mothers who lived in drought, famine, poverty, or war? Would their children live or die?

Every time I considered what I could do, my thoughts went back to my mother-in-law Brenda's trips on behalf of the United Nations World Food Programme. In many cases, the organizations she had visited that were receiving food assistance also sponsored a women's enterprise project to help women make an income. Brenda had brought me baskets, necklaces, scarves, and other items made by the women she had met. I loved my gifts, but I was infuriated by the thought of these talented women trying day in and day out to sell their beautiful hand-crafted goods to a small pool of aid workers. There had to be a larger and more sustainable market. Most of these women were mothers like me. Mothers responsible for making a living, and for keeping their children safe and stable in an ever-changing and sometimes harsh world. Women like Argentine's mother, who had found a way to protect her daughter from the harms of war by carrying Argentine on her own back and hiding her away. As a mother, I wanted to reach out to women like Argentine, to her brave mother, to the women in the burkas, to the women Brenda met in the Ethiopian village, and make a connection that might be meaningful to their lives and to mine.

Of the estimated 1.3 billion people living on less than $1 a day, women make up 70 percent. That's 900 million women trying to get by (and get their children by) on less than $1 per day. The United Nations estimates that of the world's 27 million refugees, almost 80 percent are women. Over 600,000 million women in the world are illiterate due to their lack of access to education. In many developing countries, women are not allowed to own property, are denied access to credit, are trafficked as sexual slaves, and become infected with HIV/AIDS at a rate two times that of men. The women of the world needed their own 911 call.

I've heard Nobel Peace Prize winner Muhammad Yunus

speak, and he calls the poor "the Bonsai people." "It's not the seeds," Dr. Yunus insisted in his address to a packed ballroom in Denver at the Social Business and Microeconomic Opportunities for Youth conference. "We all come from the same seeds. It's the pots." Too often in the history of the world, human potential has been minimized, choking off growth, especially for the world's women. Indeed, all too often people in developing countries and even in poor urban and rural America are limited not by their own capacity but by their opportunities—their pots, if you will. If you believe, as I do, that all people are created equal—with equal capacity to learn, earn, and live—then why are there vast divides on this small planet in people's income, health, and education?

Opportunities.

It's hard to fathom getting by, day after day, on a dollar or less. Which meal would you choose to eat? Or could you eat at all? Try to imagine 1.3 billion of anything. Maybe there are that many snowflakes in a storm or drops of water in the ocean, but I can't fathom that number in terms of human beings. With approximately 6 billion people in the world, that means one in every six does not have his or her most basic needs for food and shelter met. But two of the other five don't fare much better. Close to half the world, nearly 3 billion people, lives on less than two dollars per day. Women and children are the worst off in this equation, with children being the most likely to die of poverty. According to UNICEF, 26,500 to 30,000 children die each day due to poverty.

I first saw a woman's world through the "poverty lens" as a case aide at Lutheran Social Services of Illinois, in Macomb. When I needed a social work practicum to complete my degree, a woman I'd babysat for during college arranged for me to work as a case aid for the Families First program. The Illinois

Department of Children and Family Services (DCFS) referred families to Families First when there was a suspected case of child abuse or neglect. If the child did not appear to be in imminent danger, DCFS would assign Families First "home visitors" to work intensively with these families in their homes for three months to try to prevent outplacement of the child in foster care. My first solo case—I'll call her Jenny—was haunting. I received a late-afternoon call from DCFS about Jenny. She was charged with child neglect because it was February and Jenny and her sweet three-year-old daughter were sleeping in Jenny's car. The two were homeless and at risk of being separated by the foster care system if Jenny didn't find a safe place for her daughter to live immediately. Families First was called in as a last-ditch effort to help Jenny secure adequate housing before she lost custody of her little girl. While the regular caseworkers went home to their families for the evening, I chauffeured Jenny around town to the few emergency shelters and social service agencies. We finally convinced the staff at the Salvation Army to give Jenny a voucher for a week at the local roach motel to buy us some time.

This experience was a jumping-off point for me. I had lived in a very fair world until I met Jenny. My life, all twenty-one years of it, had been pretty easy—sheltered, even. The long evening of driving and begging for accommodation ignited my passion for my less fortunate sisters. And while it would be another twelve years before this passion would grow into a business, I knew then that a woman with no money could end up with few options on short notice. Room to grow can be cut off quickly. We have to work together on stitching up a sounder safety net.

After my anxiety attack, I relied on my own safety net of women to get me back on track. I had always avoided the

Mary Kay, Pampered Chef, and Tupperware parties. I'd dodged many obligatory suburban gatherings where I knew I'd be a pariah if I drank my girlfriend's wine and ate her snacks but didn't fill out the order form for the latest overpriced candle. I declined invitation after invitation to avoid the temptation of peer pressure to spend on things I couldn't afford. I stayed home while my suburban sisters sampled Tastefully Simple, Silpada silver jewelry, CAbi fashion, Creative Memories scrapbooks, and the Wine of the Month Club. But my anxiety attack had led me into an unexpected depression. Suddenly I longed for any reason to get together with girlfriends as often as possible— even over wine and unnecessary purchases.

Partygoing led me to party hosting, which somehow turned into party selling. I signed up with The Body Shop at Home to be a home party sales consultant. I had always loved The Body Shop for its feisty and unconventional founder, Anita Roddick. I liked its products, its policy of not testing on animals, and its commitment to helping low-income communities globally through its community trade program for acquiring raw ingredients. It didn't take long before I'd hooked a gaggle of local ladies on Body Shop lotion. Those ladies helped my sales reach $10,000 in one month for products they could buy for less, with no shipping and handling charges, at The Body Shop store just ten miles from our neighborhood. Apparently the magic lay not in the lotion but in the location—the home.

After a couple of months peddling lotion, the project Brenda and I had discussed three years before about helping the women of the world seemed almost doable. I revisited my idea of importing and selling products made by the women Brenda had met. I had long ago suggested that her committee buy and resell the products made by women's enterprise projects where the WFP gave food assistance. Now I thought that instead, I should personally try to do it. After all, what if I really could sell things made by women who needed opportunities? What if my souvenirs from Brenda's travels to Africa could turn into sustainable livelihoods for the women she'd met—women whose fates had haunted us both? What if I could rally my Body Shop believers into shopping women out of poverty? What if I could tap the talents of my closest girlfriends to bring this idea to life? I've always said that there is nothing short of a brain trust of moms at my kids' bus stop. What if my bus-stop brain trust worked together to change the world while the kids were off at school? If we could make a difference for even one woman, the idea was well worth a try.

I decided to use the wake-up call of my panic attack and the tragedies that coincided with my early years of motherhood as my call to action to help the women of the world. If the world was going to be better for me and my children, I needed to band together with women I'd never met in places I'd never been to make sure life was made better for them and their children.

I began to research and read. I wanted to learn everything there was to know about the concept of "fair trade." The fair-trade movement in the United States dates back to the late 1940s, when two nonprofit organizations—Ten Thousand Villages (originally the Overseas Needlepoint and Crafts Project), a group within the Mennonite Central Committee, and SERRV International, which first aimed to help post–World War II refugees—began to import crafts from artisans in developing and postwar countries to sell at homes, churches, and fairs. The groups aimed to raise money to help the artisans. Initially, the quality and marketability of the crafts were not concerns at the forefront. Because it was based on charitable rather than business concepts, the fair-trade movement in the United States spent its first fifty years growing at a somewhat sluggish pace.

Not assisting artisans to learn the current market trends kept fair-trade products largely out of the mainstream markets in the West. There is no doubt that pioneers of the movement, including Ten Thousand Villages and SERRV, have had a vital impact on the lives of artisans in developing countries over the long term. Their grassroots volunteer efforts in churches around the United States have also educated thousands of people on the economic needs of artisans in the developing world. And both of these organizations have set the standard in trading ethically, creating benchmarks for how artisans should be paid and treated. The problem, as I saw it, was in the products.

I call the problem the Carved Giraffe Theory. I don't know anyone with a carved giraffe at the top of her birthday wish list, and carved giraffes are rarely the "go-to" gift for Mother's Day or any other holiday. Even I, with a keen interest in all things African, have never felt a longing for a carved giraffe. My beef is not with wooden giraffes specifically. My problem is with not teaching artisans in the developing world what mainstream consumers are buying so that the artisans can increase their business and therefore reduce poverty in their lives and communities. Because fund-raising is a nonprofit's real income, nonprofit fair-trade organizations did not require their artisans to grow and change with the market. And so artisans made more giraffes, which sat in church basements across the nation until next year's sale.

I wanted my company to be different. I would focus on products that women in the United States wanted. If I could help poor women artisans produce purses, jewelry, and apparel according to current fashion trends, we could open new avenues—we could grow sustainable fair-trade enterprises with fresh, new rotating styles, which would mean new work each season. I wanted to train consumers to buy the fashion-forward items they would usually purchase from the mall from us instead, thereby helping to shop their less fortunate sisters out of poverty.

The Internet became my connection to women across the world whom I had never met. The first organization I contacted was The Gemini Trust, one of the groups Brenda had visited in Addis Ababa, Ethiopia. The Gemini Trust was founded in 1983 by an American pediatrician, Carmela Green Abate, to assist very poor families with twins. In the slums of Addis Ababa, twins are prevalent and are often born premature and with low birth weights. Thirty percent of all twin babies die before their first birthday; each day is a struggle to survive. Malnourished mothers can't provide sufficient breast milk for the babies and sometimes turn to bottle-feeding, often with disastrous results. Bottle-fed babies can suffer bouts of diarrhea and vomiting from their mothers' mixing formula with unsanitary water, resulting in malnutrition and increased vulnerability. Often, the babies' families just do not have enough food. Gemini worked to combat infant death as well as to provide overall health, hope, and dignity to these families. In addition to providing health services, Gemini aimed to reduce poverty with income-generation projects. I worked with Carmela to purchase ninety necklaces from the Gemini Trust women's enterprise initiative, a small group making handicrafts such as baskets and Ethiopian crosses. I explained that I didn't know if American women would like my idea or the products. I tried to quell expectations, explaining that I might only be able to buy this one set of necklaces. Carmela responded that it was as many necklaces as the women would sell in a year, so whatever I could do was fine.

For my first round of products, I purchased from two other women's cooperatives abroad and from four women's nonprofit welfare-to-work programs in the United States, including the Women's Bean Project and The Enterprising Kitchen. Jossy Eyre founded the Women's Bean Project in Denver in 1989 to help women end the cycle of poverty and unemployment. Jossy had been a longtime volunteer at Denver's only homeless day shelter for women and children, The Gathering Place. While The Gathering Place helped meet women's basic needs for food, shelter, and safety, Jossy felt it was only triage. She wanted to help women make lasting changes in their lives through employment. Jossy bought $500 worth of beans and put two homeless women to work packaging the beans into soup mix. She believed that teaching workplace competencies through a business would help women break free from their backgrounds of chronic unemployment and poverty. From its first batch of dried beans, the Women's Bean Project was carefully nurtured into a thriving social enterprise that has touched the lives of hundreds of Colorado women.

Before founding The Enterprising Kitchen in Chicago, Joan Pikas was teaching literacy classes and preparing adults to take the GED high school equivalency exam and growing ever more frustrated with the process. "A number of people taking the classes were close to illiterate or hindered by learning disabilities. They probably could not pass the exam, and yet they were putting their life on hold until they did," Joan said. "They needed another way out of poverty, so I started thinking of how I could help them get to where they needed to be." Like Jossy, Joan thought the key to turning women's lives around was meaningful employment and job skills that could lead to sustained independence. Joan started by teaching the women to package organic grains, but she didn't find much of a market for the product in the city. Then a friend suggested she switch to soap making. It turns out, making soap from organic botanicals and essential oils isn't that difficult. And so Joan taught women—women who were homeless, on welfare, or coming out of abusive relationships—how to make soaps and how to make new lives. Women like Shawna.

Shawna was my age, but she had six children ranging in age from six to twenty-three. Back when we were both in high school, while I was having fun with my friends, sixty miles away Shawna had become a mother at age fifteen and was living in a rough neighborhood in Chicago. Young motherhood and not graduating high school closed doors to Shawna, and her subsequent choices left her life spinning further out of control. By the time she arrived at The Enterprising Kitchen she had struggled with addiction, lost her children to protective services at the Department of Children and Family Services, and lost hope in her future. The Enterprising Kitchen helped her get it back. "I am in the process of regaining custody of my children from DCFS. I've been introduced to a different kind of love and support than people get coming from my type of background," Shawna said about her experience at The Enterprising Kitchen. "A lot of people think The Enterprising Kitchen is just about soap, but they don't have a clue. It's about restoring and re-creating lives. I've seen women housed and start back to school. I've seen little miracles here, and that means I'm one, too." Each bar of soap I purchased for my new company came signed with the name of the woman who made it. Shawna signed her soaps with pride.

With products piling up on my dining room table, I tried out my idea on any friend willing to look and listen. "I don't know," Halie said, unenthused, carefully inspecting my tabletop presentation of fair-trade purses and jewelry I was test-marketing. "I like The Body Shop stuff better."

Halie wasn't a close friend, but she was one of many acquaintances who'd been willing and, to my surprise, excited to have me come sell lotions in her living room. I'd hooked her on The Body Shop's values and free shipping on reorders, and on the soothing moisture of cocoa butter. Now I was hoping to hook her and all of my other girlfriends and customers on my scheme for changing the world.

Global Girlfriend launched at a large party at my house on May 16, 2003. My friends Robin and Stephanie served the wine, Cheryl fixed the displays, Courtney designed the logo and the invitations, Mary-Mike acted as cashier, Dottie and Laurie greeted people at the door, and Ann sent flowers from New York. My new global girlfriends from seven women's groups provided the first products, and close to a hundred friends and friends of friends showed up to shop, learn, and support women they'd never met. Aside from seeing babies born, I had never witnessed such an exciting act of human connection. Women truly were acting locally for their girlfriends globally. We sold almost all of the ninety necklaces, plus pretty much everything else on hand, that first night.

This is what I love about women. There is an unspoken sisterhood that's unstoppable. Okay, we girls have been accused at times of being catty, or gossipy, or even bitchy. I'm not disputing that as a gender we are full of human nature. But we are also full of human kindness, and when it counts most, that's the trait I see trump all others. That night, for me, Global Girlfriend became a way to see hope in the world. A way to connect with my girlfriends at home and to connect with girlfriends from faraway places—knowing that as women our lives are more the same than they are different. While we may be separated by oceans, languages, or just life's circumstances, there are no barriers to caring about one another. Mother Teresa of Calcutta once said, "If we have no peace, it is because we have forgotten that we belong to each other." Global Girlfriend was a new way for women around the world to belong to one another. Mother Teresa also said, "We can do no great things, only small things with great love." We had started something small but with a loving intent, and that intent was soon bursting beyond my living room.

# 3

# FRIENDS IN LOW PLACES

❧

Do what you can, with what you have, where you are.
—THEODORE ROOSEVELT

Amazingly to me, the front doors to the homes of the warmest hearts in Colorado swung wide open for me and my bins of women-made treasures. I had worried that getting people to invite me to share my message with their friends might be difficult, but I hardly had to make an effort before the invitations were almost too plentiful to keep up with. Women were not only willing but hungry to get involved—they understood and longed for the global sisterhood that came from bringing together a community of girlfriends to touch the lives of women halfway around the world. They were no longer willing just to stand on the sidelines as spectators to the television versions of women's lives in far-off places; they were ready to find ways to connect across the miles. Each item for sale became more than a thing—it became a wish of goodwill for each woman who had touched it.

I hauled bins, boxes, and bags of goods in and out of my white Dodge minivan to home parties, street festivals, and church holiday fairs until I no longer needed the gym to get my workouts. Needing help to keep up with my new hectic schedule, I recruited my friends to join me in my grassroots marketing campaign to reach women on the sales circuit I fondly nicknamed "living rooms, hot pavements, and church basements." My neighbor Mary-Mike was soon spending a few days a week in my basement entering sales into our new QuickBooks accounting program and helping me tag inventory. While I signed on to credit-card offers and cash advances to fund the new stream of products I was stacking on my dining room table, countless girlfriends opened their living rooms. Women of all backgrounds were eager to join my efforts. I was welcomed into the homes of amazing women like Erica Shafroth, who helped found Mothers Acting Up; Vetcra Bank executive Betty Aga; stay-at-home mom Carla Cowan; public relations professional Molly Wolf; Colorado chair of Mothers Without Borders Whitney Mackintosh; pediatric nurse practitioner Lisa Kantor; preschool teacher Jill Redlinger; corporate lawyer Laurie Mehew; hospital chaplin Dottie Mann; and countless neighbors and friends like Stephanie Salter, Cathy Maiocco, Carrie Bohan, Barb Harwell, and Candice Reed, who wanted their friends to learn how to help.

I flew my idea to my hometown of Hinckley, Illinois, and conducted a big party at the home of my best friend from high school, Dana Inman. Then on to the big city of Chicago for an upscale event with Brenda's friends in the conference suite of her Wabash condominium building. Then, in Wellesley, Massachusetts, Mary-Mike's sister-in-law Ruthanne Neville volunteered to take products to her friends' homes once a week to support women. Small town to big city, and back to the suburbs; the enthusiasm for Global Girlfriend was overwhelmingly contagious from the start. I felt like I was in the old Fabergé shampoo commercial where the girl flips her lush and lovely locks back, exclaiming, "I told two friends, and they told two friends, and so on, and so on, and so on. . . ."

While many of my new customers were not familiar with the concept of fair trade, they clearly understood, as women themselves, what earning an income could mean to any woman, but especially to a woman living in poverty. I often ask women what they would do if their income doubled tomorrow. This is a pretty compelling question if you really think about what a doubled income might mean to your own life. What improvements would you make in your lifestyle? Would you buy a new house? Or add new flooring or a new roof to the house you already own? Would you buy a new car? Would you send your child to a better school? Go back to school yourself? Feed your family more steak and less hamburger? (Unless you are a vegetarian like me and eat neither.) Would you buy better medical and dental treatment or better insurance to provide those things when you need them?

Now imagine you are a woman living on less than two dollars a day in rural Africa, or in a sprawling urban slum in Cambodia, with limited access to clean water, an inadequate food supply, and not enough money to afford your child's school uniform or even pencils. How would your life change if your income doubled or even tripled? What if your two dollars a day grew to four dollars, or eight, or twelve? This may not sound like much money at first glance, but when taken in a local context, it may be exactly what you need to send your child to school, to treat dirty water so it is safe to drink, to not be haunted by hunger, and to afford basic health services. What if, for the first time in your life, that income was steady and based on your being rewarded economically for your talents and effort?

That is what the fair-trade business model does for women in poverty.

Simply put, fair trade means that disadvantaged artisans and farmers earn a fair living wage for their work and are equipped with development strategies to foster prosperity and reduce poverty. The World Fair Trade Organization explains fair trade as "a response to the failure of conventional trade to deliver sustainable livelihoods and development opportunities to people in the poorest countries of the world; this is evidenced by the two billion of our fellow citizens who, despite working extremely hard, survive on less than $2 per day." While I came from a nonprofit background, working in child welfare and education, I liked the idea of choosing business as a tool to help end poverty. As women, our informal work—such as caring for children and elderly family members, cooking, cleaning, producing food, collecting fuel and water, and even making traditional crafts— has long been undervalued in the global economy. Even women's way of looking at the world has been undervalued in the workplace. Women are more likely than men to choose collaboration over competition and to consider others' needs before their own. These qualities have long been seen as weaknesses in the workforce, but I believe they are in fact women's greatest strengths. If together we can harness the power of partnerships and work collaboratively, we have the collective power to bring forth a new global economy that values the people behind the products we buy. And since in the United States 85 percent of all brand purchases are made by women, she who holds the purse strings really can change the world. I saw Global Girlfriend as a step toward a new "she-conomy."

Our fair-trade model is based on three simple principles. First is transparency. Global Girlfriend openly shares the stories of every group making our products and believes that the only way buying habits change is when people see the things they buy as not just "things" but as the people behind those items. This gives women the chance to connect, to learn about women's lives abroad and see their hard work and talents flowing out through the beautiful products they made, and to know that each purchase directly affects the life of the woman who made that product. Second, and most important, is how Global Girlfriend pays our women partners. At the time Global Girlfriend places each order, we wire transfer a 50 percent deposit of the order total to the women's bank account. Paying up front for our orders ensures that women do not have to put out their own money and resources for the materials (be it beads, yarn, fabric, or jewelry components) needed to make the products. We don't want women to choose between feeding their families and buying materials. Then, when the order is ready to ship, we pay the remaining 50 percent and the shipping so that the artisans are paid in full upon their delivery of the goods—if we never sell one of the items, that is our burden, not theirs. Third is what we pay. The goal is never to get the cheapest price for an item, but to arrive at a fair price for both parties that considers the material costs, the transportation costs, and the time and labor it takes for an artisan to produce the product. We use tools like the Fair Wage Guide, a free online resource to help artisans and craft buyers calculate cost and determine a fair wage, to look at what is a living wage in a local context. Often I've found that smaller women's groups devalue their work and actually need to charge more, not less, for their products.

We also help equip our women partners with basic business skills so that they can value their work, find ways to pool their purchasing power for raw materials, and collectively harness the power of the market to build their small businesses. Global

Girlfriend staff provides product design and technical assistance, and training in costing, export, and general business skills in order to help women's young businesses take hold and flourish. We do this because working is satisfying, and earning a living that allows you to care for yourself and your family on your own terms brings human dignity no matter who you are or where you live.

The women I met in the homes of girlfriends around Colorado introduced me to amazing women abroad. For example, Cheryl Pillay from South Africa. Cheryl was from the capital city of the KwaZulu-Natal region, Pietermaritzburg. In 1992 the old Pietermaritzburg prison, run-down and abandoned, was converted by several area churches into a center to help women in the community who were suffering from a growing AIDS epidemic, homelessness, high early pregnancy rates, and domestic abuse, and to empower them to be self-sufficient. Although this effort, called Project Gateway, was helping women, Cheryl saw that the center lacked meaningful employment opportunities. In 2000 Cheryl founded a women's economic development project called Zandla Xpressions. She set up a small space within Project Gateway to train women in both craft and business skills. Most women who came to Project Gateway were not ready for Cheryl's training until their immediate, short-term needs for food and shelter were met. As the women had those needs met by the other services, Cheryl would work with them not only to create products, but also to improve their perceptions of their self-worth and their abilities, and she encouraged the women to become agents of change. Cheryl knew that even women ravaged by poverty and abuse could reinvent their lives. She herself had broken free from an abusive marriage and had found the courage to rebuild. After meeting Cheryl through a referral at a home party, I bought as many of the crocheted copper wire bracelets and brooches from Zandla Xpressions as my budget would allow.

Next I added items from Au Lac, an artisan cooperative in Vietnam. Vietnam was a country I felt compelled to help. I guess as the daughter of a Vietnam vet I wanted to be part of a new generation of bridge builders, forging a continued peace through partnerships. I was introduced to the cooperative by a Catholic nun in Denver who was from Vietnam originally and traveled to her home country to work with women artisans and provide pastoral care to a group of handicapped women. Ms. Ta Huyen My, Au Lac's warm and energetic coordinator, provided me with pictures of many, many products to choose from. The group had a wide array of hand-embroidered silk handbags, scarves, and small pouches. They made ornate handbags from carved water buffalo horn and the mother of pearl from seashells. They crafted home décor items including shiny lacquered boxes and photo frames as well as natural bamboo bowls, salad servers, trays, and boxes. And they even made women's silk apparel—everything from jackets, pants, and dresses to pajamas. When I mentioned how prolific their designers were, she thanked me, saying she did much of the design work. She also warned me that there were better times of the year than others for them to complete orders. Since most of the women were also farmers, crafts were a way to supplement their farming income. She wanted to be sure I understood that the women would need to tend their fields during rice-planting and harvesting seasons. I understood.

In November of my first year in business I was introduced to Gertrude. Gertrude Protis Kita of Usa River, Tanzania, was my table neighbor at the Evergreen fair trade holiday fair, and it took some work to get to know her. Having finished draping her long banquet table with wildly colorful batik cloths and laying out piles of beaded bangles, letter openers, and ornaments, Gertrude sat down to watch me with suspicion in her eyes. I had covered my table in a crisp white drape with antique-looking jewelry stands and shelves all painted white on which I displayed my girly array of handmade baubles. As I worked to ready my table for the sale, I greeted Gertrude and her American friend Helen Walker Hill. I introduced them to Global Girlfriend and asked Gertrude about Tanzania, the women she worked with, and her products. When she didn't warm to my small talk, I grabbed my purse from under the table and bought some bracelets to wear. Gertrude thanked me with a slight smile, but as the customers poured in she was back to her game face. The fair was like market day in Arusha, the nearest large city to her town, Usa River. With Helen's financial sponsorship, Gertrude had come all the way to America in hopes of selling her bracelets. I was also selling bracelets. Clearly I was the day's competition, just like back home in the market stalls, and we would not be friends today.

Undeterred, throughout the fair, I made occasional small talk with Gertrude and Helen. I bought more bracelets on the last day of the sale and a beautiful piece of brown cloth Gertrude had beaded with a Maasai pattern. When the sale finally ended, I approached Gertrude and said I would like to work with her and carry her products at Global Girlfriend so that she would have a market here after she returned to Tanzania. Gertrude's products were well made. They were distinctively African, with traditional Maasai patterns, but had texture and style that I thought American women would appreciate when looking to add a global flair to their wardrobes. Most of all, I just liked Gertrude. She was spunky and competitive with an entrepreneurial spirit I was convinced would make her successful. In business it is not enough to be willing to work hard; it is not enough to be a skilled craftswoman; it's not even enough to be a talented saleswoman. For women in developing countries who want to find a wider market, it's important to be all three, plus a little lucky. Gertrude was hardworking, talented, and an excellent saleswoman; but she got the chance to come to America because she had been lucky enough to meet Helen. I was lucky to meet Gertrude, and I knew it.

"We need work," Gertrude shared, finally understanding that I wanted to be her partner, not her competitor. "The women need to feed their families."

Gertrude had a family of her own to support. Born just one year after I was in 1971, in Pare, near Mount Kilimanjaro, the second of six brothers and three sisters, Gertrude was raised in the small community of Usa River, Tanzania. Usa River is a thirty-minute drive from Arusha, where most of Tanzania's adventure tourism starts due to its proximity to Mount Kilimanjaro, Mount Meru, the Ngorongoro Crater, and the vast Serengeti. Gertrude's father, a charming man and a leader in the community, worked as a safari guide. Gertrude was lucky enough to attend school as a child, and after she finished she took a safari job, like her father, with Abercrombie and Kent, a famed African safari outfitter. But in 1994, she became a single mother to her firstborn, Christopher. Single motherhood is hard no matter where you live, but it brought new challenges in Usa River. To make some extra money when Christopher was very young, Gertrude started beading handicrafts using the skills she had grown up with. She once told me, "My hands can do anything with beads." She made beaded bangle bracelets, necklaces, ornaments, and earrings. She sewed wrap skirts and vests of dark fabric and beaded bright East African patterns in geometrical shapes and zigzag lines on the body of her apparel items. She skillfully crafted traditional wedding collars, which are intricately patterned necklaces beaded on a firm wire frame that sit wide around the neck, sometimes reaching all the way to a woman's shoulders. Gertrude met Helen when Helen visited Usa River on a church mission. Gertrude hosted a beading class in the local Usa River church for the visiting missionaries. Helen, impressed with Gertrude's skill and outgoing personality, encouraged her to pursue finding a market in the United States for her beadwork as a way to support herself and her son, Christopher. While Gertrude sold her beaded jewelry to safari tourists, the local market was unpredictable and didn't always produce a steady income. Believing deeply in Gertrude, Helen had paid for her trip to the United States to try to market her jewelry.

"I love handwork," Gertrude explained, "but sometimes we don't have any orders. I choose to work with single mothers because I am a single mother. I feel this work helps us a lot with our life and our children. Bless you for bringing us more friends in Colorado to support our work and our children."

"I will buy all the bracelets you have left with you now and place an order for more to be made when you get back home," I offered. Gertrude liked the offer very much but stopped short.

"You cannot buy them today," she said sharply. "You can buy what I have left after my last American sale." Helen had arranged for the pair to attend two more church-based holiday sales, and Gertrude wanted to be sure she had the inventory. I was actually very relieved. Once I had put the offer out there to buy all of her bracelets, I noticed a large box overflowing with bracelets peeking out from under her table. My funds were limited, as they were coming directly from Brad's and my bank account or from one of the credit cards I had opened to bootstrap my new business. I was worried about what sort of bill I had just racked up with my altruistic "I'll buy them all" Daddy

Warbucks proclamation. I prayed the next two shows would be a huge success for her.

One of the most treacherous pitfalls in running a fair-trade business is the temptation to put your heart before your pocketbook. Everyone who starts a fair-trade business does so because they want to help the people they work with. But it is so important to always follow good business principles in order to stay afloat. This includes not overspending on more than you are capable of selling, choosing products wisely, asking for high quality standards from your product partners, and sticking to your budget. For me, wanting to help generously had to be balanced with the self-discipline necessary to grow a strong healthy business, one that could sustain future orders and produce future sales for Gertrude and the rest of the women we were working to support. I was lucky that Gertrude went on to do well at her other sales, and I learned a lesson in trying not to promise more than I could personally deliver.

One week later, on her way to the airport, I met Gertrude in a Wild Oats parking lot along I-70 to exchange my cash for her bracelets (a fair amount for both of us). As we opened our trunks to transfer the goods, it wasn't exactly the picture of a law-abiding business transaction. But our meeting in a cold and snowy winter parking lot was the start of a long friendship. As Gertrude embraced me for a warm hug before pulling away in Helen's car, I felt my first intimate connection with one of the women I longed to mean something to.

The more events I went to, the more products I needed. Within the first year, we grew from working with seven groups to working with fifteen groups, and we had products coming in from ten countries. Packages started arriving on my doorstep several times a week. I would pull into my driveway from preschool or the grocery store and before I could open my car door, my neighbors would be walking up my front drive. "Hey, did you see you've got a package?" Laurie would greet me. "Who is it from?" Amy or Kim or Debbie would be only steps behind Laurie. No matter my other plans or the threat of melting ice cream, I would leave the groceries in the car and let my toddler forgo her nap, and my girlfriends and I would start slicing open boxes to see what was inside. Since I did all of the ordering myself, you might think I would know exactly what was coming. But that never seemed to be the case. Some products turned out just as I had expected, but more often than not in the beginning, they were different from the sample or photo I had ordered from. Tote bags I thought looked beautiful in digital photos turned out to be large enough to carry my laundry (and maybe a small child) inside. This taught me to always ask for measurements. Once I ordered a necklace made from crocheted copper wire that looked unique and appealing, but in reality it felt like some sort of medieval torture device. But worst was when some natural jewelry from Africa, made with seeds and pods, sprouted bug larvae on the ride over to the United States. Women, and U.S. Customs, hate live bugs in their jewelry.

My kids especially liked the packages from NEED. Each was wrapped in itchy burlap fabric, hand-addressed with black Magic Marker, and plastered with dozens of stamps covering two sides of the package. I would carefully peel off the foreign stamps with pictures of tigers and Gandhi, dishing them out to the kids and grown-ups alike. Unfortunately, in the beginning, what was inside the box was less fascinating than the package itself. NEED, the Network of Entrepreneurship and Economic Development in Lucknow, India, was founded by Anil and Pushpa Singh. The Singhs started NEED to help marginalized women in their community, especially poor women and widows, strengthen their position in society. Anil, an Ashoka Fellow, was as passionate as any man I had ever met about women's economic empowerment. (Ashoka is a global association consisting of more than two thousand of the world's leading social entrepreneurs.) When Anil proposed leaving his stable job in the government to start an empowerment project, Pushpa supported him wholeheartedly. An educated woman with a master's degree in psychology from Ranchi University, Pushpa was inspired from an early age by her social worker father. Pushpa and Anil were a perfect team, with Anil building the organization and Pushpa working directly with the women: recruiting them for training programs, offering them support in their personal lives, and helping them work through the program to establish their lives independently. In our first phone exchanges, Anil explained his cause with passion. "E-Stacey," he said, adding a long *e* sound to the front of my name, "women must suffer with much drudgery here. In the patriarchal communities of rural India, a divorced woman is often ostracized from the community and, without a husband or father to rely on, becomes destitute. We have seen so much hope from women who can earn their own income and help themselves to survive."

Years before the Nike Foundation created the powerful video "The Girl Effect," which swept the Internet (a must-see video for anyone who cares about the future of girls and women, at www .thegirleffect.org), Anil explained to me the simple math of how helping one woman can change her community. "Kala was very poor with two children who were always sick from drinking the bad water," Anil explained. "When she started working at NEED, she earned enough to afford to get milk from the woman with the buffalo every morning. Soon her children were healthy from the milk and could attend school. Kala had more time to work while the children were at school, and she could buy the water buffalo milk two times a day. Other women at NEED also could afford the milk from the income they earned from working, and the woman with the buffalo could soon afford to buy two more buffalo. All of the women could afford to shop for fresh vegetables more often in the market, and this helped the women who farmed the fields. Everyone's life was made better by one woman's opportunity to work." Anil's simple equation—woman plus fairly paid work equals prosperity for her community—became a cornerstone of my commitment to this work. When Kala took up crafting jute bags, she took the community up with her.

I told Anil and Pushpa that I would buy some samples from NEED just to get an idea of their work. This was a naive decision. My first package from them was for over $500 worth of random assorted products, including jute notebook covers, roughly finished bags, a women's sari, apparel pieces too tiny to fit most American women, holiday ornaments, and many small embroidery samples we never were able to sell. This was disheartening to me, but I understood that Pushpa and Anil had seen my openness to samples as a chance to make a sale and to show me everything their women could produce. But just as I had learned the lesson of not overpromising with Gertrude, with NEED I learned to put a limit on the amount and type of samples I would accept from any of the groups. At the time, $500 could make a significant purchase from one of my groups, so it could not be wasted on products we were not likely to carry. Still, there were gems hidden in the large burlap bundles. Pushpa, Anil, and I learned from this experience what good partnership required. A fair-trade partnership like ours is based on neither side taking advantage of the other, on working together toward one goal—designing and crafting a product that will sell in the marketplace—so that ultimately the artisan feels a positive economic impact by the market access we create. I learned to clearly define what samples I would accept and how much money I had allocated for a sample budget. Pushpa, Anil, and the women at NEED learned to use their traditional skill sets to make samples for Global Girlfriend according to our designs and what we felt could be successful with U.S. shoppers. It was important to me that, despite some early setbacks, Global Girlfriend support the women at NEED who were taking risks to change their own lives.

One of those women was a twenty-eight-year-old I will call Soriya, from a village near Lucknow. She came from a loving family of supportive parents, four sisters, and one brother. When Soriya was nineteen, and in her first year of post–secondary school studies, she was wed through an arranged marriage. While she had wanted to finish her education, Soriya was opti-mistic about her new husband. He had a government job that provided sufficient income to maintain their small two-person family. But within two years her situation had changed drasti-cally. According to Soriya, "My hopes were crushed when I re-alized that my husband had no respect for me and showed little concern or affection toward me." Her husband had become involved in gambling, and his gambling debt grew to 50,000 rupees, which was far more than what he could pay back. "The depth of his indifference was proved one day when he demanded that I should earn an extra income working as a prostitute, to pay back his debt. His plan was to present me to his friends and relatives in lieu of the money he owed to them. Being shocked at his demand, I turned to my mother-in-law for sup-port, but upon hearing her son's order, the older woman deemed it a reasonable request and strongly defended his demand. I was scared, angry, appalled, and ashamed. Later I came to know that it was she who advised her son with this idea. I knew that

I was in danger and that my reputation, dignity, and social status were at stake, but I decided adamantly to draw the line. I refused to sacrifice my dignity, pride, and body for the sake of some extra money. In the middle of the night, I fled to the home of my parents. I trekked about thirty kilometers through the darkness of the night," Soriya recalled.

With this courageous act, Soriya not only defied her husband, but also rejected her society's mandates that women obey their husbands no matter what. Welcomed back warmly by her parents, Soriya was worried. She had never worked outside of the home, and she knew that her parents could not afford to feed another person. Luckily, Soriya met Pushpa. Pushpa encouraged her to seek training and employment at NEED, which lit an entrepreneurial spark within Soriya. She started by making jute bags, and then mastered *chikan* embroidery—the special embroidery used on the skirts and tops Soriya was helping NEED produce for Global Girlfriend. Now skilled and earning her own money, Soriya proved on the night she left her husband that she was strong willed and determined and refused to be let down. I did not want to let her down either. We ordered three styles of skirts and even tried simple yoga pants in the first apparel order Soriya worked on for us at NEED.

Meanwhile, my girlfriends on this side of the Atlantic were making things happen. I had seeded my most trendy friends—Ann, Ruthanne, Robin, and Stephanie—with jewelry and handbags. These girls were the fashion mavens of their neighborhoods, and people noticed what they were wearing. Happily for me, the people who noticed Ann included editors at *In Style* magazine, where she worked as an advertising sales director. An editor friend of Ann's named Erin admired a beautiful hand-beaded bracelet I had sent Ann as a gift and said that if I would like to send her some samples she would consider a feature piece in the magazine. The bracelet was made by a craft cooperative of women in Nepal. Nepali women have been weaving beads traditionally for centuries. As the Himalayan passage between China and India, Nepal has a rich handicraft heritage. Kunja Artistic Bead Work (or KABW) is a cooperative that utilizes traditional beading skills as an income-generating source for women in need. Weaving or stringing tiny glass beads, women create beautiful and timeless pieces. I sent Erin a bracelet. I could barely believe the break when she called to tell me we would have a piece of jewelry in *In Style*'s big ten-year anniversary issue. Erin asked me what order information I wanted next to the product. I wasn't sure. My home phone number seemed wrong. My AOL account e-mail address also didn't seem very professional. Instead I gave her the URL for my fledgling Web site, globalgirlfriend.com. "Do you have online ordering?" Erin asked.

"We will before the issue comes out," I assured her.

Time to tap the bus-stop brain trust again. I had set up a simple Web site with information about hosting local home parties through a do-it-yourself template on Network Solutions. Luckily, my friend Traci Takaki's sister Kim Malueg owned a Web development company with her husband, Kurt. Kim worked quickly to develop a gorgeous and trendy site that built on the logo that my graphic designer friend Courtney O'Shea had sketched out and scanned in her basement a year earlier. We added photos and stories of the women and lots of information about our cause. I called on Robin George, one of my fashion maven friends and a talented photographer, to quickly photograph all of our products in her basement studio. I set up merchant services with the bank, and with a couple of weeks to spare, Global Girlfriend was an official e-commerce business.

Our success in *In Style* brought customers from around the

country to our Web site. When an unforeseen majority of these new customers asked about a catalog, I fibbed and said our first catalog would be coming in the fall. Now I had to make a catalog. Again, I recruited Courtney to do design. I wrote the copy, and poor Robin was forced to be not only photographer but model too. She set the shots with me standing in as the dummy model. Once she was happy with the shot, I would jump out, she would jump in, and I would click the camera shutter to complete the photo. My friend Betsy Wieserma introduced me to Jason Scherer, a print broker willing to help me print and mail for less. And with that we mailed our first catalog to over five hundred new Global Girlfriend customers.

That holiday season, catalog in hand, Global Girlfriend had a booth at the Denver Junior League holiday mart and, with the help of some Junior League friends, was chosen to be featured on our local NBC station 9 news. In January I decided that we should build on the contacts we had made through home parties, the catalog, the Junior League, and the media by hosting an International Women's Day event on March 8. International Women's Day was founded in 1908 when fifteen thousand working women in New York took to the streets demanding shorter work hours, better pay, and voting rights. Two years later, in 1910, at the Conference of Working Women in Copenhagen, it was adopted worldwide as a day of both celebration of women's achievements and rebellion against the inequities still faced by too many women around the world. I had learned through the women's groups I worked with that in other parts of the world, International Women's Day was a highly anticipated and celebrated holiday. I wanted this day of recognition to stretch to my dot on the map. My girlfriends agreed. That March, twenty local women's organizations and over two hundred women converged on St. Philip Lutheran

Church in Littleton, Colorado, to view the documentary *Peace by Peace: Women on the Frontlines*. The film was narrated by Academy Award–winning actress Jessica Lange and profiled women peace-builders in five nations: Afghanistan, Argentina, Bosnia-Herzegovina, Burundi, and the United States. Engaged and interested women walked from table to table at our Women's Organization Expo to learn about the work of groups like the Urgent Action Fund for Women's Human Rights, Girls Inc., The Gathering Place, Mayan Weavers, the Women's Bean Project, and more in their own effort to find opportunities to get involved locally. Everyone enjoyed free cheesecake. I opened the official program by thanking the many contributors to the event, then sharing my dream with the audience: "My greatest wish for each of you is to be blessed with women in your life who lift and inspire you the way these women inspire me every day." I continued, "While International Women's Day has been celebrated since 1908, this may be the first time many of you have done something to mark the day. It is for me. I hope it will be the first of many we all celebrate together. You are making a difference for women worldwide just by being here tonight, by listening to women's stories and recognizing the challenges they face. But together we are more than just a gathering of women here in this room; your presence here tonight is part of something much larger happening today celebrating women the world over."

Our event was a beautiful community wish for the women of the world. It was a marker in the life of my business as women came together and embraced the many ways we can collaborate, as nonprofits, businesses, concerned citizens, and enlightened consumers. Women came to learn, but they also came to shop, embracing the reality that they could change lives through their purchasing power. Clearly these women grasped that what happens in the lives of the least fortunate of us profoundly impacts the global life of each of us. They wanted to create the "she-conomy" that made their dollars count for women everywhere. I felt an unleashing of the collaborative spirit of women bringing forth a new way of working together for a fairer world. Yet I found myself wishing to experience women's lives in faraway places for myself. I wanted an even deeper connection so that I could speak from experience to my customers and supporters who longed to know about their sisters' lives on the other side of the world.

# 4

# GOD TURNS HIS HEAD ON
# THE INDIAN HIGHWAY

❦

*Life is either a daring adventure or nothing.*
—HELEN KELLER

My mom was clinging to her seat, one hand clenched on the car door handle with the other, white-knuckled, grasping the firm fabric bench seat, as our driver, Vikrim Tiwari, dodged our car in and out of traffic like a slippery meatball in a swirling plate of spaghetti. We outmaneuvered fast-moving cars, three-wheeled cycle-rickshaws, ox-drawn carts, and the occasional suicidal bike rider. "God is everywhere in India," Vikrim exclaimed, then paused with a mystical smile before adding, "but he turns his head on the Indian highways."

Finally on the ground in India to work with my girlfriends firsthand, I was now dreaming of being home safe with my kids and out of the New Delhi traffic. Life in Delhi felt so aggressive. Everyone in India I worked with had always seemed so calm and cordial in our phone and e-mail communications. I had pictured a spiritual haven in my mind—the India of my yoga practice. Or maybe the high-tech, highly evolved India of Tom Friedman's best seller *The World Is Flat,* with an enormous emerging middle class, all with good jobs at a call center. But now, driving the Delhi city streets brimming with poverty and desperation, I felt like I'd landed in a Charles Dickens novel.

Beggars approached our car at every stop. Some stepped up with forlorn faces and holding out a malnourished child or one missing a limb. Small children performed elaborate circus-style acts along the medians, then pounded onlookers' windows to collect a fee. Whole families bathed in roadside puddles. Women in soiled brightly colored saris scavenged through mounds of garbage with hand rakes looking for bricks, bits of plastic, and scraps of wood to shackle together as shelter.

It shouldn't have shocked me. After all, I had come to India to see the poverty. I wasn't here trekking or on a spiritual journey to Dharmsala. I wasn't a telecom executive or a call center guru on my way to Bangalore. I was more of an anti-poverty crusader, and even more of a mom with a basement business half a world away. But as the traffic scramble sped up, I secretly longed for an expedient arrival back into the peaceful arms of the upscale Hotel Nikko. I caught myself glancing away from the window, focusing instead on small talk with my mom and on Vikrim's numerous cell phone conversations about his unrequited love. While God was turning his head to the Delhi traffic, he had also missed the people on the curb. Uncomfortable or not, I needed to see them.

In our Western world, it is often too easy to not really see the ugly truth of what people endure. Sure, we watch the news, we read books and articles, and we see dramatic photos of children living in squalid conditions on commercials for worthy aid organizations. We feel bad. And then we go on with the rest of our day. I am not saying that everyone should spend their time standing around, wringing their hands in worry—after all, that is hardly what the women actually living in some of the poorest places on earth are doing. But it seems that we are almost immune to suffering unless it directly impacts our lives or our families. With all the images of unnecessary suffering, we are inoculated into inaction because we feel nothing we could do personally could make a dent in the larger problem.

The hardest reality in India was that the poor here are chosen. They come from the undesirable castes that are built into the Indian social structure. To me the caste system is reminiscent of the racial segregation in the United States that was still in place less than sixty years ago. Choosing people's worthiness by the color of their skin, their birth parents, or the caste they were born into is simply and fundamentally wrong.

I thought I was prepared for the poverty I would see in India. I was not. Watching people eke out an existence in the streets of this megacity brought me to tears. It made my efforts feel so tiny, as though they were futile in the face of so much desperation.

Still, I thought of the story of the boy on a starfish-covered beach who stood throwing the starfish back to their ocean home one at a time. When an old man came along and said, "There are too many, boy; you'll never make a difference," the boy picked up another starfish, tossed it back into the ocean, and replied, "I did for that one." Helping even one woman here would make a difference.

Extreme poverty, the poverty professor Jeffrey Sachs calls "poverty that kills," is both unnecessary and preventable. Close to half the world, nearly 3 billion people, lives on less than $2 per day, and 26,500 to 30,000 children die each day, from preventable disease, or no access to clean water, or simple starvation. This situation is like a global human holocaust where we close our eyes while innocent people die of curable diseases like malaria and dysentery, and from lack of food.

Even after countless hours of advocating for women living in extreme poverty for over three years, my first encounter with the downtrodden of Delhi was wrenching. Watching tiny girls with dirty clothes and faces begging for rupees, I tried to imagine them as my own daughters. While my sweet daughters, Cali Ann and Ellie, were home safely tucked in bed, these daughters of the world may have never had a safe place to lay their heads.

I was glad to have my mom along with me as a witness and a sounding board. We would be spending half a month together traveling in India and then Nepal, and I felt very lucky to be spending the most time I had spent alone with my mother since I left my childhood home. I stared out the window, past the crowds, and remembered our arrival a few nights earlier. Our landing in New Delhi in the middle of the night had been surreal. That may be how everyone feels after their first eighteen-hour flight, but it also may just be India. I had expected people—lots and lots of people filling up every square foot of space. But upon our landing, the Indira Gandhi International Airport was fairly empty, and aside from the low-hanging ceiling, I didn't feel the crushing lack of personal space I had been warned of by friends who had visited India. Through the airport windows I could see a small crowd of taxi drivers anticipating a late-night fare off of a full international flight, but other than the small taxi line and the people I'd flown in with, it was a quiet and neutral entrance into one of the most exotic places in the world.

After a long customs line in arrivals, with visas stamped and luggage collected, our group of sponsored buyers was rushed past the ambitious cabdrivers and hurried into a parking lot of small waiting cars the Indian Export Council had arranged. In the chaos of the moment, I was motioned into the backseat of one car and my mom whisked away in another before we knew what was happening. The caravan quickly rode the fence line that led off of airport property and onto the NASCAR-esque raceway that is the Indian highway.

My heart pulsed with mild panic, first about being separated from my mother. You don't want to lose your mother in India. It's just not good. Especially when the most adventurous trip either of you has been on in the past might have been a twenty-hour car ride to Disney World. Second, my life was suddenly in the hands of a driver I did not know, who was weaving wildly in and out of brightly painted trucks dotted by rickshaws and roaming cattle. My brain was trying desperately to keep up with my eyes as a strange new world whizzed by my window. Each thought was abruptly interrupted by the constant beeping of our car horn—our small vehicle's only defense against the barrage of trucks that rule the Delhi roads at night.

Unlike me, Debbie Farah was at home in the chaos. Debbie had made this trip possible for me by introducing me to Kevin Stephens, the man in charge of recruiting buyers on behalf of the Indian Export Council. Sitting in the front seat of our compact car, she seemed to barely notice our near misses at every curve. She didn't mention the dangerous driving, or the men urinating openly along the roadside, or the cows roaming freely in a city of 14 million people. She was at home in India, a place she had visited often and had come to love, and whose beauty, poverty, and contradictions drew her back.

Debbie's gesture of inviting me along was true to her inclusive nature and personal philosophy of fair trade. Like me, Debbie had started her own fair-trade business, Bajalia Trading Company, to help people in poverty. She specialized in products from women in war-torn Afghanistan. Debbie's parents were both born in Ramallah, Palestine, and she was a first-generation Palestinian-American. Her heritage blessed her with two languages, Arabic and English, as well as a deep love of international travel and diverse cultures. On past trips to India, Debbie had spent most of her time in the Kutch region, working with rural communities of women on traditional embroidered textiles. She was excited to be spending this trip in the bustling city.

Our convoy arrived safely at the hotel, with our driver pulling in directly behind my mom's carload of foreign companions. After we dumped our suitcases in the corner of our room and brushed our teeth (remembering of course not to use the tap water), my mom fell immediately asleep and began to snore— something I didn't know she did after not living in my parents' house for many years. I tried to rest up for what the morning would bring, but I found that my mind kept churning. I thought about the women I had worked with whom I would finally be meeting face-to-face on this trip. I was excited to match real women with the images I had built in my mind, but I was also nervous about how they'd perceive me. Who was I, after all, to appoint myself their spokeswoman in America? Would they expect too much, believe I could do more than I actually could for them? Or might they not really need the support I had come to believe I was helping to provide? I decided to keep my expectations simple, hoping to gain new insight into other women's lives, discover some great new products, and leave India with enduring friendships.

Out the window, in the hazy morning sky a small twirl of smoke cascaded up from the sidewalk below. From our room the view was of a sea of tall buildings, the impeccably kept grounds of the Hotel Nikko, and the poverty that lived on the sidewalk just beyond the hotel gate. People were toting water in worn plastic containers, carrying bundles of all sorts of things, and one woman was burning a fire to keep warm right on the cement walking path.

After a buffet Indian breakfast, we boarded our chartered bus for the Noida exposition center and got our first real look at India by daylight. Here I found the scene I had been expecting the night before. Daytime in Delhi was a mass of moving exhilaration. Contradictions greeted me at every turn. Poverty and majesty seemed to walk along holding hands in Delhi.

Our bus sped past fine hotels, busy market stalls, red-light districts, grand temples, and squatter camps until we turned onto the brand-new Noida Expressway leading to the convention center. The building was impressive from a distance. Large, with world flags flying out front, it looked like a testament to India's presence in the modern business world. But as the bus swung into the north end drive we could see that the back of the building was unfinished. Rows of bamboo scaffolding lined the back side of the building, and teams of women with large baskets on their heads were climbing the scaffolding to deliver bricks to masons one basketful at a time.

I was baffled by the lack of labor-saving technology. Debbie laughed at my naïveté. "Why do they need machines when they have so many people who need work? Cheap labor built everything you see here." Even the most modern building was built on the backs of the poor.

India has the largest number of poor people of any country in the world. Of its nearly 1 billion citizens, it is estimated that up to 400 million, just shy of half the population, live below the official Indian poverty line of $1.25 a day. While the growth of India's middle class due to better jobs linked to the global economy and urbanization has been impressive, the main cause of poverty is still the high rate of illiteracy and a population growth rate that exceeds the country's economic growth. In the uneven distribution of India's capital resources, women and children once again fair worst.

Inside the expo center, the bustling trade show was inviting, with two floors and many, many rows of vendors with beautiful block-printed textiles, beaded baubles, leather goods, lace, jute, clay, and a smorgasbord of unique products. We met a buyer for Wisteria catalog who knew just where she was going and which vendors she wanted to see. Not knowing any of the vendors at the show, my mom and I wandered a bit aimlessly, looking at all of the finery. In the first few aisles, I went into booths offering lovely products that had the earmarks of historically women-made crafts. We picked up beaded jewelry, hand-embroidered scarves, and quilted throw blankets. Revealing too much in my introduction, I told the savvy salesmen that I ran a fair-trade company and worked with women's groups, helping them earn fair wages. Of course, every man said that all of his producers were women and he paid a fair wage and I should buy, buy, buy. When I asked if we could come visit their groups while in India, their stories changed slightly, and my mom and I knew to slowly back out of those booths.

Two days of the show went by without our finding the women's cooperatives we had been told would be represented, and I was very disheartened. Attending the show had been part of our obligation to the sponsored trip, but I was ready to get on with our own agenda of visits I had arranged for the days following the show. I had not come all this way to be lied to by aggressive Indian men. On the first day, I did place a small order with a group of disadvantaged women producers of hand-block-printed gauze fabric sewn into small gift pouches for jewelry organized by some young designers at the National Institute of Fashion Technology. NIFT designers were tapping the traditional crafts of the different regions of India and helping artisans to meld tradition with modern design. Women in a rural area outside of Mumbai made the fabric. But on the whole, it felt like we had spent the rest of our time strolling up and down the aisles with little hope of finding women artisan groups. Most of the booths housed representatives from small factories, run and staffed by men from throughout India. We did not find the women's cooperatives and NGOs (nongovernmental organizations) I had expected.

A few steps down an aisle we had already walked a half dozen times, I noticed a striking woman with a southern Indian flair to her sari and her jewelry. Her sari was boldly colored in turquoise and hot pink, and her arms were adorned with chunky metal cuffs and bangles. A little metal chain and ring decorated her nose, and her huge dark eyes were warm and welcoming. Standing next to her, greeting people, was a young woman of Indian heritage who was clearly an American. She introduced herself as Priya Patel. How had I missed these gals in the sea of men? I quickly learned that they had been having as dismal a show as I had. No one was looking for what they were selling—women's economic empowerment. We were both in luck.

Founded in 1995 by Anandiben Patel, the Gramshree Trust was created to empower underprivileged women through education and enterprise activities. Initially, the trust focused on advocating women's rights, but Anandiben soon saw that the real need was for respectable work for women. Over time Gramshree grew to provide handicraft training as well as to fund a marketing division aimed at selling the women's crafts outside of the local community. Priya had volunteered for six months helping Gramshree Trust in Amnabad through the American India Foundation. She had been helping with design, capacity building, and markets; this show would be her last week with the group before returning to the States. She was extremely helpful in interpreting my simple sketches and placing my order for the women's appliqué handbags.

Boarding the bus back to the hotel, I felt better. At least we had met two women's groups to work with. And tomorrow's plans were also promising. Mrs. K. Satyasri would be arriving at the hotel to meet us the next morning after her almost twenty-four-hour commute to Delhi from Narsupur in the Andhra Pradesh region of India.

The climate of the Andhar Pradesh region is very volatile, often causing life-taking hurricanes, cyclones, and damaging floods that rob people of their homes, crops, and livestock. Narsupur sits on the west bank of the Godavari River at its delta into the Bay of Bengal. Mrs. Satyasri's cooperative draws its name from its location as well as from the skill that has been passed down in the area for over a hundred years: lace making. The Godavari Delta Women Lace Artisans Co-operative Cottage Industrial Society was founded in the 1970s by Mrs. Satyasri's mother, the late Mrs. K. Hemalatha. Irish missionaries had brought lace making to the region in the 1800s, and the craft has been a staple income generator for local women ever since. But since the withdrawal of the British from India in 1947, and with few outside market opportunities, women had trouble selling enough lace to make ends meet. For two years, Mrs. Hemalatha had journeyed on foot to local village lace artisans to learn of their plight and their needs. After a long petition process through the Indian government, she was finally allowed to register her cooperative as an official nongovernmental organization in 1979.

In her charter, Mrs. Hemalatha wrote, "Being womenfolk we are looked down on in society as sub-human beings. There are certain taboos and customs which are hindering the growth of the women. Generally a male is treated as superior to a female." She worked tirelessly for years to change this. When she could no longer run the cooperative due to advanced age and poor health, her daughter took up the torch.

It was no wonder I was confused about the call I received that morning from the front desk. "Mrs. Edgar, two gentlemen are here to see you." I could not figure out who those gentlemen might be. In the lobby, two men stood sheepishly by the front desk, holding a large army green duffel bag. Somehow I knew they were my visitors.

"Miss Stacey?" one of the men asked as I walk toward them.

"Yes," I answered.

"Prakash," he replied, holding out his hand to shake mine. "This is my friend Prasad." I greeted the men and introduced my mom, still unsure of who they were or why they were there.

"I am the husband of Mrs. Satyasri," Prakash continued. "Unfortunately, it is very dangerous for a woman to travel the rails alone, so we came to meet you and show you the women's crafts." I was disappointed not to meet Mrs. Satyasri. Knowing her mother had traveled by foot all around their region, at first I was surprised that she couldn't come by train alone. But as an American woman who felt free to move about as I pleased, I rarely thought about my safety when traveling. Sure, I was cautious and didn't walk alone down dark alleys at night, but I felt free to go where I pleased without feeling threatened just because I was a woman. Women in India and other places in the world do not necessarily share my sense of entitled security. I understood that one of the two had to stay home to take care of their family and the extended family of the women in their cooperative. Despite my disappointment, I was impressed by Mrs. Satyasri's loving marriage and that her husband, Prakash, was equally dedicated to the women's cause.

Admittedly, I was disappointed that so many men seemed to be wiggling into my "up with women" India trip. But I was honored that they had come so far just to meet me, and I was eager to see the samples stowed in their green duffel. We sat down on one of the formal couches in the marble-floored lobby to visit. As soon as Prakash began unzipping his bag, two hotel staff moved in to scold him and instruct me. "I am sorry, miss; merchandise exchange is not allowed in the lobby. Please feel free to invite the gentlemen up to your room."

Once upstairs we invited Debbie to come view the samples. While neither man's English was perfect, they communicated well, and I found that once out of the public space, they seemed far more at ease. Prakash gave us a detailed history of the co-operative and shared the stories of some of the women. I was especially struck by the story of a woman I'll call Mrs. Chivukula (Prakash referred to all of the women formally). Mrs. Chivukula had been married and had two daughters, Daksha, age eleven, and Padmakali, age eight. She had only gone to school through the fifth grade and had married at a very young age. Her husband had been a mason and moved around a lot doing construction work, leaving the family often. Even though he had regular employment, he made very little money, and the family struggled economically. While her husband was away, Mrs. Chivukula tended to her girls and to the family's meager home, and made lace items—a craft she had been taught by her mother. To her shock, her husband contracted HIV/AIDS and became very ill. While traveling for his construction job, Mrs. Chivukula eventually learned, he had slept with many women, including prostitutes. Mrs. Chivukula had contracted the virus as well. When her husband died of the disease, Mrs. Chivukula was penniless and struggling to survive. Then she found work at the Godavari Delta Women Lace Artisans Co-operative, and the group even helped with her expenses, feeding her and her family and helping with school fees. Though she suffered with her disease, the cooperative provided a family, an income, and support.

We spent at least two hours visiting and looking through samples. I took lots and lots of photos of the samples to get ideas for products we might be able to order or at least design from. I loved looking at what skills the women had and what patterns they already knew how to make and then thinking about how to change or combine elements into new designs. For example, taking the pattern of a beautiful shawl and the colors of a top, and asking the group to combine the two into a new shape like a handbag or a tote that would appeal to women in the United States. By the end of our sample show, Prakash was modeling for me, trying on women's hats and scarves, and I had placed an order for some bags I sketched out using elements drawn from their samples. The two men were delightful.

After saying good-bye to Prakash and Prasad, we got ready for our next visit to the outskirts of the city. A friend of a friend of a friend, Anita Ahuja, founder of Conserve India, would take us to meet with her women's economic development project in a garbage dump.

Anita Ahuja was proper and poised. She had the stride of an English duchess as she crossed the lobby of the Nikko and a soft handshake and a soft voice to match. We knew only a little about each other's projects, but the potential for partnership was immediately clear. "I love what you are doing with Global Girl-friend," Anita said as she greeted me by the lobby entrance. "It seems as if you know what I know—that you can build a business enterprise that provides a social service. I see many ways we can help the women find a wider market for their crafts." I liked her immensely and instantly.

At Brad's company holiday party a month earlier, he and I were somehow seated with the president of his company, David Smith, and his wife. The Smiths had recently visited India and were friends with the U.S. ambassador to India. As it turned out,

Anita and her husband, Shalabh, also knew the ambassador. Six degrees of separation or just a small world after all, several weeks later I sat in Anita's car, bumping over potholes on the gravel road parallel to the river of pollution soup that led to the garbage dump where Anita was changing women's lives.

The caste system in India is one of the most oppressive social structures in the world. The Dalit caste (which sounds like the "delete" key on your computer keyboard and in essence means the same thing) is the lowest, and those born into this caste are considered "untouchable." Anita, my mom, Debbie, and I arrived to visit some "untouchable" women at an east New Delhi garbage dump by way of a modern Land Rover, but soon found an impoverished community whose every resource had been eked out from items others had thrown away.

As we turned off the pitted gravel road into the dump, there were rows of makeshift shanty houses on our right and a field of drying dung patties to our left. The rambling rows of houses were shackled together with discarded scraps of plywood, Styrofoam, plastic sheeting, and bricks unearthed from the trash heaps. We got out of the car and walked a narrow path between the dung field and a brick wall that led to Conserve India's outdoor plastic collection courtyard. We passed two women on their knees slapping wet cow patties into a metal bowl, where they shaped the steamy dung into piles to dry in the sun before they were burned as cooking fuel.

But what at first glance appeared to be one of the most desolate places imaginable to live quickly unveiled to me its enterprising underbelly. Like ants moving a mountain, the women of the community had begun an innovative business using the plastic bags that abounded at the dump. They used the bags to create a revolutionary new recycled plastic fabric that was being sewn into handbags worthy of any high-end department store.

Anita and her husband, Shalabh, had been unable and un-willing to leave the lives of these women to fate, deciding instead to invest their own lives, and life savings, in the people and things the rest of the country considered "garbage." Anita saw the rising problem of plastic waste littering the streets of India's major cities and set out with the personal mandate of bringing a green movement to her country through recycling and waste management. Though Indians were once known for using baskets, tins, and other reusable carriers for trade, the rise of the middle class had caused a sharp increase in the amount of plastic consumed by the country. When Anita founded her NGO, Conserve India, in 1998, India had become the third largest consumer of plastic (behind only the United States and China), buying 5 million tons of new plastic annually. Unfortunately, much of that ended up as trash, especially in the form of plastic shopping bags.

Anita's original idea for Conserve India had been to go into schools and start recycling collection centers. Most Indian households did not recycle at the time. By bringing an education program into the classroom and asking the children to bring their families' plastic waste to school for collection, Anita thought she could not only start widespread recycling throughout Delhi but also help shape a new generation of Indian citizens committed to sustainable practices. But the program was not well received—the caste system caused problems. Children from upper castes were not allowed to touch trash. Their families would not allow them to do "the work of a ragpicker" by carrying bundles of plastic waste to school.

Disheartened but undeterred, Anita changed her target audi-ence. She went to where the plastic garbage was—the city dumps. Whole makeshift towns had been built there from trash, and whole communities were subsisting on what could be found within the mounds. In the dumps, there were no jobs, no schools, and, to a large degree, no hope. Anita began working with some of the women on what they might be able to make from the plastic trash. She thought bringing employment to the women of the dump using the discarded plastic might start to solve both waste management issues and extreme local poverty. Anita washed and cut bags that she then tried braiding, weaving, and sewing together, but she could not create a style of bag she liked or had confidence in. She knew that there had to be something special about the product they made because otherwise no one would buy an item made of garbage by poor women. She shared her frustration with Shalabh, an engineer, who offered to play around with the plastic to see if they could mold it into another form. By 2002 the Ahujas had invented a new material they called HRP (handmade recycled plastic), in a kind of "up-cycling." Up-cycling is meant to not only recycle a product, but also to make it into a better, longer-lasting item than it was at the start. Making HRP is a process that converts used polyethylene bags into a "renewed" innovative material with significantly different properties and great visual appeal, without the use of any additional color or dyes.

Anita led us through the courtyard doorway where eight women warmly greeted us. As a rainbow of plastic sheets on clothing lines strewn across one side of the courtyard flapped in the breeze, one of the women dotted each of our foreheads with a red saffron dot and placed a lei of fat marigold heads around our necks. Anita accepted the saffron but waved off the necklace of flowers. I appreciated the lovely floral scents rising off my neck, as it helped to clear the scent of the cow poop field from my memory. After some interpreted introductions and a couple of snapshots, the women went back to work and Anita continued sharing their story.

"We started with a group of just twenty-five women. The women did not know how to use even a pair of scissors, let alone a pencil. Our first literacy lesson with the women was for holding scissors and learning to cut in straight lines," Anita shared as I watched a cutter named Rava Devi trim the torn edges from each bag in her pile of plastic. After bags of all shapes and sizes are collected from the trash heaps, they are washed. Then the torn or damaged edges are cut off, leaving only the usable pieces, which are then sorted by color into bins. "They also did not know how to recognize colors—basic knowledge that you and I take for granted. The one thing they did have in common was that everyone here knows about Bollywood. Women and men love the Bollywood stars. They know the names of all the actors and actresses, the film names, and the songs from the films, so that gave me the idea to name every shade after a Bollywood star," she continued.

Anita had magazine and newsprint clippings of famous Bollywood actresses taped above collection boxes for sorting the plastic by color. She chose photos of each star wearing the particular color designated for each sorting bin. "For instance, this blue is Shareena," she said pointing to the cutout of a lovely long-haired belly dancer wearing a turquoise sari.

As we walked from the collection boxes over to the cement basins where women were cleaning the plastic bags Rava and the others had cut, Debbie whispered in my ear, "Take off your flowers." Debbie seemed to get hot easily and had already taken the ring of marigolds off her neck and wrapped them around her wrist. Did she want me to do the same so that she would not be the only one not wearing flowers? Confused by her odd request, I listened to Anita as she went on to explain the next step in the process.

"These ladies then wash the plastic once it has been cut and hang it out to dry." As we approached the two women washing bags, I noticed them laughing and smiling, seeming to tease each other.

"Anita, can you ask them what is so funny?" I requested.

"She says that her friend is lazy and always gives her the dirtiest bags to wash." Anita chuckled along with them. The two women continued to tease each other and laugh and talk. As we followed Anita, observing the process and seeing just how many hands touched each step, I couldn't stop thinking how much the women reminded me of Mary-Mike and me sitting on the floor of my basement, tagging new products by hand, and her saying to me, "You always give me the ones that need to be refolded— just kidding." With her tagline of "just kidding," you knew she was not. Girlfriends really are the same the world over.

When I asked what a difference working for Conserve had made for Rava, she answered, "Since I am working here, the condition of my house is good. I have rent of thirty dollars a month. If I stop, the condition will become bad. This work lets me feed my children and live properly." At Conserve, Rava makes three times more than she did before she joined the group, when she tried to survive on ragpicking without knowing what she might find to sell, use, or trade. We wandered around the grounds of the dump, meeting the ragpickers and being followed like the pied piper by a parade of children curious about the strange foreign visitors. None of them wore shoes, and Anita told me there was no school for them to attend.

After our tour we bid good-bye to the women at the dump and hopped back in the Land Rover to travel a few miles into an industrial area of the city to Conserve's office. Debbie turned to me. "Why didn't you take off the necklace when I asked?"

"Why did you ask?" I replied.

"In the Hindu culture, those strands of marigolds are

offerings to the gods," she said. "Accepting one and wearing it around is saying you are better than they are. Right, Anita?"

My heart sunk. That was why Anita hadn't accepted a lei in the first place. "It's okay," Anita comforted. "But I don't want them to think that I am any better than they are. I don't want them to think that I can solve all of their problems or have all of the answers for their lives," she explained. Anita's statement was profound. I spent a lot of time worrying about how to help more and how to solve problems, and the fact is I don't have any better answers than the women have already found for themselves. I am just blessed with more access to opportunity. If I can simply open the door to my part of the world for these women, the people who buy the women's products can then make the real difference.

When we reached the Conserve offices, women and men were busy sewing, inspecting, and packaging the final products. Anita introduced us to her head of quality control, a woman named Bharti. Bharti was very young when she joined Conserve. She was from a small village outside Delhi and unfortunately was born with a disorder that affected her speech. Disabilities in India seemed to draw more undue prejudice than in the United States, and Bharti's condition caused her to be discriminated against. Bharti started working with Conserve in its quality assurance department as one of its first team members. With Anita's reassurance and praise, she became an expert in quality control and an integral part of the department. Bharti's steady job helped her earn a much-needed income to pay for the regular checkups and treatment she needed to stay healthy and to keep aspects of her condition at bay.

Then Anita shuffled us into the showroom. As Debbie, my mom, and I entered the room, we each let out an audible gasp. Suddenly it sounded like we were watching the most spectacular fireworks display we'd ever seen. Each of us rushed to touch our favorite styles, snatching them from where they perched on their display shelves with all the accompanying "oohs" and "aahs" of coming face-to-face with awesome beauty. Stylish handbags in structured forms were splashed with distinctive patterns, stripes, and bold solids; they could easily have sat beside designer bags on the shelves at Nordstrom. All of them were made from the plastic trash. "It is amazing," my mom said, shaking her head, "that these have come out of there." She's not usually an overly emotional gal, but I saw tears welling up in her eyes. I think we were all struck with the enormity of what the women had accomplished. I had no doubt that our customers back home would be equally impressed.

Circled around Shalabh's desk, we shared a carry-out meal of the best Indian food I had in India, while I worked on my order with Anita. It would be the largest order I had placed from one group for my company so far—$6,000 worth of recycled plastic handbags. While that may not sound like much compared to the large orders being written by big importers over at the Noida show, it was substantial for Global Girlfriend, and I think for Conserve too.

"This is a good start," Anita told me. "I have high hopes for our partnership."

"Me too," I assured her.

"I want people to look at fashion differently, but especially to look at poverty differently," she said. "I hate that when you say something is a recycled product, people think it should be worth less, not more. The same is true of these poor women; they are worth more than how society treats them."

If there was one thing that stood out to me in India, it was how the poor seemed to be treated as if they were disposable. The discrimination they faced was blatant, yet these tenacious souls charged on, making something from nothing. And Conserve was not the only organization Global Girlfriend was working with in India that was helping both women and the environment.

Assisi Garments in southern India had just begun producing a line of 100 percent organic cotton tops and skirts for us. While Anita had started Conserve to solve an environmental issue but ended up making an even larger social impact for women, Assisi Garments was founded in 1994 by an order of Franciscan nuns in Avinashi, India, to help poor and disabled women and ended up impacting the local environment for the better. The cooperative was the dream of Sister Vineetha, a visionary nun who began by training and employing just eight women—three who were disabled and five who were desperately poor—who needed a safe haven and a skill to earn a living. Young disabled women of India are often deemed unfit for marriage, leaving many condemned to a life of suffering. Unable to support themselves, they struggle to survive in a culture that does not accept their differences. The group began by taking in small jobs from the surrounding garment factories. As the women's sewing production evolved, so did the organization. Sister Vineetha and her order recognized the demand for jersey garments and saw an opportunity to increase the work for the young women they supported through the use of organic cotton. They knew farmers in India were suffering from cancers and illnesses linked to conventional cotton farming, so the sisters had their seamstresses use organic cotton instead of conventional cotton to sew cotton jersey garments in a workshop they established.

The World Health Organization estimates that as many as twenty thousand deaths and 3 million chronic health problems are caused by poisoning related to agricultural pesticides globally each year. Conventional farming of cotton plants uses more chemicals per acre than any other crop, and the runoff from these pesticides enters the water table that we all share. The women used organic cotton grown by a cooperative of three hundred organic cotton farmers in Maharashtra, India. Over time, Assisi swelled from helping eight women to assisting over two hundred poor and disabled women learn a trade, have a safe place to live and the food and medical attention they need, earn fair wages for their efforts, and develop a plan for their future. I felt fortunate to work with producers who have control of the manufacturing process from seed to sewing machine.

Similarly, our partners at Freeset in Kolkata (Calcutta) were using eco-friendly jute as the basis for a bag business that was rescuing young women from the city's red-light district. Freeset is located in Sonagacchi, the largest, and most infamous, sex district in Kolkata. Within a few square miles, more than ten thousand women line the streets, selling their bodies to the thousands of men who visit daily. Most of the women are trafficked as girls from Nepal, Bangladesh, and rural India. For others, poverty has left them without options. In India, prostitution is big business and thrives on exploitation and slavery, robbing the poor of dignity and innocence. Freeset was started in 2001 by a couple from New Zealand, Kerry and Annie Hilton, who packed up their four children and moved to Kolkata to live and work among the poorest of the world's poor. They soon discovered that their new neighbors were thousands of women forced into prostitution by trafficking and poverty. The Hiltons knew that to bring these women real freedom they would need more than charitable donations; they would need a sustainable business alternative that gave women the chance to earn a living outside of the red-light district.

The Hiltons, in partnership with Priya Mishra, a local Indian doctor, founded Freeset, teaching the women to sew and screen print stylish jute carryalls that carried women out of prostitution. According to Dr. Mishra, "It was hard work teaching unskilled women to sew at a quality acceptable for the export market. Some could barely use a pair of scissors, and in those early days the average daily output was less than two bags each. Would you believe some of the bags were sewn inside out and upside down!" But the team persisted in patient training and refining because of what the business was doing for young women like Menaka.

Menaka was born in Bangladesh. When she was twelve, Menaka and her family were forced out of their home, along with other Hindu families. They managed to escape to a refugee camp on the border of India. Menaka made friends with a thirty-year-old woman in one of the nearby houses she used to sneak into to use the toilet. The woman often asked Menaka to go to Kolkata with her. Menaka always refused, until one day she had a fight with her sister. Without telling her parents, she left with her friend. Menaka's friend took her to Kolkata's largest red-light district and sold the twelve-year-old to a brothel owner for 1,000 rupees (roughly $22 U.S.). A customer of the brothel stole her innocence, and her young life changed forever— all from a decision to take a road trip with a woman she thought was her friend.

Many of the women who worked at Freeset shared a similar story, but working for this new enterprise, they were writing new stories for their future. Menaka used to stand with thousands of other prostitutes, but she was brave enough to change her life by leaving the brothel to join Freeset. Over almost ten years, Freeset grew from 20 women to over 140 women set free from forced sex work by fair-trade employment. Freeset also gave women around the world an opportunity to set a woman free from prostitution by simply buying a handbag. I found this freedom through employment and the opportunity to become an abolitionist through consumerism simple yet enormously powerful ideas. I loved the fact that changing your tote bag could change a life, and I was reinvigorated to keep sharing that message with Global Girlfriend customers.

By the end of our time in India, my mom and I were feeling both at home and inspired. We loved seeing fair-trade employment in action and enjoyed our tourist adventures as well as dining with new friends at places like The Olive Bar, bartering at the Dalihat market, and visiting a tailor's shop to bring back traditional Indian outfits for my kids. Vikrim took us to see all the religious and historic sites like the Red Fort, the Qutb Minar, the Lotus Temple, and the Krishna Temple. We saw the most beautiful side of India and the most beautiful side of her people. I felt invigorated by the tenacity of our business partners. On my first drive through India, all I could see was nameless poverty, and it made me feel paralyzed. Now I could see real women, who despite extreme obstacles made meaningful lives for themselves with what they had. We had shared smiles and laughs despite language barriers. None of the women here expected me to solve her problems, as I had naively worried they might. They had learned to be tremendous problem solvers just to survive. What they wanted from me was to tell others about them. To show others what they could do and to help open the door to new connections that would bring them more work. They wanted nothing but a hand up.

But one worry was clouding what had truly turned into an auspicious trip—political unrest in the next country on our

itinerary. With all of our traveling, work, and touring, we hadn't
had much time to watch TV, and I had been trying to keep up
with the situation in Nepal via the Internet. Each night when
we returned from our daily adventures, I would walk up alone
to the hotel business center, where I would pay my few rupees to
a girl with a cash box and then sit down to dig into my e-mails.
I would skim the bolded list of unread e-mails for three ad-
dresses: my husband Brad's, Sanita's, and Chandra's. We would
be staying at my friend Sanita's home in Nepal with her family.
Sanita's family founded and ran an NGO called Kumbeshwar
Technical School, helping women in a fair-trade business that
produced knitwear. Sanita was the first member of the Khadgi
family I was introduced to online through the World Fair Trade
Organization. Because her brother was getting married on the
morning of our arrival, my friend Chandra from another fair-
trade group I was already working with in Nepal, Sana Hastakala, would be picking us up from the airport. Brad's e-mails
sounded worried. "The State Department is warning against
travel to Nepal," he had written earlier in the week. "Please be
sure it's safe to go." I knew he didn't want to tell me not to go
to Nepal, but he was concerned.

Two nights before our departure, we sat down for the first
time to the Indian nightly news. The anchors reported that the
growing unrest was moving from the countryside into Kathmandu. The broadcast showed video of a stone-throwing mob
in Kathmandu's historic Durbar Square, and my mom looked
over at me, poker faced, and asked, "We still going?"

"I think so," I replied. "Let me e-mail Sanita."

In the days preceding my trip to Nepal, the U.S. State Department put out a warning advising Americans not to travel
to Nepal due to heightened violence between Maoist rebels and

the Nepali government. After crowds stoned each other in Durbar Square, Nepal's controversial King Gyanendra put the country on curfew three days before my mom and I planned to arrive. The entire population in the Kathmandu Valley was ordered to stay inside from dawn to dusk in the king's effort to thwart pro-democracy rallies in the streets. King Gyanendra's government even went so far as to arrest vocal citizens and leaders who spoke out against his rule. The king faced the threat of the Maoists, but also the unrest of his former followers now tired of his heavy-handed unilateral reign. With no other way to prevent public outcry, the king held the country under his thumb with a military-backed curfew.

If the curfew wasn't lifted soon, my friends would not be able to pick us up at the airport, and there would be no taxi service as an option. Worse for the Khadgi family (the family we would be staying with), their son Saytendra's wedding was scheduled for 6:00 A.M. on the morning of my arrival. This day, and the early hour, were found to be the most auspicious day and time for the couple's nuptials by the family astrologer. It could take months before the next auspicious date could be found if the curfew was not lifted. The country and the Khadgi family were holding their breath, and so was I.

In addition to the tensions in the country, there was also the problem of rolling power outages. E-mails from Sanita had been intermittent and sometimes took a couple of days to arrive, depending on how long Sanita had power each day. I hoped this message, and her reply, would travel fast. I wanted to know what was happening without letting on that we had any doubts about making the trip. I wanted to go, but I wanted to respect my mom's feelings about the trip as well as be sure I wasn't lying to my husband when I said it would all be fine. Back in the business center, I logged on to my AOL account and sent Sanita a quick and vague note:

*Dear Sanita,*

*Greetings from Delhi! I am just checking in on the political situation in Nepal. We have seen a lot on the news here today about the violence and curfew. I am very excited to see and meet all of you on Monday. Please let us know if there have been any changes. I am able to check my e-mail once a day.*

*Best wishes,*
*Stacey*

Almost immediately, while I was reading my other, less urgent messages, the famous AOL "you've got mail" voice alerted me to her reply.

*Dear Stacey,*

*Namaste! We are pleased to receive your mail. Hope you are having a good time in India and everything in your trip is going well. We are having some political problems, but please do not worry—your schedule has not changed. Mr. Chandra will come to pick you at the airport. Hope everything will be fine. Hope curfew will be lifted.*

*Looking forward to see you soon!*
*Sanita*

Hope everything will be fine? Hope the curfew is lifted? Not exactly the resounding reassurance I had hoped for, but it would have to be enough. And travel warnings or not, I was excited to visit the country some had dubbed Shangri-la.

Unfortunately, to get to Nepal we first had to pass back through the Delhi airport. This time the airport was full. The mash and movement of people and baggage mixed with the scent of Indian food, heat, and raw human smells made me a little light-headed. We hauled our heavy luggage into the long security line and waited to send it through the conveyor and then scurried to our gate.

On board our Jet Airways flight I felt a wave of relief pass over me as we sat calmly and comfortably in our seats. I thought about the lessons I had learned in India. Poverty, though pervasive, can be surmounted. The women working at Conserve, Assisi, Freeset, and Godavari reinforced my belief that fair businesses really can change lives by providing jobs with sustainable incomes, fair wages, and dignity. Seeing prosperity felt like seeing the seed of my dream from the basement in full bloom. All of these great organizations had started small, as a simple effort to help just a few women, but had grown to help hundreds of women over time—just like Global Girlfriend was doing. Most important, in what first seemed like a beach full of washed-up starfish I now saw instead an ocean of opportunity to make a difference, even if it was just for a few women at a time. India had been a journey worth making. Now I sat wondering what lay in store for us in Nepal.

# 5

# NAMASTE NOTIONS

❧

*There are two ways of spreading light:*
*to be the candle or the mirror that reflects it.*
—EDITH WHARTON

Whether by luck or by divine intervention, the curfew was lifted the day before we left India for Nepal. Nepal is a landlocked country bordered to the north by China and by India to the east, west, and south. The total population of Nepal is estimated at around 30 million people, with much of the population concentrated in the fertile Kathmandu Valley. Despite its unrivaled beauty, the country faces many challenges, beginning with the political unrest we were flying into. Adult illiteracy is high, with two thirds of female adults and one third of male adults considered illiterate. The country lacks enough employment to meet the needs of its growing population, and over half of the country's citizens live on less than $1.25 per day. Similar to in India, the Hindu caste system is prevalent in Nepali society. And, according to the U.S. State Department, between ten thousand and fifteen thousand Nepali women and girls are trafficked to India and then sexually exploited each year. As we flew closer to the country, its famous breathtaking Himalayan mountain range, whose peaks skim the heavens, came clearly into view.

"Look, look," said the Nepali man seated between me and the window. "See?" he asked, pointing enthusiastically into the blue.

Parallel to our plane's path was a most spectacular view of the top quarter of the world's tallest mountain. Excited, I almost knocked the sweet lime drink from my mom's hand as I turned to show her my seatmate's discovery—Mount Everest. I reached into my purse for my camera, and little Flat Stanley came spilling out, along with the rest of my bag's contents. My Nepali neighbor reached down to help me sweep my goods back into my bag, and he grinned widely when he saw Stanley, asking, "Who this?"

Like many second graders around the United States, my daughter Cali Ann had read the book *Flat Stanley,* about a boy who is made flat, mailed to visit his friends far away, and then mailed back home from his adventure. Each student in her class was given their own Flat Stanley to mail out to a friend or family member far away. Stanley would then be mailed back and posted on the Bradford Primary hall map. Cali asked me to take her Flat Stanley along on my trip to India and Nepal. She wanted him to meet my friends, but I think Stanley was also sent to remind me of Cali while I was away. In India I had taken photos of Stanley dining, shopping, and wearing my lei of wilting marigolds from Conserve.

I handed Stanley to my new Nepali friend, and captured their meeting on my digital camera. I then took a dramatic photo of Mount Everest, with growing anticipation of getting on the ground. "Namaste," my neighbor warmly exclaimed with his hands folded in a prayer position. He handed Stanley back to me, and I carefully tucked him into his special pocket.

"Namaste," I replied for the first of many times.

Suddenly we were below the clouds and I could see green-tiered fields, square redbrick buildings with Asian rooftops, and a prominent white hill dotted in color looking at us with huge knowing eyes—it was not actually a hill at all but the famous Buddhist holy site Boudhanath Stupa, the holiest Tibetan Buddhist temple outside Tibet. The Stupa glowed white, and as the plane drew closer to the runway we could see the eyes of the Buddha, which were painted on all four sides, looking over the Kathmandu Valley. Colorful prayer flags were so plentiful that from above they looked like confetti floating all around the ever-staring eyes. Despite our knowledge of the country's current problems, I was overcome by a feeling of om, a deep peace that comes from being just where you are supposed to be in the world. Om is a Sanskrit word, used often as a chant in yoga and meditation. There is no exact definition for the word, but it is said to be a sacred exclamation at the beginning and end of a prayer or a mantra. In the quiet and civilized immigration line, I looked around at the stunning hand-carved poles and desks that made up the Tribhuvan International Airport, and out the windows at the city scenes set with a Himalayan Mountain backdrop, and could not help but feel Nepal was the sacred exclamation to our trip.

Just outside the airport doors, Chandra Kachhipati, executive director of Sana Hastakala, spotted us immediately even though we had never met. "Namaste," he greeted us, and loaded our bags into his small red hatchback. Then off we went through the Kathmandu streets to visit the Sana Hastakala shop and sewing center. The traffic in Kathmandu was manageable and much less stressful than the traffic in Delhi. We passed a man on a motorcycle driving with ten live chickens, five tied on each side for balance, hanging upside down from their feet and flapping around as he drove feverishly past us. Though we were in a large city, it felt calm and the pace more sedate than in bustling Delhi. Buildings were primarily rectangular multistory constructions, and the landscape surrounding the city was hilly and green. But the pollution seemed thicker here than in India. I knew from living in Colorado that sometimes the valley below the Rocky Mountains could become a pollution bowl that traps carbon emissions. The Himalayan Mountains had the same effect on the Kathmandu Valley, causing the excessive human-generated carbon emissions to hang over the city, especially in the evenings.

Pulling into a small drive opposite the Hotel Himalaya, a prominent landmark near Sana Hastakala's storefront and workshop, Chandra welcomed us inside the garden gate. My mom and I followed him through a small and brightly flowered garden courtyard, which led to a cement hallway and into Chandra's office. He removed his shoes at the doorway before entering, so my mom and I did the same. Sitting behind his desk, a young woman named Manjushree was typing at the computer but rose quickly to welcome us. "Namaste," she said, bowing.

"Namaste," I replied, starting to get the hang of this Nepali hello.

Over multiple cups of delicious chai (a warm, comforting mixture of assam tea, milk, and spices like cardamom), Chandra explained the history of Sana Hastakala and the artisans they work with. Founded in 1989 with seed money and technical support from UNICEF, Sana Hastakala had grown over the years into an independent and formidable fair-trade organization, advocating for the rights of the poor and providing incomes for over fifteen hundred artisans around the country. Sana Hastakala means "small handicrafts" in Nepali. Many of

Sana Hastakala's artisans were members of women's collectives located in very remote villages far from the Kathmandu Valley. The Sana Hastakala shop had opened both local and export markets the artisans could never have accessed on their own. Global Girlfriend began working with Sana Hastakala in 2005 and had found great success with several of their women's cooperatives, especially KABW. Bimala Rai, one of the bead artisans, had been working making beaded jewelry with KABW for eighteen years. She shared with me, "Before I joined KABW, I was totally unskilled and never had my own income. KABW provided me a platform to learn skills and become an earner to help support my family."

Bellies full of tea, we walked upstairs, above the office and the shop, to visit the women's sewing center. While many of the artisans Sana Hastakala supported were out in the villages, there was also a great need for employment in Kathmandu. Disabled women were some of the most discriminated against in the entire Nepali population. Sana Hastakala trained a group of disadvantaged women, two of them with severe hearing impairments and others with mild physical disabilities, to sew products and special orders in a nice open workshop above the storefront. Many of the projects involved innovative ways to use other artisans' hand-woven fabrics in new trendy products. For example, fabric made of allo (a natural fiber that grows in the high Himalayan regions of Nepal) was cut and sewn into handbags, slippers, apparel, and bags and accessories that were adorned with the rudraksh seed, which is associated with the heart chakra in Hindu spiritualism.

On the day of our visit, nine seamstresses were busy sewing tan fabric men's wallets with red trim. There was a blue message in Nepali screen printed on each wallet. Manjushree explained that the message was a warning against the dangers of

HIV/AIDS. A health organization would be distributing the wallets to Nepali truck drivers, along with condoms, to try to curb the spread of HIV/AIDS among long-haul truckers, who too often brought the disease back home to their wives.

I took a chance and grabbed Flat Stanley from my purse, then asked the women to gather together for a photo with him. They all giggled, and I asked Manjushree to explain to them about this little paper man, and how my daughter had sent him. I clicked their photo, then took one of Chandra and Manjushree posing with Stanley.

In addition to the women who worked in the in-house production unit, Sana Hastakala supported women artisans throughout the countryside, most of whom were able to work from their homes. In many cases, Sana Hastakala's support had made women the breadwinners in their families. Thirty-six-year-old Mina Kumari Maharjan was from a farming community. She worked in the field during the farming season with her husband, but it did not pay enough to meet the family's needs or send her sons to school. Mina started making felted items from local wool for pouches and bags I ordered for Global Girlfriend. Soon her income was better than her husband's and she was able to send both sons to school to get an education. "Mina Maharjan wanted you to know her sincere thankfulness for the great support in buying her felt handicrafts for Global Girlfriend," Manjushree told me as we walked to their store.

Downstairs, the shop was a treasure trove of new crafts to discover. Along the entry wall, soft, brightly colored pashmina stoles were stacked in cubicles next to sheets of handmade wrapping paper, journals, and cards. The far wall was covered in felted bags, rugs, pencil cases, and hats, with baskets of felt key chains and hair accessories lining the floor below. And the displays in the center of the shop held an abundance of beaded and silver jewelry, brass singing bowls, spiritual statues, woolen sweaters, and hand-painted Maitali arts. Maitali is the colorful Nepali painting women traditionally do on their houses in rural areas. The scenes depict women's work, like fetching water or cooking food, or are simple representations of animals like turtles and birds. Maitali artisans were now painting these cultural designs on small boxes, trays, and mirrors. Manjushree pointed out all of the crafts made by women's groups, which was almost everything but the metalwork and carvings. Chandra brought me sample after sample, while I photographed each piece and took notes on the artisans who had made it, noting descriptions and prices. When I asked Chandra for his view of fair trade, he said, "The essential part of running a fair-trade business is developing a better work culture, one where producers and marketers work together for mutual benefit, like a family. Then work becomes about more than money—it's about pride." I couldn't help but notice the word *family* in his description. In India, I had looked into the eyes of the little girls begging in the streets and pictured them as my daughters. Global Girlfriend could only become stronger if the company and our customers envisioned the women making our products as our sisters.

As the sun set outside, and the lighting grew dim in the shop, Chandra said we needed to leave for Kiran and Gita Khadgi's house before it grew too dark. My mom and I each paid in Nepali rupees for the load of products neither of us felt we could live without. I had selected a generous amount of samples for Mary-Mike and me to comb through back at home, but I also bought gifts for my family, my friends, and myself. Sana Hastakala's crafts were rich and detailed. Ikat scarves, felted bags, warm knitwear, hand-beaded jewelry, handmade paper, and pashmina stoles were just too beautiful to pass up. Back in Chandra's hatchback, we couldn't stop talking about all of the talented artisans he had collected. Embarrassed by our gushing, he started to point out sites as we left Kathmandu to travel three miles, into the ancient city of Patan.

Patan is one of the three royal cities of the Kathmandu Valley. Kathmandu, Bhaktapur, and Patan all have ancient royal palaces and grand temples. Situated along the southern banks of the Bagmati River, Patan was a colorful landscape of brick buildings intermingled with abundant fields growing local vegetables like cauliflower, peas, cabbage, and eggplant. In Patan, also known as Lalitpur or "the beautiful city," Hindu temples and Buddhist monuments with guardian deities and ornate carvings were set inside of the four Ashoka Stupas that marked the corners of the Patan district. The four Buddhist Stupas were said to have been erected in 250 B.C. by the Buddhist emperor of India, Ashoka.

As we wound deeper into the oldest parts of the city, the buildings seemed to close in as the street became more and more narrow. Many people were closing up their shops for the day. At the base of each brick building was a set of old wooden or metal doors painted in bright, and often chipping, colors like turquoise, green, and salmon pink. There were food shops, vegetable stands, small drugstore-type stalls, and tailoring shops. My favorite was the butcher shop, where a man with a low table displayed a singed leg of something with the skin removed but the hoof still attached. Two-way traffic gave way to a one-car lane. Luckily, most of the other motorized transportation was motorcycles, so they could slip by us easily in the slim spaces (only about 5 percent of the population in Nepal owns cars). When we did finally meet up with another car, the other driver had to back up until we both reached a wide enough place in the road for us each to pass.

When we pulled up at Kiran and Gita's home, the sounds of jubilant wedding celebrants spilled out of their doors and windows. The 6:00 A.M. wedding had happened, and almost thirteen hours later, the guests were still enjoying the party. Chandra opened the front door knowing that there was no need to knock, and that even if we did the chance of being heard was slim. Piles of shoes filled the front entryway rug, and we stepped gingerly between pairs, trying not to trip. We set our bags on the cool hard stone floor, slipped off our own shoes, and walked toward the commotion in the living room. Laughter and revelry turned to enthusiastic greetings from the crowd, some of whom were gathering their coats and saying their good-byes just as we were saying our hellos.

"Namaste," Kiran said. He bowed and then shook my hand. "Namaste," I replied as he then proceeded to introduce my mom and me to a dizzying lineup of wedding guests.

No matter your faith, it's impossible not to feel the divine interceding when every man, woman, and child greets you with prayer hands, a bow, and the word *namaste*. More than a Nepali hello, namaste means (loosely translated), "The divine light of God that lives inside of me sees and acknowledges the divine light of God that lives inside of you." I couldn't help but think that maybe if we in the United States spent more time greeting people with such a powerful statement, we might spend more time actually looking for the light in others. The light of my Nepali friends shone brightly, making it easy to see the best in each of them.

As the party crowd cleared out, the room, once warm with bodies, cooled quickly in the winter chill. Upon first inspection, the Khadgi family home seemed large, until I learned just how many people lived in the house—at the moment, twelve family members plus multiple others occupied eight rooms. The number grew and shrank depending on who needed a place to stay. Kiran led me over to a sofa where an older gentleman sat wearing a tall round felt hat, one similar to what the Shriners wear while driving their funny go-carts in Fourth of July parades. "This is my father, Mr. Siddhi Bahadur Khadgi, founder of Kumbeshwar Technical School."

Kiran's father was truly a visionary in his community. For many years he had owned a successful organic fertilizer business in Patan. The fertilizer came from grinding up animal skeletons after the animal had been butchered for food, and turning those bones to meal, which could be fed to chickens or sprinkled on fields to yield a more hardy crop. Every day, Mr. Khadgi rose early in the morning to drive his truck throughout the Kathmandu Valley to make pickups from the local butchers, farmers, and families. Because he started his workday so early, he often saw the very poor street sweepers out finishing their work before the rest of the town stirred. Most street sweepers were of the very lowest, Pode, caste in Nepal—Nepal's own "untouchables." While they were called street sweepers, that was just a euphemism. They were actually expected to clear the sewers of human waste. In return for a hard night's work doing the community's dirtiest job, the sweepers received leftover food from houses around which they cleaned. They barely had clothes, and were often sick due to the poor-quality and unhygienic food they ate and the squalid shacks they shared with livestock. And while Patan had a freshwater spring tap from which citizens could gather safe drinking water, people from the Pode caste were not allowed at the tap. Recognizing that the members of the Pode caste were valuable people in their own right, Mr. Khadgi could not bear to sit by any longer while his neighbors suffered. He no longer wanted to pretend that their suffering didn't exist. It seemed to me that when Mr. Khadgi started helping the poor in his community, he began truly living namaste—seeing and acknowledging the light in people the rest of the community had chosen not to see.

He started helping by simply accompanying a few street sweepers to the springwater tap, breaking the taboo and allowing them to drink freely. This action was met with great animosity, but Mr. Khadgi stood his ground and continued to invite the sweepers to drink. Eventually, the community taboo was broken, and the street sweepers were able to get water like others in the community. Then Mr. Khadgi opened a small day-care center in his home for the sweepers' children. The day care eventually grew into a primary school, with local women teachers. Finally, knowing that the women and men of the Pode caste needed real employment opportunities, Mr. Khadgi started a vocational school teaching knitting to women and carpentry to men. To accommodate all of his students, he built onto the back of his family home. What started as a simple kind gesture had grown into a highly respected NGO providing free primary education for over 250 children; vocational training in knitting, carpet weaving, jewelry making, and carpentry; an orphanage caring for twenty orphaned children; and a production business where people could find sustainable employment.

After we had a long visit with Kiran and his father, Kiran's daughter Sanita showed us to our bedroom. Having noticed that my mom had been shivering in the living room, Sanita delivered an electric space heater to our door. "This will help you stay warmer while you sleep," she offered, and then said good night. We happily plugged in the heater and crawled into bed, only emerging to unplug the heater, which vacillated between humming loudly and glowing brightly. We slept soundly and cozily under thick comforters stuffed with recycled fabric.

The next morning, we rose early and walked with Sanita to the "old house," the former family home, which Kumbeshwar Technical School (KTS) had taken over. As the organization grew, the family gave up more rooms to the knitwear production, school, and carpentry training. Eventually the family built a new house for sleeping, but many of the family and staff meals were still cooked by Gita and shared at the old house, which was now the school. Sanita gave us a tour of the classrooms, the day care, and the many production units where women were making the products Kumbeshwar sold. The number of women who touched one sweater, the item Global Girlfriend had been buying from KTS, struck me. I had decided to add knitwear from KTS soon after I designed our first simple organic apparel pieces made by Assisi Garments. I wanted to take Global Girlfriend into women's clothing because it is something that American women purchase every season. I loved telling customers, "You can change a life by simply changing your clothes." In the case of KTS knitwear, each sweater actually touched several women's lives. First a spinner spun raw wool into yarn, and then the yarn was dyed in a large copper pot that sat in an outside courtyard. The woman dyeing the yarn sat above the heated dye vat, spinning a wheel that kept a large skein of yarn moving through the dye for an even color. The dyed yarn was hung out to dry in the sun on rows of laundry lines. Once dry, the skeins were wound into balls by six women sitting with yarn winders on the KTS rooftop. Finally, the yarn balls ended up in the knitting room, where several women knelt on cushions knitting over two-foot-high worktables.

I tried to forget my fear of heights as we climbed the metal ladder to reach the women on the roof. We were greeted warmly by the group, and given an empty table to use as a chair. Sanita and Rina Bajracharya, the knitwear production coordinator, pulled out sweater after sweater to show me. After some prompting from the group, I became a model for the day, trying on each style and spinning from woman to woman for their reaction. All of the women in the knitting room had gone through the school's free knitting classes, which were open to all women in the community whether they wanted to work for KTS or just learn to knit for their own families. Some women preferred to work from their homes, where they could be with their children and attend to their housework, knitting when they had extra time. The women who worked in the knitting room did both knitting and quality control for the home-based knitters.

Rina had started with KTS as a home-based knitter right out of high school but slowly grew into a respected leader among the women and was promoted to a management position. After working at KTS for some time, she was wed in an arranged marriage and had two children, a son and a daughter. After taking some time off when her children were first born, Rina went back to her knitting work, which made her mother-in-law very angry. Her mother-in-law did not feel women should work at anything other than caring for their family. Both Rina and her husband came from poor and traditional tribal Newar carpentry families, in which only the men worked. But both families had struggled to meet their basic needs. Rina wanted to contribute to a better life for her children, and her husband supported her work at KTS. Typically, once a woman is married, her mother-in-law directs her new daughter-in-law's work in the home. Rina was breaking tradition by working at KTS, but over time her in-laws saw the impact of her earnings on the whole family. Eventually, Rina won over her in-laws by providing well for them, and even got her mother-in-law and sister-in-law to join a knitting training class. They loved it and began knitting at home for extra income.

Unlike the majority of knitters at KTS, Rina was lucky to have a supportive spouse. Many of the women were single mothers or in abusive marriages. Sharashwoti Shakya, the knit-wear production assistant, was born in the village of Lubhu. Her family arranged a marriage for her with a divorced man in Patan so she could move to the city. Her husband was a carpenter who drank too much. She had to care for him, her three children, a stepdaughter, and her mother-in-law. The family was living hand to mouth when Sharashwoti learned knitting from her friends, and one of those friends introduced her to KTS. She joined KTS knitting at home, and after her husband died, she was fully responsible for her family's livelihood. Sharashwoti was a hard worker and soon became a valuable staff member whom KTS relied on to train other women.

At one o'clock each afternoon everyone broke for lunch. Gita spent most of her day cooking. She served breakfast, lunch, and dinner to at least fifteen people every day. At lunchtime, some of the KTS staff joined the family for a midday meal. I counted over twenty people at each of Gita's spectacular lunches; meals that seemed to me would take the effort I associate with a family Thanksgiving feast. But Gita seemed to cook and serve her guests with ease, and enjoyed nothing better than dishing up second helpings and hearing the rave reviews of her satisfied diners. Gita reminded me of my great-grandmother Elizabeth, who had made noon meals for the staff of my family's business when I was very young. Before I was school age, I remember my mom taking me to Grandma Elizabeth's house when the town's noon whistle blew. Grandpa Clark, Grandma Irene, Uncle Gale, Aunt Christine, and my dad would meet us there for a home-cooked pot roast or chicken dinner that most women today would only consider cooking on Sundays. I saw my great-grandma's same love of caring for her family with meals in Gita.

I also had some of the best laughs of the trip eating at the Khadgi kitchen table. The first night we ate dinner with them, Gita made roasted chicken to accompany her traditional lentils, rice, and vegetables. "No chicken for me," my mom said, nodding off the looming serving spoon in Gita's hand. "I'll have the vegetarian like Stacey."

Kiran looked up from his plate, laughing even before he delivered his punch line: "Diane, you scared of that avian flu?" Everyone cracked up. My mom was indeed scared of the bird flu circulating in southeast Asia at the time of our trip, but she took a piece of chicken anyway to prove Kiran wrong.

Then there was the evening Gita made rice noodles in broth for supper. One of the two old "aunties" who lived with them sat directly across from me, struggling with her soup. She had a personality that couldn't keep her from smiling, despite the fact that she was missing her top two front teeth and three teeth directly below on the bottom. Each time she slurped in a spoonful of slippery noodles, a few slid out through the gap where her teeth had once been. Everyone laughed along with her as she playfully made a game of her eating challenges. The Khadgi family had embraced me like a long-lost cousin who'd finally come home, but I saw that this was the way they enveloped everyone who crossed their path. This didn't seem to be unique to the Khadgis either. Everyone we'd met in Nepal had welcomed us into their offices, homes, and lives like extended family. It was hard to believe there had been any unrest in this country that was one of the most charming and welcoming places I'd ever been. It was even more unbelievable to me that one man's decision to help a poor neighbor get a simple drink of water had evolved into a social business employing 1,756 women in knitwear production in the Kumbeshwar facility and in homes throughout the Kathmandu Valley. Mr. Khadgi was a prime example of one person's small action making a huge difference, and of passing that principle down to two generations of his own family, who were now committed to carrying on the work he started.

While our time with the women and staff of KTS was heart-warming, we quickly became used to the bone-chilling cold in the KTS cement-block office, always remembering to wear mittens and thick socks. Very early each morning, before the workday started, Sanita took us to visit temples and sights. Kiran went with us the day we visited Durbar Square in Kathmandu, because he felt we needed his protection. Due to the recent rioting, armed guards stood behind sandbag barricades around the square, ready to take on protesters. Kiran scolded me when I naively snapped a photo of one of them. He warned that I'd lose my camera to the Nepali army, but fortunately the guard I photographed either did not notice or did not mind.

Before the trip I had given Sanita a list of other groups I wanted to visit while in Nepal. She had acted as my social secretary, scheduling every meeting, while her dad took the time to drive us to them. I was especially excited to meet with the staff of the General Welfare Prathisthan (GWP), an organization I had been buying from for about a year.

At our second annual International Women's Day event back home, almost a year before the trip, I decided we should focus the program on the horrific crime of human trafficking. With growing momentum from our inaugural IWD event, several additional organizations helped to sponsor the day. The White House Project and the Rocky Mountain Riveters, in particular, helped me rent out Denver's Oriental Theater and buy the rights to show the Andrew Levine documentary *The Day My God*

*Died,* and we marketed the evening as "a unique event providing global insight with local reach." Again, over two hundred women attended, but this time the feeling was different from the general celebratory atmosphere of the previous year's IWD event. The film profiled several young Nepali women tricked by traffickers and sold into prostitution. Anita was sold at age twelve, Sita at age fifteen, and Gina was only seven when she was sold and raped by fourteen men on her first day at the brothel. The stories shocked the audience, even though they knew the topic of the film in advance. Women left the theater crying, and those who stayed sat sobbing. Obviously, no one felt like shopping or eating cheesecake after the film. Women had loved last year's topic of peace, but the horrors of trafficking were almost too hard to process.

The U.S. State Department estimates that worldwide as many as 1 million children are forced into sexual slavery each year, and up to two thirds of them become infected with HIV/AIDS. Some girls are sold for less than $100 U.S., according to Human Rights Watch. I felt like no matter how hard the subject, the crime was too horrible not to know about. The NGO profiled in the documentary, Maiti Nepal, does amazing work to rescue girls from their captors, and to bring traffickers to justice. I loved Maiti's founder Anuradha Koirala's words: "First you have to learn to take them as your own child. Then you will feel the sorrow, and then the strength comes out from you to protect them."

What came out of our second International Women's Day event for me was a meeting with two women who had dedicated their lives to the cause. Modern-day abolitionists Sarah Symons and Kenlyn Kolleen both run U.S. nonprofit organizations that raise money for anti-trafficking initiatives in Nepal. Sarah founded The Emancipation Network in Massachusetts after seeing *The Day My God Died* at a film festival, and we met by phone through the film's director, Andrew Levine. Kenlyn lived right up the road from me in Boulder, Colorado, and ran Free A Child, a project empowering young women to stand up against traffickers in rural Nepali villages. Free A Child ran its education program through a larger Nepali NGO—General Welfare Prathisthan. She knew that GWP wanted to expand their income-generation program for girls who had been rescued from brothels, and for those who were at greatest risk of being the victims of traffickers. Kenlyn thought Global Girlfriend would be the perfect partner. Our International Women's Day event proved to me you could never stop learning. I had set out to educate others about girls in Nepal, but learned more from Kenlyn and Sarah about trafficking than I had known myself.

We would not have time to travel six hours outside of Kathmandu to visit the young women's crafting center, but I was happy to get to visit the GWP office, learn about their many programs for people in poverty, and meet some of the staff. I had been importing their handmade paper products since meeting Kenlyn, and I wanted to learn firsthand how they felt the income-generation project was progressing.

We were welcomed with a customary cup of warm chai, and we settled in to listen to the staff's specially prepared presentation. They shared that in Nepal, between seven thousand and ten thousand children ages seven to seventeen are tricked or bought or kidnapped from their families to work as sex slaves in brothels in India. Thousands more are trafficked into domestic servitude, factory work, and other forced labor. Most of these children come from poor families in rural areas and have little or no formal education. Through their partnership with Free A Child, the GWP staff had provided outreach programs to over 7,000 people, and skills training and income-generation projects to over 350 young women. They were very happy with our orders and our support of these girls. The paper-making project we were working with was small, serving only twelve to fifteen young women. Other income-generation projects GWP was running were aimed at meeting needs in the local economy through projects like sewing local apparel, ginger farming, raising goats, and poultry farming. The paper project was helping some of the most rural women, and they were quickly becoming prolific in their production. Global Girlfriend customers were drawn to the brightly colored journals and note cards these women were producing, and as with Freeset bags in India, I felt like each purchase punctuated these young women's emancipation from forced sex slavery.

When it was time to leave, the entire staff of about twenty rushed out the door of the meeting room without one of them saying good-bye. This did not seem like the typical Nepali hospitality we had grown to love. Mahesh Bhattarai, GWP's director, talked to us a while longer and then said, "Please come; we have a small surprise waiting for you downstairs." When we walked down the stairs and out to the street, a large red ribbon was draped across the doorway of a small shop.

"This is the new shop of Girl's Friend Nepal," Mahesh announced proudly. "Named for Global Girlfriend, friend to our girls in need."

He presented me with a large pair of scissors and motioned that should I cut the ribbon to open the store. "Here we will carry the women's beautiful handwork and also give free condoms to anyone who needs them."

I was overwhelmed by the gesture. Inside the small ten-by-ten-foot storefront, freshly painted white shelves were filled with brightly colored journals, note cards, and paper lanterns.

The women's work was stunning, and their storefront a huge accomplishment. I was so proud. Kiran had to practically drag me away when it was time to leave—I could not stop admiring their work and taking countless photos. I only hoped that we could honor their cause the way they had honored mine by building them a larger market and drawing awareness to the plight of these world daughters.

Kiran, trying to keep us on schedule and feed us before dropping us at the airport, encouraged us to say good-bye to the people at GWP. My mom and I were not very hungry, but we realized how important it was to share meals in Nepal. We would have one more meal with Kiran before flying home, and he wanted it to be special. Unlike the rest of our meals in Nepal, our last was eaten at Mike's Restaurant instead of in Gita's kitchen. Mike's sat directly across from the fences that secured King Gyanendra's palace in central Kathmandu. Most of the tables, topped with blue-and-white-checkered tablecloths, were in an open courtyard. Kiran usually liked to eat outside when he dined there, but it was cold this January morning and he picked a table inside. Thinking "Mike's" was a funny name for a restaurant in Kathmandu, I asked the waitress who Mike was. "Mike from Minnesota," she answered, smiling. According to our waitress, Mike had been a Peace Corps volunteer who just could not bear to leave Nepal when his two-year placement ended. While I missed my family and was happy we would be heading home that afternoon, I understood why Mike would choose to stay in Nepal. I wanted to be able to bring just a bit of this family feeling back home to my customers and my friends. If Global Girlfriends could see themselves in this family, at the dinner table, with Kiran and Gita, with Sanita, Chandra, Sharashwoti, Bimala, Mina, and all the other women of Nepal, that might just change the world. You can let harm come to strangers, but you will protect your family at all costs. The women of Nepal were now sisters and daughters in my family and I would do whatever was in my power to protect them from sexual slavery, abuse, and poverty. Back at home I would ask our Global Girlfriends, our loyal customers, to do the same. Leaving to go home to my family, I knew I would always have a home and a family to return to in Nepal.

# 6

# BELIEVE

❦

*There are only two ways to live your life.
One is as though nothing is a miracle. The other
is as though everything is a miracle.*
—ALBERT EINSTEIN

A graceful slender woman with a Scottish accent approached me with tears in her eyes. Mary-Mike followed close at her heals, clutching the new sample of the newsprint Anarkali hand-bag from Conserve. My heart warmed thinking that my talk about our work must have touched this woman. I had been asked to be one of three keynote speakers for the RE/MAX International Corporate Women's Day event and had just come off the stage. I had asked the crowd to circulate samples of jewelry and handbags while I spoke. It seemed the purse in Mary-Mike's hand had spoken to this woman.

"I have to have that bag," she pleaded.

"Oh, I am so thrilled you like it." I was always gleeful when someone loved one of the women's items. "But this is our only sample, and our shipment won't arrive for a couple of weeks. I can take your number and call you as soon as the shipment comes in if you'd like."

Now the tears began to gently roll down her otherwise

flawless face. "I was so moved when I saw your photos of the women in India. My husband was in the oil and gas industry and worked in India. He had such a great love for the people."

I thought I understood, but then she elaborated, "My husband was killed in a motor vehicle accident in India several years ago now. He was so big and sweet, I called him my Santa. Today, April 19, is the anniversary of his death." Now Mary-Mike and I had tears in our eyes. She continued, "So when I saw this picture of Santa Claus on this bag from India, on this day, I could feel him right here, as though he sent you to me." Sure enough, upon closer inspection I saw that the top corner of the bag had a small Santa peeking out from amid all the Hindi script from the daily *Hindi Times* that had been heat processed into the plastic fabric of the handbag. I had never seen Santa on a Hindu paper before and never have since.

"It's yours," Mary-Mike and I said almost in unison. Obviously this connection was larger than any reason we would need to keep this sample, and we were honored to feel like Santa's very own elves as we handed over the bag. This encounter proved to me, once again, that the connection we all have to one another is amazingly powerful and that nothing happens in the universe by chance.

In fact, the universe had brought many unexpected gifts to my business and to me. Ming Tan was the first in a series of random Friday phone calls I like to call the "Freaky Friday" calls. Ming, the executive director of the Como Foundation, which was founded by the owners of the luxury Como Hotels and Resorts chain, called to give me some money. Ming had found me through a colleague in her office who had traveled with Ruthanne, Mary-Mike's sister-in-law, to France. She wanted to give Global Girlfriend a grant because the Como Foundation's mission was to fund grassroots organizations that work to improve the lives of women and girls. I was almost sick to my stomach as I explained that we were a for-profit company (a position I have advocated for passionately in fair trade) and therefore unable to accept charitable grants. While I believed strongly in using a business model to support women in building their own businesses, the offer of free funding versus tapping my personal savings was very appealing. Ming, a great listener, hesitated only a moment before asking, "If we can't help you financially, then what else can we do for you?" I sat silent trying to think, not wanting to pass up her offer.

"I see you have a basic clothing line," Ming said. "Who does your fit work?"

I guess I did the fit work, with the help of my tiny Indian seamstresses. Me, a woman who could not sew and had never taken a design class, was doing both the design work and the fit work. So the fit work was really not too good. In our first tops, the armpits sagged while the bellies were unflatteringly snug unless you were a fifteen-year-old. Everything was sized small, for littler people than American women, but I thought we could improve this over time.

Ming mentioned that Como happened to own a majority share in Armani Exchange in New York and she was based out of their offices. "We could do a pro bono round of fit work on your next season of apparel if you'd like," Ming said casually, as if she had just asked if I wanted a soda instead of a miracle.

"Yes!" was all I could say.

Armani Exchange did a full round of technical fit work on a perfect-size-eight woman. Two skirts, two dresses, two tops, and yoga pants were trimmed, taped, cut, pinned, and marked in black Sharpie marker until the fit team was satisfied. Then drawings and measurement charts were constructed for each product, along with before and after photos of the clothes on the fit model. Detailed alteration instructions were computer generated by the Armani Exchange fit team and then sent on to our apparel group Assisi in India. The Armani team's generous knowledge-sharing helped dramatically change the fit of our clothing. The artisans benefited from learning how a large global company like Armani Exchange does their fit work and measurements. With better-fitting clothing, we sold more—growing our apparel orders for the group from $5,000, to $18,000, to eventually over $100,000, helping us provide more jobs and have a larger impact on the women of Assisi.

On another early Friday morning I got a call from Heather Alexander at *Organic Style* magazine. As I waited for her to ask me to buy advertising space, Heather said, "You were nominated by your friend Mary-Michael Simpson for our Women With Organic Style contest and have been chosen as the winner of the Aveeno Woman With Organic Style award." I know there was a long and awkward pause on my end of the phone as I tried to process Heather's message. She continued, "We would like to fly both you and Mary-Michael to New York in two weeks for our awards ceremony at Jazz at Lincoln Center. The evening will begin with a cocktail hour, followed by the ceremony, where you will receive the award, ending with dessert and a performance by Alison Krauss. In other words, it will be a late night." After one more pause, Heather asked, "Can you come?"

Her words snapped me back into reality and I quickly answered yes and gushed with excitement and disbelief. After talking through a few more details like flights and hotels, Heather added, "I personally admire what you're doing. Giving blesses not just the recipients but you as well. I can't wait to meet you in person." With that we hung up, and I frantically dialed next door to Mary-Mike's house.

Overflowing with gratitude for her nomination, I shared the news of our impending, fully paid adventure to New York. Mary-Mike started laughing and said, "April Fool's!" My heart sunk. I hadn't realized it was in fact April 1, April Fool's day. Was the joke on me? "April Fool's, right?" This time she said it not as a statement, but as a question. At times the ultimate skeptic, she was sure I was playing an April Fool's joke on *her*. When it was clear that this was no joke, she began screaming so loudly I could hear her not just through the phone, but through the walls of our houses.

Our evening in New York at Lincoln Center was like a page from a fairy tale. Dressed in formal wear, we hobnobbed with *Organic Style* editor Jeanie Pyun and publisher Maria Rodale. We posed for photos with celebrities including Rosanna Arquette and Alison Krauss to the clicks and flashes of a mob of media photographers. Once inside the intimate theater setting we watched Helen Hunt and Jerry Seinfeld's wife, Jessica, receive awards; Helen for her work with Heal the Bay, a California effort to clean up polluted coastal waters, and Jessica for her nonprofit Baby Buggy, which collects and recycles used baby goods for New York mothers in need. Other winners included Ann Withey, creator of Annie's Homegrown organic foods (makers of my kids' favorite bunny-shaped mac and cheese); Fran Pavley, a California assemblywoman fighting for clean air; Zana Briski, director of the Academy Award–winning documentary *Born Into Brothels* and founder of the nonprofit Kids with Cameras; Stella McCartney, for her line of socially conscious couture fashion; and my social work idol, Marian Wright Edelman, founder and president of the Children's Defense Fund, who spent a lifetime pursuing justice for every child.

Hard ladies to follow. But when it was my turn onstage, I no longer felt nervous. Even looking out at Jerry Seinfeld sitting in the second row directly in front of me wearing his timeless Seinfeld grin, all I could think of was the women who made the products Global Girlfriend sold. I told the audience that this award was an unexpected honor that I was accepting on behalf of the tenacious women I work with. I was just a woman with a basement full of plastic bins. The women fighting for opportunities for a better life for themselves and their children, no matter the harshness of their circumstances, were the real women with organic style.

As the saying goes, blessings beget more blessings. As a result of the *Organic Style* awards, three Colorado publications decided to feature stories about Global Girlfriend. My local newspaper, *The Columbine Courier,* ran a nice article titled, "You Go, Global Girlfriend!" Then *Colorado Expression* printed a story in their enterprise section, "One Local Woman Makes Life Better for Many Women Around the World." Finally, Denver's premier city magazine, *5280,* did an article called simply, "Fair Trade Fashion."

The week after *5280* hit the newsstands I got another call, on a Friday. Allison Trembly was the marketing director at the new Belmar Whole Foods in Lakewood, Colorado. She had read the story on Global Girlfriend straight from her magazine rack in the store and wanted to know why we weren't selling to Whole Foods. "Um, because we have never sold wholesale, I guess," I stammered before recovering. "But we want to sell to Whole Foods! How do we do that?" For no reason at all, other than that she is a wonderful person, Allison took me under her wing and stewarded me through the process of getting our products approved for Whole Foods.

Whole Foods is a wonderful company to work with. Founded in 1978 by then twenty-five-year-old John Mackey, a college dropout, and twenty-one-year-old Renee Lawson Hardy, the original store was a small vegetarian grocery store called Safer Way. John lived above the store until he was kicked out of his apartment for storing food there, and then lived for a while in the store itself. In 1980 two more partners came on board and the foursome renamed their blossoming Austin, Texas, organics business Whole Foods Market. Whole Foods has grown to be the leader in organics, with over 270 stores nationwide and in the UK.

It was a lengthy process getting Global Girlfriend items into Whole Foods; it took almost six months before any clothing or handbags actually hit the shelves. I needed UPC bar codes, cost files, and more sophisticated story tags for the products. We included a hangtag on every one of our products that told the customer exactly who made the product they were purchasing and why buying Global Girlfriend products made a difference for women worldwide. Most important to Whole Foods was their lengthy vetting process, during which we shared as much information as we could about the women we work with and how we were helping their livelihood. Because the Belmar store was most interested in carrying our line of organic cotton women's apparel (now with a professional Armani Exchange fit!), I had to get all of our proper organic certifications in line. Luckily, our partners at Assisi Garments had gone through the SKAL certification process (now called GOTS certification— the Global Organic Textile Standard), and all I had to do was get copies of their organic certification. I also registered Global Girlfriend apparel with the U.S.-based Organic Trade Association. Once we were approved in the system, Allison introduced me to the store's apparel buyer, Natasha Calvert, and we were a go. Belmar Whole Foods launched our products with an in-store fashion show and a large display in May 2006. Again, my girlfriends filled the room, turning out to see what they had helped to build with their grassroots support. What had started as one big home party for friends and friends of friends was now debuting at a major national chain. Global Girlfriend was working with a solid twenty-five women's organizations around the world and directly impacting the lives of close to thirty-five hundred women artisans. A $2,000 tax refund had—in three years—turned into over $250,000 in sales of women-made, fair-trade goods. Partnering with Whole Foods would soon double those numbers.

This isn't to say that things with Global Girlfriend always went smoothly. Importing was my greatest challenge. Shipments came in wrong, and I struggled with how to teach the women what I expected from them. There was always a delicate balance between helping and business expectations. While my only reason to be in this business was to help women expand their market, thereby expanding their income and opportunities, to do that, the women needed to learn what the market would tolerate in terms of styles and quality. It was hard, with many groups, to explain why the product ordered couldn't vary in color and size. Or why if I ordered a hundred black and white bags, twenty of the ones they shipped could not be pink and blue. Most of these women had been selling in their local market, where every customer was different and didn't mind variation. It was fine to allow some variation early on when I was doing home parties and women thought a little imperfection was quaint, but once we were selling to larger retail partners and online, the expectation of our customers was that all like products would actually be alike.

I also struggled to communicate the right shipping, labeling, and documenting procedures to my artisan partners. This was not their fault; I didn't always know what to tell them to do when it came to U.S. Customs. On my first shipment from

Conserve I received a marking notice from U.S. Customs because each bag did not have a label sewn inside that read "Made in India." Not knowing the country-of-origin tag was required on all products, and naive as to what it meant to get a marking notice, I almost had another anxiety attack when the stern customs officer threatened to burn my shipment due to lack of origin tags. Customs gave me a one-time-only extension of three days to mark each bag myself, warning that future unmarked shipments would be burned. Another time, some handbags arrived covered in cockroaches, which I discovered only after ripping into two boxes in my living room. Home fumigation had not been written into the Global Girlfriend budget.

Sometimes I would drive an hour out to the airport to pick up a new shipment to find that it barely fit in the back of my minivan, even with all but the front seat pulled out. After the first few times this happened I should have hired a trucking company to deliver the goods when they arrived, but I was too cheap and didn't mind hauling the load myself. One time, though, I really couldn't squeeze the boxes into my minivan. I convinced the woman at the cargo bay what a good cause she would be supporting, and she helped me open boxes and load things into the van without the excess packaging (I also convinced her to keep the boxes at the dock). With hardly a line of sight out of any window but the front windshield, I drove away overstuffed but triumphant at having saved $250 in trucking costs.

On one cargo run to the airport I answered my cell phone to find the voice of a very angry man on the line. "What is Global Girlfriend?" he practically screamed at me, then cutting me off before I could begin to answer. "I have never, ever used your services but have a charge on my credit-card bill from Global Girlfriend."

"Are you married?" I asked calmly.

"Yes, and my wife—" he began, but this time I cut him off.

"We sell purses and jewelry made by low-income women worldwide, sir. Could your wife have purchased a handbag from our online store?"

"Oh," he said, still annoyed but breathing an audible sigh of relief. "Yes, I'm sure she did just that." And without another word, he hung up.

And then there was the time we had a mysterious early-morning 911 phone call from inside our brand-new office. With the growth of the business, which included a three-day-a-week work commitment from Mary-Mike and the addition of two friends, Kathy and Jeanine, to staff customer service and order packing, we needed more space than my half basement provided. I rented the main floor of an old Victorian-style home in Old Downtown Littleton, with a real phone system, our own phone number, desks, shelves, and a fax machine. We were all feeling pretty grown-up in our new space until the freaky phone call.

One morning around 7:15 A.M., I got a call at my home from an officer at the Littleton Police Department. "Ma'am, there has been a 911 call from inside your office. Are all of your employees accounted for?"

They were. No one was at the office. I told the officer that a woman named Glenda lived in the apartment above our office, and he should check to be sure it wasn't her who was in distress. "I'm calling you from inside Glenda's apartment, ma'am," he replied.

I was stumped, but also a bit scared. With Brad already headed to work, I dropped my kids at Mary-Mike's, grabbed her husband, Greg, for support, and zoomed to the office to meet the police. We all stepped lightly inside as two officers slowly looked in and around every doorway and closet and behind every desk and shelf. The space was not that big, so it didn't take long. All clear, was the verdict. A bit shaken but relieved, I walked out onto the front sidewalk and was chatting with the officers when one said, "So what do you really do at Global Girlfriend, anyway?"

This was a weird question from a man who had just looked through all my clothing and purse bins and around my UPS boxes and searched my desks. "We sell all the stuff you just saw— fair-trade women's accessories and clothing made by women's cooperatives in developing countries," I answered.

"Oh, I saw that," he said. "I thought you might be importing something more like Ukrainian brides or girlfriends." He chuckled in a half questioning way. I assured him that we just had girly purses, not girls. We were adamantly against sex trafficking. After the police left, Greg wondered out loud if there had ever been a 911 call at all, or if this was just the police looking into the legitimacy of a business with the name Global Girlfriend.

Sometimes it was hard to tell what was a lucky break and what might not be. Allison and Natasha, pleased with how well our things had sold in their Whole Foods store, set up a dinner meeting for me with Kathy Oglebay from the Whole Foods national office. Kathy agreed to meet us at Boulder's unique Dushanbe Tea House for dinner. Jeanine and I drove up to Boulder on a cold November night and walked into the Tea House to find Kathy, Allison, Natasha, and another Whole Foods regional buyer named Wendy already seated. After a round of introductions, Allison explained how she had found Global Girlfriend and gave Kathy some history on how the line had been performing in their store for the past seven months.

"We already have a fair-trade brand, World of Good," Kathy said abruptly and changed the subject.

I felt like I had been punched in the gut. Here we were buying dinner and she wasn't even open to *considering* Global Girlfriend for other Whole Foods stores? I remembered the first time I heard of World of Good. I was working a booth at the 2004 Sustainable Resources Conference at the University of Colorado in Boulder when a woman told me about a friend of hers named Priya Haji in Berkeley, California, who had an idea similar to mine to work with not just one fair-trade group but many around the world. In early 2003 when I started Global Girlfriend I knew of fewer than fifty small fair-trade businesses importing from developing countries. Almost all of these companies were working with a single group or at least a single country, and most had been founded after a trip to that country or service in the Peace Corps or as religious missionaries. Ten Thousand Villages and SERRV were the only larger groups I knew of that were combining products from all over the world. Priya wanted to bring fair trade into the mainstream markets, just as I was working to do, by pooling the crafts of disadvantaged artisans under a new, hip brand. Aside from the fact that she was working with both men and women, and that I had started a couple of years before her, the main distinction between our two companies was that Priya wasn't funding her new venture on her credit cards like I was. As an MBA student at the Haas School of Business at Berkeley, Priya had won a business-plan contest and secured venture funding to start her enterprise. She e-mailed me early on when she was a student forming her idea to inquire about my business. I always enjoyed other women's interest in Global Girlfriend, but I didn't think much of it at the time—until the World of Good brand was popping up around me like dandelions in an unkempt yard. My competitive ego was reeling, while the voice of my Zen inner social worker reminded me (using a cute childhood tune), "That's what it's all about."

Business may be about competing and gaining market share, but fair trade is about making people's lives better. Surely there was room for many business-minded do-gooders in the industry. And space for their products on the shelves at Whole Foods.

After eating and making small talk, Jeanine saved the day by asking, "Stacey, didn't you bring photos of your trip to India and Nepal?"

"I did," I exclaimed, trying not to dump my food in my lap or spill Kathy's drink as I shoved my MacBook between our plates and opened my iPhoto library.

Kathy was moved by the pictures. I flipped photos and told stories about the groups, and pretty soon she asked to see our catalog, then our prices, and then she turned back to Allison for that sales information one more time. With my mojo back, I finished the evening with a straightforward pitch. "I am a big fan of World of Good. I think there is more space for ethical companies trying to make a difference for people who need a voice and a market; Whole Foods should not limit themselves to supporting just one such company. You carry so many different brands of spaghetti sauce, chocolate bars, and yogurt— why not lots of fair-trade goods?" Kathy went on to be not only my largest customer, but also my greatest advocate within Whole Foods and, over time, a good friend.

Then, when it seemed things couldn't get any sweeter, another Friday phone call came in. This time it was Donna Owens, a freelance journalist from Baltimore assigned to interview me for *O, The Oprah Magazine*. If little girls dream of meeting the

Wiggles or Dora the Explorer, I think big girls dream of meeting Oprah. Big-girl businesses certainly dream of having any sort of mention in her magazine. Over and over as my business grew, friends said, "You should be on *Oprah*," or "I've e-mailed Oprah about what you're doing." I would always smile and nod, knowing that the chances of getting a tiny company like mine noticed by Oprah were somewhat like those of being invited for tea with the queen of England. On the moon. And while this wasn't a meet and greet with her majesty the queen of daytime television herself (or the queen of England), it was the next best thing. Donna was articulate and enthusiastic. She was such a skilled interviewer, I barely knew when she was asking a question and when we were just talking like long-lost girlfriends. She magically turned a 250-word piece titled "The Greater Goods" in the May 2007 issue of *O* into a cyclone of activity at our 5533 Prince Street office in Littleton.

As soon as the *O* issue hit newsstands in mid-April, I could barely keep up. My staff, my family, every friend and her teen daughter were called on to help pick and pack orders, answer customer calls, reply to e-mails, and haul carloads of packages to the UPS store for delivery to customers. Stores were also inquiring at a rate I could not keep up with, and I quickly recruited one of the savviest women in my neighborhood, our former school PTA president Alison Evans, to come on board and be our wholesale director. On a few of our busiest days, as a roomful of helpers tripped over one another in a flurry of order activity, Mary-Mike would break out singing her own version of a seventies hit. "O O O She's magic! you know, never believe it's not so!" And the room couldn't help but sing along in a tribute to Oprah. When I sent copies of the magazine to Ms. My in Vietnam and Mrs. Satyasri in India to show them their products profiled next to the article, they sent me back proud

photos of their own with the women holding up the copy of
O *Magazine* I had sent. My girlfriend Robin even got a credit
next to the product photos she had taken for me in her basement.

May 4 of that year was a Friday. It was my son Dakota's
birthday, so I was hoping I had enough help to get the orders
out for the day and to hurry to the store to buy a cake before
he got home from school. I wouldn't be baking this year. In the
midst of our Oprah order packing chaos, we all decided to ig-
nore the ringing phone and let it go to voice mail as we
worked to call it a day. When I finally waded through boxes to
my desk and checked the messages using speakerphone, we all
heard a deep voice like a radio announcer say, "Hello, I'm Tim
Kunin from the GreaterGood Network. I read about you in
*Oprah Magazine* and I'd like to buy your company." All action
stopped.

"Obviously he has no idea what we do!" Sweaty, barefoot,
and ready to buy that birthday cake, I laughed off the call and
went on loading boxes into my car.

Tim was persistent. First thing Monday morning he called
again, and this time I answered the phone. He explained that
one of his employees' wives had noticed the article about us in O
since the title was "The Greater Goods" and Tim's company was
GreaterGood. In a long discussion, Tim introduced his company and walked me through all of his cause-related "Click to
Give" Web sites, including The Hunger Site, The Breast Cancer
Site, The Rain Forest Site, The Literacy Site, The Child Health
Site, and The Animal Rescue Site. Tim explained how every
visit to the sites triggered a donation to charity, and on top of
that, every purchase made in the online stores created an additional donation to causes GreaterGood supported. The sites'
multilayered format made a huge impact in four ways. First,

GreaterGood sold advertising to many outside companies for placement on GreaterGood's Click to Give home pages. A person could go to the sites every day and click a large button at the top of the page to give to the cause they cared about (feeding the hungry on thehungersite.com, sponsoring free mammograms on thebreastcancersite.com, giving books on theliteracysite.com, etc.) by simply clicking the button and viewing the advertising after the click. Advertisers paid a charity royalty, 100 percent of which went to GreaterGood's charitable partner for that cause, every time a person clicked. Millions of clickers every month provided meaningful donations to their core charity partners like Mercy Corps, Feeding America, Room to Read, and others. Clicking was a quick, free, simple action people could take to make a difference.

Second, each Click to Give site also had a shopping site of related products. People interested in animal protection, or world peace, or saving the rain forest could then shop for products that were designed around these causes. For every product sold, GreaterGood gave an additional donation to the charitable partner of the site the product was purchased from.

In order to broaden the number of nonprofits and projects they were supporting, GreaterGood added a Gifts That Give More program. Clickers and customers could purchase gifts that supported specific projects, like sending a girl to school in Afghanistan through Greg Mortenson's Central Asia Institute or sponsoring a mobile health clinic through Partners In Health in Haiti, and 100 percent of their donation to that project would go directly to the charity. GreaterGood charged absolutely no administration fee and actually donated the credit-card processing fees for all Gifts That Give More. That year GreaterGood.org, the company's nonprofit foundation, gave almost $2 million to nonprofits they believed in.

The fourth way they made an impact in the world was through the items they bought. Tim and his team believed deeply in buying fair-trade products from artisans in developing countries. While they carried a host of fair-trade and commercially made products across the sites, Tim's heart and drive were in the products that gave back. Fair trade on Greater-Good had the potential to make an impact twice, first by supporting the artisan who made the product, and second by generating a donation to charity when the customer bought a product.

"I could make a women's fair-trade brand," Tim explained, "but I like yours. I like what you've done, your products and your passion. Let me come to Colorado and let's talk."

"Tim, I have no intention of giving up my business," I said boldly but respectfully.

"I'm not asking you to give up your business. You *are* your business," Tim assured. "I want you. I just want to put the working capital into Global Girlfriend so it can reach its full potential for the women you champion. How about I just come out to Colorado and we can talk?"

I told him I didn't want to waste his time, but he reassured me there were no strings attached. Since he had asked twice, I agreed to meet with him if he came. Tim said he was traveling that month to Ethiopia but would get back to me about a date. Most of the month went by without another word. I was sure he had changed his mind. I went back to business as usual.

Then during the last week of May I answered the phone to the same announcer voice. "Stacey, it's Tim," he said. "I'm back from Ethiopia and coming to see you tomorrow."

Holy short notice! We all scurried to "professionalize" our office/warehouse mess and prepare for our visitor.

Tim breezed in from Seattle for a whirlwind day at Global

Girlfriend. I was not sure how I would know him when I picked him up at the airport, but I found him immediately by the base-ball cap on his head displaying The Hunger Site logo. I had expected a businessman come to woo me. Instead, Tim wore faded black chinos and a dingy white polo shirt that looked as though he'd worn it every day of his trip to Ethiopia, and had a curly dark beard and a messy mop of matching curly hair spilling out from under his well-worn hat. Tim had owned the Seattle-based GreaterGood company since 2001, when he bought it after the company failed financially. In 1999 he had started his own for-profit business called Charity USA working with charities. Charity USA was an online affiliate marketing Web site where he partnered with large companies to give a donation to charity ev-ery time someone shopped on their sites. If you wanted to shop online and make a difference, you could first log on to Charity USA, then find a list of your favorite stores and click through to that store's Web site to shop. Your purchase would be tracked, and that company would give a donation to charity through Charity USA. The site also sold advertising space. GreaterGood was operating a similar model in the late 1990s but had been funded with almost $20 million in venture funding, while Tim had bootstrapped his company with his own money and a small investment from his father. When the dot-com bubble burst and GreaterGood burned through its venture funding, Tim and his friend Greg Hesterberg saw a great opportunity to buy Greater-Good and combine it with what Charity USA was already doing. GreaterGood had more employees than Charity USA did at the time, so they decided to leave the company headquarters in Se-attle. Tim had been making a cross-country commute from his home in Boston for years now when he wasn't traveling to meet with artisan partners around the world.

He greeted me with both a handshake and a hug, and off we went for a long day of looking at products, learning about our artisan groups, reading press clips, lunching with my little staff, and visiting our Whole Foods display. Finally we sat down and he tried to convince me we should marry. I was enticed by the thought of having a real warehouse and getting the pallets of clothing out of my garage so Brad could actually park inside. I loved the idea that we might be able to add a charitable donation to every product and also offer opportunities for Global Girlfriend customers to donate charitably to help the women we support through GreaterGood's Gifts That Give More program.

Tim and I shared a passion for helping through business. He understood, as I did, that business could be a tool to bring sustainable fair-wage employment to disadvantaged artisans in the developing world. We also believed that for-profit businesses could be great partners to nonprofit organizations. Nonprofits are essential in providing services that business cannot, but business is the best vehicle for marketing products and building sustainable incomes for the poor. The two together—business for jobs and nonprofits for services like health care, clean water, women's rights, and community building—are a perfect marriage. Global Girlfriend had been giving a portion of our sales back to our charitable partner Women for Women International to support the services they provided women in war-torn countries. We provided a market and generated an income, and then gave donations to charity with that income to provide the services business alone could not bring to a community. By partnering with nonprofits that provide essential services to the poor, we were able to double our impact. GreaterGood's support and programs would only further that goal.

As much as I loved providing an income to women world-wide, I also loved the thought of being paid for my work. Five years of working for free and paying all the bills can be strain-ing, even when you are passionate about what you're doing. I had poured every dime we made back into the business and toward purchases so we could grow and make the company viable. Tim's proposal would provide me with a salary, and take over the staff's salaries as well. What I didn't want to lose was control of whom we supported and what products we carried.

Tim and I both recognized that with the Whole Foods part-nership, our strong women-focused mission, and great media attention, Global Girlfriend was positioned for tremendous growth. As I drove Tim back to the airport later that evening, he talked incessantly about the possibilities until suddenly he went silent in the passenger seat. I saw his head bob and hang down chin to chest as he fell fast asleep. I wasn't offended; I was glad he felt comfortable enough with me to give way to his Ethiopian jet lag.

While I didn't accept Tim's proposal that day, I did accept his invitation to visit him in Seattle to get a better understand-ing of his company and his intentions for mine. When I went to Seattle a few weeks later, I was blown away by what Greater-Good had built. A buzzing hive of sixty some employees, Greater-Good had product loaders, copywriters, product buyers, a tech team, accountants, photographers, graphic designers, and more—all clearly dedicated to a shared social mission to make the world a better place. I was welcomed warmly, and everyone seemed as devoted to my cause of helping women in poverty as I was. Tim agreed that nothing in Littleton would change except our increased budget and decreased order boxing. My staff would be kept on and paid better. I would remain the president of Global Girlfriend, making all decisions, and our very defined mission of helping women work their way out of poverty would remain intact. By summer's end, Global Girlfriend was the newest division of the GreaterGood Network.

# 7

# OH LA LA, FAIR TRADE

Fashion fades, only style remains the same.
—COCO CHANEL

With our improved apparel fit provided by Armani Exchange and the capital backing of our new parent company, Greater-Good, I set out to prove to our expanded customer base (provided a la Oprah) that being fair was always in fashion. In 2007, the same year we merged with GreaterGood, one of my favorite go-to brands, the Gap, was in the news for exploiting children in India. Britain's *Observer* newspaper first broke the story that children as young as ten years old were working sixteen hours a day for no pay embroidering garments for the Gap. In the report, the *Observer* quoted one child as saying, "I was bought from my parents' village in Bihar and taken to New Delhi by train . . . They had loudspeakers in the back of a car and told my parents that, if they sent me to work in the city, they won't have to work in the farms. My father was paid a fee for me, and I was brought down with 40 other children." Another boy told the *Observer* that if the children cried they would be hit with a rubber pipe or punished by having an oily cloth stuffed in their mouths. While Gap North America president, Marka Hansen, reacted quickly, explaining that the Gap was unaware of the situation, which had been caused by a rogue subcontractor in India, and while the Gap quickly terminated that relationship and did not sell any of the goods in question, the average American consumer got a startling look at the problem of child labor at a global level affecting one of their favorite brands.

As a mom (one who loved the Gap) I needed to know that nothing I wore was to the detriment of children just like mine, but from poor countries. True style is being true to your belief system. While it has been said that women will sacrifice anything for fashion, I don't believe that women are willing to sacrifice their moral compass for a cute pair of jeans. The Gap didn't think so either, and they instituted a strict code of vendor conduct, employing ninety compliance officers around the world to be sure their factories adhered to their no child labor policy. The Gap instituted a no tolerance policy across their supply chain. But they were not the only company appearing in headlines about poor labor practices; several other large corporations were all exposed for poor labor practices including forced labor, trafficking, and child labor. Again, most of these companies employed foreign subcontractors, but the burden is still on the company to know that the people making their garments actually benefit from having them as employers. The whole point of having a job is for personal and financial gain. The only way to provide this in the apparel industry is to fairly compensate workers for their efforts. If you believe that it is wrong to exploit children and workers, then you must look into the labor practices behind the garments you wear.

With heightened consumer awareness about sweatshops and child labor, Global Girlfriend and other fair-trade brands had the perfect opportunity to give consumers an alternative with organic, fairly traded apparel—garments aptly termed "clean clothes." The Clean Clothes Campaign was stared in Europe in 1989 to educate and mobilize consumers around the rights of workers in the garment industry. Clean clothes were garments produced using nonexploitive, fair labor practices; safe working conditions; and fair compensation.

Europe has been a leader not just in fair-trade apparel, or clean clothes, but also in many aspects of bringing fairly traded goods to the mainstream. Europe's formal fair-trade movement took root about twenty years after Ten Thousand Villages and SERRV started the U.S. movement. Oxfam, Europe's first alternative trading organization, was founded in 1942 but expanded their sales of artisan crafts in 1965 with their "Helping-by-Selling" campaign, offering imported handicrafts in Oxfam stores in the UK and through a mail-order catalog. In 1969, an organization named Worldshop opened its doors in the Netherlands with stores staffed by teams of volunteers. More recently the movement to promote fair trade had spread to the political fabric of the European Union. By 2000, public institutions across Europe were purchasing and serving Fair Trade Certified coffee and tea. Six years later, the European Parliament unanimously adopted a resolution in support of furthering fair trade throughout Europe. Considering Europe's progressive embracing of the fair-trade movement, it was no surprise to me that an annual European Fair Trade Salon was being initiated, with the first to be held in France.

At my friend Sarie's prompting, I attended the salon, which was in Lyon. Sarie, one of the first women I worked with internationally when I founded Global Girlfriend, was hosting a booth to showcase her fair-trade products. Nawangsari Setyowati, Sarie for short, was the founder of Arum Dalu in

Indonesia. Sarie began her fair-trade organization in the early 1990s to help improve working conditions in her craft-rich country while raising the environmental awareness of the women artisans. Much of Sarie's home island of Bali as well as neighboring islands of Lombok and Java are dependent on handicraft production as the main source of income for the community. But as resources began to be depleted due to overpopulation in large cities and through deforestation, Sarie grew more concerned with educating people on environmental stewardship in their craft production. She felt that working directly with poor producers to help them earn an income while sustaining their local resources was the only way to make a difference in her community. Resourceful and creative, Sarie and her women artisans became Global Girlfriend customer favorites.

Once again my mom joined me, and we brought my daughter Cali along with us on the trip. Our fashion scouting began in Paris. In January, Paris plays host to several high-fashion trade shows, including Prêt-à-Porter Paris and Maison & Objet. Our plan was to start our French adventure by exploring these trade shows to glean the latest fashion trends and try to translate them to garments or accessories that could be made by our women's groups. After soaking in high design, our mother-daughter threesome would then venture across the country to Lyon for the Fair Trade Salon.

Even though it was wintertime, Paris was aflutter with activity. Our hotel, the Hôtel des Grandes Ecoles, sat just off the famous Rue Mouffetard, a quintessential Paris market street in the Latin Quarter. The hotel was pink with a black metal French-style roof and looked just like Madeline's house from the famous children's books. All that was missing was Miss Clavel. Directly behind the hotel's open courtyard garden was a grammar school where we could hear children playing in the yard. Early each morning the Rue Mouffetard was lined with vendors selling fresh everything. Flowers added color to the winter air, while cheese, fish, and vegetable stands mingled with crates of wine, crusty baguette loaves, and tempting pastries. In the afternoon, outdoor cafés were filled with espresso drinkers in black wool coats and colorful scarves. The workday commute for most Parisians was on foot or by metro. With so much to see—quaint neighborhood streets, grand cathedrals, and historic architecture—the walking felt more like a museum tour than a daily grind. Even most of the underground metro stations were beautiful, with antique subway tile and golden frames around billboard ads. And the smell of something sweet baking hung in the air in almost every neighborhood.

Prêt-à-Porter Paris is a ready-to-wear fashion show featuring women's apparel and accessories from around the world. Held at the Paris Expo at the Porte de Versailles, the show was hosting a section called So Ethic spotlighting ethical fashion manufacturers. The first few aisles of the larger show were like those at the Noida exposition center in India. The same Indian vendors with booths at Noida also had booths at Prêt-à-Porter Paris. I skimmed them quickly, moving on through the large number of Chinese accessory manufacturers and small French boutique-style artisans, until I reached the So Ethic section. Most of the booths were for French companies using organic or recycled products. Others were just too couture, with the high prices to match. I had not necessarily expected to find any new vendors at Prêt-à-Porter, but it was a great show for shopping new trends and gathering ideas for our artisans. Then an embroidered skirt caught my eye.

In the last aisle of the So Ethic section was a simple booth with a naturally dyed clothing line embellished with hand embroidery and block printing. I was drawn like a magnet to the subtle colors and delicate needlework. Gemma, the booth's hostess, perked up from her chair, where she had been sitting looking somewhat deflated. "All of our designs are organic cotton made with natural vegetable dyes and fairly traded from Nepal," she said. "Women do all of the hand embroidery in their homes throughout the Kathmandu Valley." Now I was interested.

The clothing was produced from fabric colored with dye made from bark, roots, and the leaves of plants native to the region of Nepal. The Giggle brand had been formed to improve the lives of its native artisans by empowering them to find a global market for their garments, and to improve the environment by using only certified organic cotton and 100 percent natural dyes. The natural dyes marked a critical shift in garment dyeing in Nepal and had significant implications for the Nepali ecosystem. Waste from synthetic dyes are the largest chemical pollutant of Nepal's once clean rivers, and these pollutants and metals are carried downstream through thousands of miles of Indian rivers as well, potentially affecting the health of millions of people. By using organic cotton and natural dyes, and by arranging for women to embroider from their homes so they could work and still care for their children, Gemma had created a brand that was a great fit for Global Girlfriend.

Giggle was helping many women, including Saraswoti Maharjan, a married mother of two. Like many rural Nepali people, Saraswoti and her husband had been forced to move to the city because of the lack of paying jobs in the rural areas. Her husband took a job driving a taxi in Kathmandu, but they still had trouble making ends meet. Saraswoti started embroidering and knitting for Giggle at home to earn money. She was able to contribute to her family's income and use her talents as a skilled craftswoman without having to compromise her time with her children. Saraswoti's earnings allowed her to send her children to school (which she and her husband had not been able to do before), and to provide them with food and clothes. Her income had eased the financial pressures on her family, pressures felt by many of Nepal's rural immigrants. I loved Saraswoti's story because it was the story of so many women around the world, even my own. Mothers of young children are often torn about how to be with their children yet earn an income that helps the family. I wanted my Global Girlfriend customers to have the opportunity to support Saraswoti and the women she worked with, so I partnered with Gemma to import some of the Giggle line that specifically helped her women artisans (Giggle also works with male tailors and printers).

The next day at Maison & Objet, held on the opposite side of the city at the Paris Nord Villepinte, I found more treasures. Every aisle at Maison & Objet was eye candy. Elaborate displays of stunning high-end furniture and home décor made up the center section, with handcrafted items set around the edges of the seemingly endless sales floor. Everyone there was dressed to the nines in heels, tailored pantsuits or designer dresses, and perfect accessories that made the buyers look more like runway models.

In a small booth toward the back I found simple woven-grass tote bags that were dyed in shades of gold and blue and featured a provincial plaid pattern. Each was handmade by artisans in Congo and hand-carried out of the country. I did not know of anyone getting products out of Congo, a country where women desperately needed support. The Congolese people were enduring one of the most violent African wars to date. And their suffering was going largely unnoticed by the rest of the world. Since 1998 more than 5.4 million people had died in the Congo conflict, with half of these being children under the age of five. Vicious gang rape and torture continued to be a daily reality for Congolese women, and the world community was doing little to intervene.

Heroes like Zainab Salbi, founder of Women for Women International, journalist Lisa Ling, and Lisa Shannon, founder of Run for Congo Women, were speaking out and getting media attention for the women of Congo. While efforts on behalf of powerful nations were few and far between, individual women were standing up with Zainab, Lisa, and Lisa to support their sisters. Women were sponsoring a sister in Congo through Women for Women International. With just $27 per month for one year, women were supplying their Congolese sister with direct financial support and rights and leadership training, but most of all with friendship. Sponsors are encouraged to write to their sister often, sharing messages of support, encouragement, and hope. Women were also running. I am not a runner, but once a year I do Run for Congo Women. I run in solidarity, I run to raise money for the cause, and I run to endure discomfort on behalf of Congo women, knowing that when they run, it is too often for their lives. Lisa Shannon was moved to found Run for Congo Women after seeing Lisa Ling's report about the state of women's lives in Congo and Zainab's efforts to help on *Oprah*. Zainab writes a blog, which she aptly titled *The Butterfly Effect*. On her blog she explains, "The butterfly effect is a metaphor for the concept that small, seemingly insignificant events—like the fluttering of a butterfly's wings—can produce tremendous and unanticipated consequences." A handbag could not change the brutal statistics from Congo, but an income could at least help the women with their daily needs. I bought the bags, which I named the Congo Woven Carry-All—a snappy name for one of our most important new products. Each bag purchased would give our customers the opportunity to help a woman in Congo become financially independent and feel supported by the outside world.

I also bought an innovative recycled product that caught my eye, the Paris garden apron. The brainchild of Parisian designer Isabelle Teste, the aprons were produced by Indre-et-Loire, a low-income women's association in Ancenis, France. Indre-et-Loire helps women who are homeless or living at or near the poverty level transition into a more productive and sustainable life, similar to the programs we supported in the United States like The Enterprising Kitchen and the Women's Bean Project. In addition, their products contribute to sustainable development by making a statement against the systematic waste of plastic bags—the girly garden accessories were made from recycled potting soil bags. They were a cute twist on garden garbage and also hope for women in need.

I timed a call each day back home to Brad, Ellie, and Dakota to check in on them and to report on our Parisian adventures. I worried about Ellie the most while I was away, but she seemed to love having her grandma Brenda there, and not having to share Grandma with her sister. "Just don't buy too much," Brad said, reminding me that despite the merger with Greater-Good six months earlier, we were still warehousing a shipping container's worth of Global Girlfriend goods in our garage. As supportive as Brad has always been about my business, he was ready for my new parent company to take on some of the personal inconveniences, like inventory, that he had endured. He had not been able to park in his own garage for about four years. Our dining room table, clearly visible to everyone who came through our front door, was constantly covered in products, tags, ribbon, and boxes for the latest catalog. The Global Girlfriend office outside of my house never had enough space.

GreaterGood, on the other hand, had a sixty-five-thousand-square-foot warehouse in Kent, Washington. The plan was to move the retail inventory to the Kent warehouse (leaving the wholesale stock in Littleton), but we couldn't until our Web site moved to their technology platform. That couldn't happen before the holiday season, and now New Year's projects had pushed the planned move until March or April.

"By the time the artisans make the products I order here, the delivery for retail will be in Seattle," I reassured him. Brad sighed, knowing that he'd spend at least one more winter scraping ice from his windshield every morning while my boxes of clothing and handbags stayed warm and dry in his parking space.

But while not every aspect of the merger moved as quickly as we all would have liked, GreaterGood offered us opportunities for deeper partnerships with women's nonprofit projects we believed in supporting. One of the most vital partnerships we forged was with Camfed, the Campaign for Female Education. Ann Cotton founded Camfed in 1993 after visiting Zimbabwe to investigate why girls were not going to school in rural Africa. The common assumption was that families kept girls out of school for cultural reasons, but Ann found that instead it was purely poverty that created a roadblock to girls' education. Families in rural parts of Africa, as well as in other developing nations, could not afford books, uniforms, and pencils for all of their children, so most often the boys were chosen for the family's education budget, since boys had the best chance of employment after completing their schooling. And the problem was not isolated to Zimbabwe. In sub-Saharan Africa, over 24 million girls cannot afford to go to school. Girls were simply considered a bad investment for a family's limited capital. Ann returned home from Zimbabwe determined to help girls go to school. She knew that with small investments in girls' education, entire communities could become more economically productive. If girls were given an opportunity to learn and then to become economic contributors, they would bring their families, their neighbors, and their villages up with them.

Like Global Girlfriend, Camfed began in a very grassroots way. Ann made and sold baked goods to friends and family to raise money and awareness about the lack of education for African girls. Her initial efforts on behalf of girls in Zimbabwe have grown into a world-class program that has provided education to over 1 million impoverished girls in rural areas of Zimbabwe, Zambia, Tanzania, Ghana, and Malawi. Ann Cotton is proof that one person with a simple idea—that poor African girls deserve an education—can change lives. I was proud to support Camfed's work with our new partnership, providing business grants to older girls who've finished their schooling and are ready to become entrepreneurs in their communities. GreaterGood was committed to giving a donation to charity with every product sold on their sites. Global Girlfriend had the amazing opportunity to partner with a nonprofit of our choice to contribute a portion of our sales to that organization. Camfed was a perfect fit. Global Girlfriend was a business created solely to improve the lives of women in poverty, so I knew nothing made a larger impact than investing in girls' education and then investing in their small businesses. With each item purchased, Global Girlfriend began giving one dollar toward a hundred-dollar microgrant to a young woman wanting to start her own business. A microloan is paid back, but with the microgrants we wanted the women to get a leg up with an initial capital investment that they did not have to repay. Women who have received seed money and have grown their businesses in turn run Camfed's seed money microgrant program for new grant recipients, creating a bond of female solidarity that is integral to its success. The young women who launch a small business with microgrants sponsored by our customers' purchases benefit themselves, their families, and their entire communities with the income generation and even with job creation as their businesses expand. I reminded Brad often that his garage sacrifice made a difference for women everywhere and was now helping me house the products that were providing microgrants to women in Africa. As an investment banker for Citigroup, Brad conceded that these women were a bullish investment.

In the morning, my mom, Cali, and I hurried to the Gare du Nord to catch the fast train out of Paris for a ride across the French countryside to the more industrial city of Lyon. While the train was state-of-the-art, and the ride was supposed to be fairly quick considering the distance, our trip was emotionally uncomfortable. Cali and I were seated across from two Korean men with loads of strange packaged meat snacks, while my mom sat directly to my right with a family comprised of two older women who were sisters and the husband of one of the sisters. Ten minutes into the train ride, they received a phone call that sent the sisters into tears. Everyone around felt terrible, though we had no idea what had happened since we spoke only English, the Koreans only Korean, and the family group only French. The husband finally tried his best to explain to my mother that the women's third sister had just had an "accident of the heart." After a little more decoding, we all realized that the sister had died of a heart attack. I tried to pass the time looking out at the small farm villages that dotted the open fields of central France, but I could not help but feel deeply for the sisters, who let out the occasional sob. Their horrible loss made me grateful for such a special experience with my mother and my daughter.

It was colder in Lyon than it had been in Paris. After we checked into our hotel, I hopped on the aboveground trolley tram that would take me to the university hosting the first annual European Fair Trade Salon. The university was comprised of gray cement buildings and looked more like a prison than a college. It was a stark contrast to the beautiful architecture of Paris. Inside, however, there was a different atmosphere. Students manned the entrance, checking people in and handing out badges showing our names and affiliations. The salon was offering a host of lectures and discussions, but I headed directly to the exhibit hall to find Sarie. I was impressed with the number of booths. While many were for European fair-trade companies importing from the developing world similar to Global Girlfriend, and an equal number were for fairly traded commodity crops like coffee, there were a decent number of artisan groups as well, from what the conference called the "global south."

I visited the booths of several fair-trade groups I had heard of, including SEWA and Pushpanjali from India, Mahaguthi from Nepal, the Holy Land Handicraft Cooperative Society from Palestine, and Acción Creadora from Bolivia before finally reaching Sarie's booth. We recognized each other immediately. Sarie was petite and beautiful, with perfect skin, long dark hair pulled back and wrapped on top of her head, and a smile that lit up the room. She was fluttering around her booth like a butterfly, emptying a box of product samples that had been lost in transit from Indonesia to France and had arrived a few minutes before I did. Sarie stopped everything when I walked into her booth and was hugging me before I even remember confirming I was actually me. "Stacey, it is so good to meet you finally." Sarie hugged me and then looked me up and down. "So, so good, my friend."

Sarie had been a very good friend to women in Indonesia, too, women like Ibu Gusti Ayu Juwita from the rice farming village of Bone. Ibu Ayu started a small business making simple souvenirs out of pandanus leaves for the tourists staying at the hotels on the beach that was near her village. When tourists came to watch the famous Balinese Kecak and Fire dance on the beach, she would sell them her crafts, making some extra income for her family. In Bali, women spend a lot of time making various kinds of offerings to be used at their traditional ceremonies. Ibu Ayu made little Balinese dolls, decorative baskets, and small grass purses. No capital was needed, since she used natural fibers growing around her house or in the fields nearby. All the work was done in her home.

After some success at the beaches, Ibu Ayu came up with the idea to display her products in front of her house every day. This was the beginning of her first shop and where she was fortunate enough to meet fellow Balinese entrepreneur Sarie. Sarie started buying small simple baskets from Ibu Ayu to use as gift packages for the silver jewelry her cooperative was producing. After ten years of partnership, Sarie and Ibu Ayu were able to grow Ibu Ayu's one-woman crafts venture into a business supporting 20 women in her village full-time and providing part-time work for 100 to 120 more when big orders came in. The work created has become an important income source for many families in the region, creating employment for girls who have finished school but graduate to find no jobs available elsewhere. The women working for Ibu Ayu are paid daily wages, and these are living wages that are higher than local minimum wages. The women working part-time out of their homes are paid when they have finished the orders assigned to them. Orders they would not have if not for Ibu Ayu and Sarie.

I picked through the treasures Sarie continued to unearth from hidden unopened boxes in her booth, and we worked on designs of skirts and bags. The conference sessions I attended were very good in teaching me more about the fair-trade movement in Europe and the growth of the organic cotton farming industry in Africa. Just as I had become dedicated to expanding our current clothing line, I really wanted to add a line of organic cotton apparel made by women somewhere in Africa. Africa needed trade as much as or more than any other place in the world. But the organic cotton growers at the conference were selling the raw cotton, not milling it into fabric, and certainly not sewing it into garments. Finding a source for organic cotton African fabric and seamstresses to convert that fabric into new clothes would become my next quest.

Attending the salon not only helped to expand my grasp of what was on trend but also brought me three new women's groups to work with. While at points I could not help but notice the stark contrast between the opulence and comfort around me and the situation endured by the women bag weavers in Congo, or the Nepali embroiderers, or even the homeless French apron seamstresses, I still felt that fashion and fair trade were compatible bedfellows. In fact, the two worlds had to fit together to complete the puzzle of strategies for helping women out of poverty. It is the American woman consumer, or the French woman consumer, or any woman with money to spend on fashion, who must make treating women in the world fairly the cornerstone of her personal style. Each of us needs to remember that we can cause the butterfly effect if we choose to use our purchasing power on behalf of women in poverty. If we flap our little wings in unison, the world will feel our windstorm for women. We can start simply with clean clothes.

# 8

# THE PAINTED PRIEST OF LA PALMA

❦

Memories of our lives, of our works
and our deeds will continue in others.
—ROSA PARKS

He seemed to be staring at us from the time we walked by the first airport gift shop in the Comalapa International Airport. With his dark hair, glasses, and black shirt and white collar, the priest was everywhere we went. It quickly became evident that he was a local celebrity, but knowing little about El Salvador before our arrival, Mary-Mike and I had no idea who he was. Though we had been planning our trip to Guatemala for weeks, we had not had much notice before joining this trip sponsored by USAID (United States Agency for International Development) and Aid to Artisans El Salvador. Mary-Mike was extremely excited and somewhat nervous; it was her first international trip since she was nine years old and her first chance to meet some of the women she had been working hard to support. While she and I were in the midst of our travel planning for Guatemala, Lori Grey from Aid to Artisans had contacted me from her LA office about some new products she wanted me to consider from El Salvador. When she learned Mary-Mike and I were planning to visit Central America in just a few weeks, she insisted we go to El Salvador as well. She enticed me with a product line she knew I couldn't pass up.

"You will love the new recycled tire tube purses Aid to Artisans is helping one group develop," Lori tempted. "I know recycled products are your thing."

They were, and this immediately piqued my interest. "Are they made by women?" Always my next question when considering new products.

"Yes. It's a woman designer who used to have a handbag factory and is now working with just a small artisan group," Lori answered. I quickly agreed that we would go. Luckily, Mary-Mike had grown used to my habit of committing first and asking her later.

Aid to Artisans (ATA) is one of the most trusted and respected organizations in the world providing economic development for the global handicraft sector. The organization, founded in 1976, excels at linking artisans to new markets and buyers to culturally meaningful and innovative products. ATA provides low-income artisans around the world with strategies for building their businesses through training and provides market access by introducing small producer groups to importers and retailers around the world. They partner with an extensive network of artisans, businesses (like Global Girlfriend), governments, and nonprofit organizations to maximize the potential for sustainable incomes for artisans in poverty-stricken countries. ATA and its partners deliver critical product development, training, and marketing services to sixty-five thousand artisans in forty-one countries—72 percent of these artisans are women. In El Salvador, ATA had earned the USAID contract to run the craft market expansion program, which director Ana Rosa Selva and her team had grown to more than $3 million in craft sales. Some of ATA's successes in El Salvador included securing craft sales to retail giant Crate & Barrel and to the San Diego Zoo. Lori was my contact at ATA and had helped me to develop relationships with women artisans in Ghana through ATA's work with the West Africa Trade Hub. Because of my deep respect for ATA, I was excited to be going on my first ATA-sponsored trip.

I had bought the Lonely Planet guide to El Salvador the day before we left Denver and had not had time to study up on much other than what to pack. Typically, before a trip I like to read at least some of the guidebook about that country, do a little research on Google news, and memorize the names of the "must-see" sights. This time all I really knew about El Salvador was its location and that I had vague teenage memories of news reports about the country's long and bloody civil war in the 1980s. I tried to use the flight from Denver to San Salvador to learn all I could about El Salvador and its history, studying my guidebook and talking to my Salvadoran seatmate, who was on his way to visit his family for the first time in nine years. He had left El Salvador for America to secure a better-paying job and send money back home to his family. I learned later that remittances from Salvadorans working in the United States are an important source of income for many families in El Salvador. UNDP surveys indicate that about 22 percent of families in El Salvador receive money from family members working in the United States. Situated in Central America on the Pacific Ocean and bordered by Guatemala and Honduras, El Salvador has a beautiful tropical landscape that combines inland mountains and unique black sand volcanic beaches. The war between the government and coalition rebel groups lasted from 1980 to 1992, leaving almost 200,000 people dead in this small country of not quite 6 million.

Among the dead were priests, nuns, missionaries, and aid workers who had advocated for the rights of the local poor. Archbishop Óscar Romero fought fearlessly against oppression, poverty, injustice, and the government-sponsored torture and assassinations plaguing his country in the late 1970s. In 1980 Archbishop Romero was murdered at the front of his church as he conducted mass. Painted images of his face have become one of the main handicrafts available throughout El Salvador. His was the face represented so ubiquitously that he seemed to be following us.

While the war was long over, the tension of political strife was still seen spray-painted by the opposition party, the Farabundo Martí National Liberation Front (FMLN), on the building walls and fences of the capital city of San Salvador. The decade-long war was between the military-led government of El Salvador and the FMLN, which comprised five left-wing militias. The United States backed the military-led government, but that government was said to be responsible for many human rights offenses. When Herbert Ernesto Anaya, head of the Human Rights Commission of El Salvador, was murdered, the United Nations, the French government, Amnesty International, and School of the Americas Watch protested to the world community. Peace between the warring factions was eventually negotiated in 1992, and the FMLN evolved from a guerrilla group to a valid political party.

Our taxi ride from the airport to the Hotel Mirador Plaza in San Salvador was dusty and lined with a strange combination of tin-roof lean-tos, tropical palm trees, and coconut stands. My favorite sight as we drove into the city were the motorcycles that sped by with a yellow box attached behind the driver's seat branded with a chicken logo—delivery of the local favorite, Pollo Campero. Pollo Campero is the Kentucky Fried

Chicken of Central America. Pollo Campero is a Guatemalan franchise, but the United States had also exported several business to El Salvador since the war ended. The most prominent was Wal-Mart. While the Wal-Mart name was not being used, the company operated sixty-five stores under the names Despensa Familiar, Despensa de Don Juan, and Hiper Paiz in this small country roughly the size of Massachusetts.

Mary-Mike and I rendezvoused at the hotel with Tim and our brand-new colleague Druce Biggerstaff. (It was Druce's second day on the job as the newest fair-trade buyer for Greater-Good, specializing in sourcing products from Latin America and Africa.) After we checked in, our hostesses from Aid to Artisans, Ana Maria, Ana Rosa, and Iris, met us in the lobby for a briefing. We were instructed never to leave our hotel unaccompanied, and with men toting menacing automatic rifles positioned in front of every business, we were not tempted to disobey our hostesses. But despite the guns and guards, I did not feel unsafe; we were just well-cautioned guests in a new land.

On the first evening of our four-day trip, the ATA staff took us to the top of a dense, lush volcano where an old coffee plantation home had been converted into a breathtaking mountain-top restaurant. As we sat outside looking across the jungle that shadowed El Salvador's small towns and villages, we dined on El Salvador's most famous national dish, the papusa. Papusas are thick corn-tortilla pockets filled with a mild white cheese and eaten with pickled vegetable toppings. They are delicious, and so was everything about our surroundings. Since our time in El Salvador was short, we used the evening to plan our visits. La Palma would be first.

La Palma was a city far from the coast, almost on the border of Honduras. It was about an hour and a half's drive from the capital city of San Salvador but an easy drive on the new roads El Salvador enjoyed since the postwar rebuilding. The community enjoyed a mountain setting that gave it cool mornings and evenings, similar to in Colorado, but warm days most of the year. As soon as we reached the city limits, everything was decorated in the famous La Palma style. Telephone poles, buildings, fences, and signs were all brightly painted with geometric shapes, abstract animals, and people.

"That is the fun hippie painting," Ana Maria said, pointing out the designs. "Almost everyone here knows how to paint La Palma style."

This colorful painting style was what we had come to see. In fact, over 75 percent of the community makes its living selling arts and crafts based on this style.

Fernando Llort, a talented Salvadoran artist, moved to La Palma in the early 1970s to escape the political unrest in the capital. He opened a small crafts shop called La Semilla de Dios, where he taught the locals to make colorful paintings using symbols that represented El Salvador. Llort continued to develop his style and eventually opened the Center for Integral Development, a school for anyone in the area who wanted to learn about art. Llort's style had become El Salvador's folk art.

We started at La Semilla de Dios, the birthplace of Llort's work. The turquoise walls were lined with shelves full of brightly painted wooden items. We toured the stations where each step in the process was carried out. First, men would take drying wood and cut it into the shapes for the item, then women would prep, draw, and paint the designs on the wood, transforming it into Salvadoran art. Many of the items had a religious theme, and we learned that the cooperative's name meant "God's seed." There was an abundance of crosses with Father Óscar Romero painted on the center. While Druce and Tim shopped, Ana Maria let Mary-Mike and me know that she thought the cooperative down the street would be an even better fit for Global Girlfriend because they were a women's organization instead of a mixed group of painters. They also offered more products that did not have a religious element to the artwork.

Just half a block down the street, Mrs. Aminta de Mancia had started her own painting business called Artesanías El Madero de Jesús. Mrs. de Mancia had been one of the first women trained by Llort in his style of painting. An entrepreneur herself, she wanted to start a family business painting but also had the goal of employing women who could work for her from their rural homes. Her son or other men with trucks would drive to the women's homes with the supplies for their painting assignments, and then pick up the finished products once a week. Because the making of her wood crafts requires the touch of many hands (carpenters, drawers, cutters, painters, varnishers, and packers), Aminta was able to provide employment to many people.

One of the artists, Maria, began working in the local corn-fields at age twelve to help support her large family. She knew of Aminta and her painting business but didn't know how to paint or if Aminta would be willing to hire her. One day, Maria took a chance and knocked on Aminta's door. Aminta took her in and began teaching her to paint. Now a full-time artisan at Artesanías El Madero de Jesús, Maria set her sights on creating a better future for her sisters. "When I first came here I did not know how to paint, but now I do and have learned that I am capable of anything I put my heart into. I want my sisters to finish school and go on to college, and with my salary we will be able to achieve that."

Mary-Mike and I had fun designing some new purse-size compact mirrors and brightly colored Dr. Seuss–style holiday ornaments with Aminta and her artists. There were so many colors and patterns to choose from, the possibilities were nearly endless. We left feeling good about the group and the purchase, not realizing we would visit two or three more businesses just like Mrs. de Mancia's and not be able to buy since there was nothing new. La Palma painting had reached full production saturation.

After a long drive back to the capital city I plopped down at the desk in our hotel room and went directly to my computer. I tried over and over again to pull up my e-mail but kept getting an error message. I thought maybe I was somehow not connected to the Internet, so just to test, I clicked into the Global Girlfriend Web site. The site had changed over, and the new GreaterGood version was showing where our old Web site used to be. I had known the move was coming, and I welcomed it. Even though our companies merged in August 2007, eight months later we were still running our Web site from Colorado, which meant we were still receiving all of the shipments at our office (GreaterGood was paying for trucking, so at least I no longer had to haul cargo in my minivan), and we were still packing the daily orders and driving them to UPS. The switch over of our Web site to GreaterGood's technology platform had taken far longer than anyone had expected, and the inventory couldn't move to their warehouse for packing and shipping until we were on their platform. A couple of weeks before the trip to El Salvador, Mary-Mike, Sheri, Alison, and I had packed up most of the retail inventory, leaving just a shell of items to fill orders in the interim, and shipped several pallets off to the Kent warehouse in anticipation of the Web site switch. But I had not been told that the changeover would happen while I was out of the country. In the site move, my e-mail address had also disappeared. With my cell phone service not available in El Salvador and my e-mail out I felt uncomfortably disconnected to my family back at home. I felt better when

I thought of the man I'd sat next to on the plane who had not seen his family in nine years. I had seen my family just two days before. Still, I was not used to not at least checking in.

Luckily, there was hardly time to worry about the site or getting a message home. We had several more artisan groups to visit, with only two days left to make our rounds. I pointed out to Ana Maria one Salvadoran fashion that caught my eye—the cute mid-thigh-length aprons all of the older women wore. It was hard to find a woman with gray hair who was not sporting a unique calico apron with whimsical rickrack trim, or one with a dainty floral pattern accented by pockets and lace. "Ana Maria, who makes the aprons?" I asked as I took impromptu photos of every lady and her adorable apron.

"The what?" Ana Maria said, with no idea what I was asking.

"Every woman walking down the street here and in San Salvador is wearing a cute short apron. Do you know where they are made?" I replied.

She could only laugh. "Those ladies just make those from scraps. You don't really want the old-lady aprons."

"Yes I do! Retro-style aprons are popular in the United States," I explained, sharing with her that my favorite store, Anthropologie, had a whole section devoted to quirky retro aprons and tea towels.

Still laughing, Ana Maria said, "I don't know; we'll have to see." She thought we might have some success finding aprons at Las Azulinas, a women's cooperative specializing in indigo-dyed garments and accessories.

Deep blue indigo dyes have been prized in El Salvador since pre-Columbian times. Spanish conquistadors called it "blue gold," and the Spanish established plantations all over El Salvador, making it the largest producer of indigo in the world for centuries. Hundreds of years later, in 2003, a long period of turmoil and civil war had ravaged El Salvador and left very few job opportunities, especially for women, but indigo was still a viable resource for income generation. An enterprising group of women artisans in the village of Santa Ana came together to put their skill and resources to work. Las Azulinas came out of their ideas and effort. Named for a regional flower, Las Azulinas celebrates El Salvador's rich heritage of using indigo as a source for unique crafts. One hundred percent of Las Azulinas's artisans are women.

While the group was small, it was making a huge impact on the lives of women like Dina Salgado de Méndez and Leonor Contreras. Dina's oldest daughter was born with Down syndrome, and providing for her medical needs had been a financial burden for the family. With Las Azulinas, Dina was able to work from her home and still care for her daughter. Leonor used her income to support her four daughters, and she was proud to be contributing to her household for the first time in her life. Her social and credit status as a working woman allowed her to qualify for small loans. "I have been able to use small loans from time to time to buy a bed and a refrigerator, improving my family's conditions."

While we didn't find aprons at their workshop, we zeroed in on a beautiful cotton knit wrap that had been richly dyed with indigo, leaving just small white starburst patterns along the bottom trim. The women worked in a lush garden courtyard with a large palm tree, climbing flowers, and a nice outdoor sitting area adjacent to the workshop that was open on one side but protected by three walls and a tin roof. Iris modeled the wrap while we wrote an order for it. I loved that Las Azulinas combined El Salvador's most precious resources—skilled women and lovely indigo.

The next morning, we headed to the home of Maria de los

Angeles de Ruffatti, the woman designing fashion-forward handbags from recycled tire inner tubes. She was the reason we had come to El Salvador. Maria and her husband were delightful. Their lovely but modest home was built around a center courtyard. Maria had been in the handbag production business for over twenty years, but during the long civil war her family was forced to close their factory, and designing took a back burner. But she still kept a photo album of every design she had ever made. Maria started our visit by showing us all of the handbag styles in a room off the front entry. We loved them. Druce made it clear that anything I did not want to carry, she would love to buy. There wasn't anything I did not want for Global Girlfriend. There is definitely some degree of competition between the buyers at GreaterGood. While Global Girlfriend was a specialized line that operated somewhat autonomously from the other GreaterGood brands, we still competed with the other fair-trade buyers for new products and new suppliers. Unlike buyers at other companies, GreaterGood's buyers are not assigned to a category of products and can instead buy whatever we think will sell. This offers unlimited freedom to be creative but it does, at times, create competition. We all sat in the courtyard and enjoyed pastries and lemonade while placing the largest order we had ever made with a brand-new group—one for over $20,000 worth of purses.

After that we traveled back to Santa Ana to visit the workshop of Uca Ruffatti, Maria's small handbag-making business. We had enjoyed seeing the Ruffattis' home and learning about the products, but it is always more important to me to see the products being made firsthand. In the first room, Maria's husband removed the lids on large barrels of indigo dye. Uca Ruffatti dyes cotton canvas in indigo to make handbags that they combine with either leather or rubber tire tube trim. The wet indigo was pungent, and we all quickly moved past the barrels into the room where we knew purse production was in full swing. This was where my jaw dropped. Inside the production room there were men at every table—men cutting the rubber, men sewing the seams, men adding the metal adornments. There was not a woman in sight other than those of us who had just walked in. I looked at Tim, Druce, and Mary-Mike in horror. Yes, sometimes there are men helping in the women's cooperatives we work with—occasionally husbands and family members—but the groups are never comprised of *all* men. My heart sank in my chest and, as inappropriate and unprofessional as it would be, I thought I might cry. I came to visit El Salvador specifically to buy these bags, which I thought were made by women. Of course, Maria, the designer, was a woman. But all of the crafters creating the bags (and benefiting from the income generated) were men. I could not buy the bags.

I went quickly from feeling like a hero to feeling like a villain. Maria did not understand the problem, but for me it was real. We didn't want to just support women designers; we needed the people doing the work and getting paid for their efforts to be women too. Global Girlfriend had to stay true to its mission of helping poor women, first and foremost, despite the allure of tempting products that helped people—just not women directly. There was a moral and political statement behind every product we sold. Global Girlfriend was trying to build the she-conomy of women helping other women through commerce. Morally, I felt we had an obligation to give women any seats we could get at the proverbial world trade table. For women, poverty means having little or no control over the income they do make. It means missing opportunities because they lack power and a voice in their community. Women the world over are undercounted, undervalued, underserved, and underrepresented.

But because they are the most deeply affected by poverty, women also hold the greatest potential to eradicate poverty. *The Economist* once called women "the most powerful engine" for global economic growth. If women were the engine, Global Girlfriend could not veer from our job to lay down the tracks for their train.

Women's rights are human rights. The Universal Declaration of Human Rights adopted by the United Nations General Assembly in 1948 outlines what is considered to be the fundamental consensus on the human rights of all people, including freedom from slavery and torture; protection by the law; freedom of movement and speech, religion and assembly; and the rights to social security, work, health, education, culture, and citizenship. Article 2 of this document clearly states that these human rights apply to all equally "without distinction of any kind, such as race, colour, sex, language . . . or other status." Even though this should obviously mean that women share these universal human rights, in many countries, tradition, prejudice, and social, economic, and political factors have combined to keep women from achieving their basic human rights.

Politically, the fight for global women's rights is still being waged, and women are not yet close to winning global equality with men. While some people, especially in developed countries, have come to believe that the battle for women's rights is passé and no longer an issue, there are still forty-four member countries of the United Nations—including Algeria, Argentina, Australia, Austria, Belgium, Brazil, Canada, China, Egypt, France, Germany, India, Italy, Malaysia, New Zealand, The Netherlands, Singapore, South Korea, Spain, the United Kingdom, and Venezuela—that will not accept and ratify the UN Convention on the Elimination of All Forms of Discrimination Against Women. This convention was adopted in 1979 and is the only human rights treaty that affirms the reproductive rights of women. It has been described as an international bill of human rights for women, but even the United States, which signed the convention in July 1980, has not ratified it because of opposition to this idea. Several Middle Eastern countries, including Iran, Oman, Qatar, Saudi Arabia, Sudan, Syria, and the United Arab Emirates, have ignored the convention in its entirety.

On UN Human Rights Day in 2006, the president of the sixty-first session of the UN General Assembly, Sheikha Haya Rashed Al Khalifa of Bahrain, said, "History is littered with well-meaning, but failed solutions. If we are to eradicate poverty and promote human rights, we need to take action to empower the poor and address the root causes of poverty, such as discrimination and social exclusion. It is because human rights, poverty reduction, and the empowerment of the poor go hand in hand that we all have a moral duty to take action." She was right. We have a moral duty to find solutions for people living in poverty around the world, starting with women.

Lori had not known the artisans were men when she suggested them. But I could not make good on an order that lay so far outside of our mission to help women. Money spent here would be money I would not have for other women in El Salvador or in Guatemala, or in the next country we would visit. I knew that keeping this order was not right. I felt strongly that my decision to avoid the "man-made" products was not sexist, but based on our commitment to a larger cause of helping women in poverty, even in the face of difficult circumstances— like telling the men at Uca Ruffatti and the Ruffattis that I had changed my mind about my $20,000 order. As much as the Ruffattis wanted the sale and I wanted to buy their beautiful bags, and although the men creating the bags were clearly deserving and hardworking, I had to consider that at the core of every product choice was the question of who benefited. In this case, my bottom line stood to gain the most, but at the expense of women, who would not get my business if I spent money on these bags. Guilty and torn by what I had to do, I told Maria I had to cancel the order.

Swiftly, Tim saved the day for all of us. "That's no problem," Tim reassured Maria and me. "Druce and I love the bags as much as Stacey does, and we welcome fair-trade products made by all artisans." Tim and Druce bought the bags for The Hunger Site, and they went on to be some of the best-selling styles on GreaterGood.

I deeply appreciate that again and again Tim shows all of us that he does not just "talk the talk," but that he truly has the greater good of people in need at the forefront of every choice he makes. If he had not been on the trip I would have had to cancel the order I made over lemonade at the Ruffattis' home, which would have been a devastating blow to the Ruffattis, to their artisans, and to me. The day's challenge, of standing face-to-face with artisans hungry for a market, getting their hopes up with a large order, and then pulling that order away made me feel horrible. It was the lowest feeling I had experienced in my work. Even with the best of intentions, I had made a horrible mistake of promising an order before I had fully looked into the group. Our policy was to have every new group fill out a detailed artisan profile with open-ended questions that usually helped us vet the gender, ages, and skill sets of new groups. Because our trip came up so quickly, I had not sent a profile. However, no matter how uncomfortable the situation, I was so glad to have been there making sure we were choosing our artisans for the right reasons.

I hoped Tim, and everyone we met in El Salvador, understood my decision, and why we could not take our mission off course. That day, my commitment to GreaterGood, to Tim, and to my new colleague Druce grew as well; collaboration between buyers had gone much further than competition, and had saved the day. I thought of the painted priest Óscar Romero and his unwavering commitment to his beliefs in rights for the poor. I bought a cross with his face at the airport on my way out of El Salvador to help me remember the example he set for the world to stand strong in support of the things you believe in.

# 9

# LIFE'S FABRIC

❦

*What lies behind us and what lies before us are*
*small matters, compared to what lies within us.*
—RALPH WALDO EMERSON

Connie Newton, a gray-haired woman in her sixties, and Jorge Salem, an employee of Friendship Bridge, hurried us down the bumpy stone street to the Panajachel dock where our boat was waiting. As Connie rounded the corner where the path met the water, we were rewarded with our first spectacular view of the tranquil Lake Atitlán. Twenty miles wide, the lake is surrounded by small mountains and dotted with villages alive with the traditions of Mayan life. My son, Dakota; Mary-Mike's son Robert; and my father-in-law, Jim, were already feeling at home in Guatemala. They had arrived three days earlier and had had the time of their lives exploring, while Mary-Mike and I explored El Salvador.

Mary-Mike and I had picked up Jim, Dakota, and Robert in Antigua in the afternoon and spent several hours on the winding ridges that twisted a path to the majestic Lake Atitlán. On the van ride, the boys shared their adventure tales of climbing a volcano and getting so close to the lava that it burned the hair on their legs. They were immeasurably impressed with a fellow hiker who had brought a bag of marshmallows to roast near the lava. They also loved riding on a packed chicken bus. The buses in Guatemala were brightly colored old American school buses that were decorated according to the driver's taste and personality. It was not clear if they got their names because you could load everything on them, including your chickens, or because they barely stopped to let riders on and off the bus, leaving passengers playing a perpetual game of "chicken" with their transportation. For Mary-Mike and me, it was exhilarating to see Guatemala through our sons' eyes.

After a long ride from Antigua to Pana we checked into our hotel. Pana is one of Panajachel's local nicknames. Its other nickname is Gringotenango because of the large number of tourists who frequent its streets. Dinner was at the edge of the lake, but we never saw the water. Looking out from the restaurant's terrace, all I could see was a black expanse that looked like the dark empty soybean field I used to see out my window at night growing up. Now, in the daylight, we could see what we had missed the night before—a virtual paradise. The twenty-mile-wide lake was surrounded by mountains dotted with villages, coffee fields, and tropical flowers. The area around the lake was as beautiful as any vacation spot featured in glossy travel magazines. If we were not here to work, it could have served just as nicely as a perfect vacation destination. We loaded the boats in slight disbelief that a place as beautiful as this could hold any problems.

The fact is, the people of Guatemala do indeed have worries and problems. For almost thirty-six years Guatemala was plagued with a civil war similar to the war waged in neighboring El Salvador. During the war, the government burned the countryside and villages to combat uprisings from guerrilla groups of mostly rural native Mayan farmers. Over 450 Mayan villages were destroyed, 1 million people were displaced as refugees, and over 200,000 people were killed during the civil war. While peace was reached in 1996, years of war left Guatemala with a high rate of poverty and illiteracy and the highest violent crime rate in Latin America. According to the Central Intelligence Agency World Factbook, 56 percent of Guatemalans presently live in poverty. Drug trafficking accounts for the heightened violence, and women have been the targets of much of the country's violet crime. The *Christian Science Monitor* reported in 2009 that the Guatemalan government claimed over ten thousand Guatemalan women had been raped in the preceding year. Even more chilling is the fact that thousands of women have been killed since the end of the civil war in what locals call *femicidio*—the cold-blooded murder of women, which has gone largely unpunished.

Connie Newton was a board member of the microfinance organization Friendship Bridge. Friendship Bridge was founded in 1988 by Ted and Connie Ning after the couple visited Vietnam and learned of the disturbing state of the Vietnamese health care system. They saw hospitals ill equipped with aging equipment to serve patients, little or no medicine, and rampant suffering from highly preventable diseases. The Nings wanted to help. They asked friends to carry medicines and medical supplies to Vietnam, and in the spring of 1990 their organization, Friendship Bridge, sent the largest shipment of medical supplies to Vietnam from the United States since 1975. Wanting to broaden its impact to finding a sustainable solution to the global poverty, Friendship Bridge changed its focus from providing medical relief to providing microcredit to women. With less than $3,000 and the cooperation of a group of courageous nuns at a convent in DaNang, Friendship Bridge launched its first Vietnam microcredit loan group. In 1998, Friendship Bridge expanded its work to Guatemala, another country ravaged by war and fraught with poverty. In May 2000, with over five thousand loans successfully in place in Vietnam, Friendship Bridge refocused its efforts on Guatemala. The program in Guatemala now has close to fourteen thousand women borrowers receiving microloans.

I first met Connie at the Social Business and Microeconomic Opportunities for Youth conference held in Denver in March 2008. John Hatch, known as the godfather of the village banking movement and one of the earliest users of a microloan model of helping poor communities, moderated the conference. John captivated attendees with the tale of sketching out his plan for village banking on the back of a cocktail napkin during a plane ride from Peru to Bolivia. John started in 1984 by working with farmers in Bolivia. A Fulbright-trained economist and international development expert, John conceived a small loan program that put the poor in charge of their own finances and their future. The program allowed poor communities to obtain loans without collateral and gave groups of neighbors the power to collectively disburse, invest, and collect loan capital as they saw fit. He called these groups "village banks." The organization he went on to found from the napkin plan was FINCA (Foundation for International Community Assistance), which has served over 1 million low-income families in twenty-three countries through microcredit. As John talked, all I could think was how much I would like to be drinking buddies with this man, or at least be the waitress who collected his scribbled-on napkins. After several introductory speeches by Denver's mayor, John Hickenlooper, and Colorado governor Bill Ritter, John introduced his longtime friend and colleague, Nobel Prize laureate Dr. Muhammad Yunus.

When Dr. Yunus founded the Grameen Bank in Bangladesh in 1976, his idea was met with nothing but skepticism. The traditional banking system echoed the beliefs of the world at large—poor women were not credit-worthy. More than thirty years later, the Grameen Bank has shown that tiny investments of capital, now known as microcredit, loaned to a woman in poverty can change lives. When Yunus received the Nobel Peace Prize along with the Grameen "phone ladies" (a group of cell phone entrepreneurs in Bangladesh that was funded by Grameen Bank microloans), it proved to the world that women were both worthy and capable.

"It's simple," Dr. Yunus told an eclectic audience of leaders, students, and politicians. "Solving poverty in our lifetime is simple."

He went on to explain what he felt was the next step in helping to end poverty: social business. When Dr. Yunus pioneered the concept of providing microcredit to poor women in Bangladesh, no one thought this simple idea of lending small amounts of $50 or $100 could change lives, but it did. And the world over, microcredit institutions grew from the singular Grameen Bank to more than thirty-five hundred microfinance institutions (MFIs) in just two decades. In its early form, credit itself was thought to be able to pull women out of poverty. And it did pull the poorest of the poor out of $1-a-day poverty, a poverty that is both painful and inhumane. But Dr. Yunus realized—as I had when I was conceiving my business—that in order to take the next step out of poverty at the $2- or $3-dollar-a day level, there must be something more. Women need not only the credit to start their own microbusinesses but also markets for their products.

Three years earlier, in 2005, I had attended the same microfinance conference on the Denver University campus and the message had been far different. MFIs were largely unconcerned with their ability to influence a market for their women borrowers. They appeared to be focused on professionalizing banking practices, regulating lending standards, and solidifying their loan repayment rates. These are good business practices for any lending institution, but MFIs are more than banks—they are financial agents of social change. I spoke with representatives of several smaller MFIs at the conference that year and they were not interested in helping Global Girlfriend connect to their borrowers who might be making crafts for potential export. Many felt that connecting a craft-making borrower to a market—while not helping a farming borrower with their similar need for a market—MFIs would be wrongly showing preference to one group of borrowers over another. That was true. But I thought they should be providing or partnering with organizations that could help 100 percent of their borrowers expand their market opportunities, no matter what they were growing, producing, or selling or what service they were providing. In my social work practice I had relied heavily on resource sharing and collaboration, and because of this background I was always looking for creative ways to partner with others (organizations, businesses, or individuals). I assumed microfinance and fair trade were a perfect example of how nonprofits and business could work together to solve both capital and market problems for poor women.

I was thrilled that the 2008 conference was different. Muhammad Yunus was saying the same things I had been thinking at the 2005 conference. Business and microfinance were perfect partners in providing sustainable employment. In fact, if you really look into the history at Grameen Bank you find that they have always provided employment and market resources in addition to microloans. While Grameen Bank in Bangladesh gave loans to women borrowers no matter their business ideas, they also gave women the chance at their own "microfranchise" with cell phones. Grameen Bank provided microloans for borrowers to purchase cell phones that could be used as private pay-phone businesses for rural communities. The women then ran with that idea, growing profitable small businesses around providing cell service in remote areas with their one cell phone and their ability to remember numbers from all over the world. Grameen had provided the capital and the concept, and had introduced the women to what they felt would be a viable market in their own communities. This is the idea that won Dr. Yunus and the "phone ladies" the Nobel Peace Prize. Over time, Grameen developed several other similar businesses, like Grameen Check (a textile business), Grameen Energy, and, most recently, through a partnership with Groupe Danone of France, Grameen Danone (a yogurt company). Grameen Danone in Bangladesh provided a market for women borrowers who owned cows to sell the cow's raw milk to the yogurt plant, and then for other women to buy their own yogurt microfranchise—a cooler with a strap, and a daily supply of fresh yogurt, which they could then use as a vehicle to sell fresh local yogurt to people in their villages at a very fair price. The milk producers and the yogurt saleswomen could tap financing through Grameen Bank to start or expand their personal piece of the Grameen Danone business. I saw that the same could be true for microfinance and the craft export businesses.

At the conference, I made plans with Connie to travel to Guatemala to help Friendship Bridge build a market for the beautiful woven textiles being produced by women they supported through microloans. In particular, I would visit a project called La Comunidad K'em Ajachel, a small local craft business that Friendship Bridge had helped four of their borrowers to launch. The concept of this project was that these four women, if guided and assisted properly, could commercialize Guatemalan crafts and cater traditional food to the tourist market. The group was given a $10,000 loan and a free storefront on Santander Street, the main tourist strip in Panajachel, for two years. The project had a rocky start when three of the four founders left the business before it became viable. The remaining borrower, Florinda Can Queche, took on the business (and the loan debt) herself to keep La Comunidad K'em Ajachel going, and through hard work she was succeeding locally. Flora was pooling handcrafted items from several of Friendship Bridge's borrowers and selling them in the small shop Friendship Bridge had provided. She knew from her own experiences the problems the weavers faced and was deeply committed to improving their incomes and lives through her business. I wanted to see if Global Girlfriend could expand their market one step further by bringing their goods to our customers in the United States. I was glad to be in Guatemala, creating the next link between microloan recipients and markets.

A warm breeze blew my hair as our boat cut a line in the glassy water to the boat dock at San Pedro, one of the many villages along the shores of Guatemala's tropical Lake Atitlán. Men fished from dugout canoes while women washed laundry in the shallows of the shoreline. Connie was greeted warmly by a woman walking from the lake with a basket of wet clothes she had just finished washing in the lake's temperate waters. As she walked up the steep cobblestone street, Connie was greeted again and again like a rock star by the tiny local Mayan women in their colorful *traje* (traditional clothing) consisting of handwoven *huipil* blouses and a *corte*—a long wrap skirt held up by a *cinta* (a sash that held the whole outfit together). *Huipils* are the traditional blouses worn by native Mayan women in Guatemala.

The fabric is first hand-woven on a traditional backstrap loom and then hand-embroidered with fine details. Connie explained that each village around the lake had a particular set of colors and patterns for their *huipils,* often making it easy to know where a woman is from by looking at her top. This tradition has changed some over time as women travel more from village to village, admire the weaving and colors of other villages, and incorporate elements into their own work.

San Pedro bombarded our senses with the sights and sounds of the *tuk-tuks* (vehicles similar to the cycle rickshaws of India), women weaving on backstrap looms, stray dogs, rows of women in brightly colored *huipil* blouses sitting beside baskets of even brighter fresh vegetables, and the smell of chicken frying at food stands around the town's square. Connie took the time to ask each woman who approached about her family or her business, all while keeping an eye out for Maria Mesías, the Friendship Bridge loan officer we were meeting in the midst of the bustling activity in the market square.

Connie walked in somewhat of a waddle in her socks and Birkenstock sandals, but as soon as she caught a glimpse of Maria, we all had to kick up our pace to a slight jog in order to keep up with her. Connie had raved that Maria Mesías was a modern Mayan woman—someone who kept tradition by wearing traditional *traje* but was also a role model for a new generation of women and girls in Guatemala. Mari, as her friends call her, first learned of Friendship Bridge in 1999 when she became a borrower in the microloan program. She and her mother had heard that it might be possible to get a loan for making their hand-woven, backstrap-loomed textiles, though they were skeptical, as neither woman had any collateral. After visiting the Friendship Bridge office to inquire about loans, Mari came to form part of Friendship Bridge's second trust bank, receiving a loan of 1,500 quetzals—around $200 U.S. Like John Hatch's concept of a village bank, Friendship Bridge formed groups of women into small collectives they called trust banks. Trust banks rely on the idea that the women will not let one another down in repaying their loans. They use the trust the women have in one another as collateral for the whole group. If one woman defaults on her loan, the entire group is accountable for that money. Therefore, they have to work together to be sure that does not happen.

Before Friendship Bridge, Mari had no way to get funding or to create her own weaving business. She was forced to work for other people—weaving, embroidering, and doing beadwork for very little pay. With her initial loan, Mari bought 1,000 quetzals worth of weaving thread and beadwork supplies, and started her own business. She hired three other weavers, earned back her investment and then some, and used the money from her first sales of her weavings to repay her loan in full and on time. She was left with a sizeable inventory of thread, free and clear, which was woven into her first profits. With her remaining 500 quetzals, Mari and her husband, Pedro, planted coffee saplings that soon bore fruit and supplemented her weaving income.

With the help of two more loan cycles from Friendship Bridge, she sold enough *huipils* to complete construction on her humble home. Mari bought windows and doors with the 900 quetzals she earned from the last three *huipils* she ever sold. A shining star in the Friendship Bridge program, Mari was offered a job as the second full-time loan officer at Friendship Bridge and accepted the position with pride.

As loan officer, Mari now travels throughout the villages that surround the lake, facilitating the monthly meetings of twenty-eight women's trust banks. She is charged with managing each bank's twenty to twenty-five borrowers, and with collecting and tracking their loan amounts and repayments. In addition to running the meetings and making loans, she provides interactive learning activities in the local Mayan language to teach women about their rights, health, and education, as well as gives advice on growing their businesses. Sometimes Mari uses games or songs, sometimes open conversations, and sometimes even role-playing activities in her lessons. Mari also sets up new groups of women in trust banks—recruiting members, conducting orientations to explain microcredit, and visiting prospective borrowers at home to develop financial profiles on their small businesses. She tells borrowers that when a woman joins a trust bank she is becoming the loan collateral for her friends, and so it is important to act responsibly and honorably with her loan and loan repayment for the benefit of the entire group.

As Mari approached, we could see that she was dressed in a *huipil* blouse from her traditional Maya Tzutujil community in the village of Santiago Atitlán. She wore her foot-loomed skirt gracefully wrapped and tucked like a sarong around her waist, the same way her mother and grandmother had done for generations.

Connie and Mari hugged, then Connie translated greetings and introductions between Mari and our group. Connie made Dakota and Robert introduce themselves, since she knew they were studying Spanish in school. We followed close behind as Connie and Mari walked off arm in arm, two girl-friends enmeshed in their own conversation. Finally, they ducked between two buildings into a narrow passage that led to the open-air center of a family home. This was where the "Coffee Flowers" women's microloan borrowers group would be meeting today.

Mari opened the meeting by asking the women and the

guests to stand in a circle for the opening song. Chanting loudly in an amoeba-shaped circle while ducking under hanging laundry and watching a scrawny chicken pecking for scraps at our feet, I sang along in my horrid Spanish to the theme song of the Coffee Flowers: "We are women, we matter, and we have the same rights as men." We heard in this song what the power of their friendship had taught them. As the verse repeated we all sang together louder, our voices traveling out of the open courtyard and down the market streets just steps away. We are women. We matter. We have the same rights as men. Simple concepts I and many other American women take for granted, but in rural Guatemala this song and the ripple of change it caused through these women was revolutionary.

Violence against women in Guatemala has historically gone unchecked and unpunished. Since 2001, the murder of women in Guatemala has grown at a gravely concerning pace. According to a report by Amnesty International in London titled "Guatemala: No Protection, No Justice: Killings of Women in Guatemala," "The alarming increase in the number of killings of women is compounded by impunity, weak laws, and a firmly entrenched 'machista' or sexist mindset." At the time of the report in 2005, 506 women had been murdered in that year alone, and none of their killers had been prosecuted. Between 2001 and 2007, the unprosecuted murder toll for women hovered above 2,000 victims. Over 70 percent of the rural population in Guatemala lives in poverty, and Guatemalan women have the lowest life expectancy and the highest maternal mortality rate in the region. They also have the worst economic activity rate in Central America, meaning there are little or no opportunities to generate income, or they are unable to earn a livable wage. Women in Guatemala do not enjoy the rights to money, property, or even to their own bodies as I do in America.

After Mari collected the Coffee Flowers' loan payments and checked in the members in her attendance book, we went around the circle and each woman introduced herself and her business. Then Mari began the education portion of their session. She handed out teardrop-shaped flower petals, each with a drawing of a woman doing something she wanted the women to discuss. She asked two or three women to work together to tell the group what was happening in the photo on their petal. In the middle of the circle Mari laid down the flower center that listed our rights as women. Some boldly and others shyly, the women went around the group explaining the right displayed on their petal. The right to earn money, the right to see a doctor, the right to be educated, the right to not be hit or abused, the right to gather as a group, and, most important, the right to be equal to our husbands. After each explanation and discussion, the petal was laid on the flower until the bloom was complete. Receiving a microloan to start a business and being a member of a group that supported them was changing long-held beliefs about what women could be or do in Mayan society. These women were blossoming, bravely changing the mind-sets of their husbands and the futures of their daughters.

Leaving the meeting, Connie said, "Stacey, ask Mari how many children she has." Before I could ask, Mari answered, smiling widely, "Two. Two boys, sons." The fertility rate in Guatemala is the highest in Latin America, with an average of five children born to each Guatemalan woman during her lifetime. Although the Guatemalan government has officially recognized that the national birth rate is high, it has done little to encourage family planning or the use of birth control among its citizens. Mari was proud both because her family was small by her choice and because she and her husband had worked together on deciding what size family was best for them. Her husband respected her and her choices. Mari was a role model with a small family, a good income, and a life in comfortable balance with traditional values and modern attitudes. She was raising two sons with new ideas about the rights, capabilities, and importance of women. I hoped I was raising my son the same way.

The next day we met the woman we'd come to Guatemala to meet, Florinda Can Queche, the founder of La Comunidad K'em Ajachel. Flora was born and raised in Panajachel. Her father, Don Reginaldo, was the only indigenous farmer in their area who refused to sell his land to rich landowners from Guatemala City, which left the family's very humble home surrounded by beautiful summer houses owned by wealthy vacationers. Flora's mother, Dona Chabela Queche, married Don Reginaldo when she was just fourteen years old, and the couple had four daughters, of which Flora was the second youngest. Neither of Flora's parents had more than a year of formal education, which limited their work opportunities to farming and weaving. Money was hard to come by in Flora's home, and at the age of seven she began learning how to weave and make beadwork from her mother and her Mayan neighbors who worked as guards and housekeepers in the vacation homes of the wealthy. Her first income came from selling bracelets she made at home with her mother and younger sister. Flora spent six years in formal education and then, at the age of nine, began working full-time as a weaver to help generate income for her family.

At first, Flora sold her traditional backstrap-loom weaving in the local market, but a European businessman soon discovered her skills. Along with several other young indigenous girls, Flora began weaving for the importer, who would order mass amounts of cloth. He exploited the girls, making them work long days, late into the night, and paying them extremely low wages. Nevertheless, for Flora, at ten years old, this was the only option for steady employment that could help sustain her family. The concept of fair trade was unknown at the time in Flora's community, and many Western businesspeople exploited Mayan labor. She worked for the merchant for three years, but over time grew strong enough to leave his employment and fight for her rights to make a fair wage.

Just like her mother, when Flora was fourteen, she was married and began a family of her own. After having three children—two boys and a girl—Flora went back to weaving and making bracelets to help support her family. She opened a small business selling her crafts at the boat dock on Lake Atitlán. She grew her business little by little, selling in the intense summer heat and the drastic rainy season. In time her business grew enough to provide work to two additional craftswomen, Cadelaria and Dona Jesús. Eventually, a group of her friends told Flora about the loans Friendship Bridge was making to women to start or expand their businesses. Flora took out a $120 loan from Friendship Bridge. She enjoyed participating in the training sessions the Friendship Bridge loan officers provided. Her loan group provided friendship and a place for women to come together to laugh and learn. Flora's loan helped her grow her crafts business, and with her profits she was able to employ five women. She saw the opportunities employment offered these women, and that it had offered her through her initial microloan, and she made a promise to herself to continue assisting talented women artisans. Her success in growing a crafts business was the genesis for starting La Comunidad K'em Ajachel. Flora and her original three partners were willing to take on the much larger debt risk in order to help their fellow indigenous Mayan artisan sisters find a wider market and fair pay. Artisans like Antonia.

Antonia began to weave when she was only nine years old. Poverty forced her to work at such a young age in order to help her family. She was responsible not only for weaving items that could be sold by the family, but for helping her mother with the daily chores of cooking, cleaning, and washing clothes. She began working full-time as a teenager, traveling an hour by foot to reach her job working for an American woman in the neighboring community of San Pedro La Laguna to help contribute to her family's income. After getting up each morning at five, Antonia would work all day and then stay up weaving until midnight. She was committed to helping her family try to escape from a life of poverty. Unfortunately, Antonia's father took advantage of his daughter's efforts. When Antonia began to earn an income, her father worked less and less, spending Antonia's earnings on alcohol and stressing the family's finances more than before she was a family breadwinner. Antonia knew she needed to become financially independent, and she eventually became the leader of a group of weavers called La Esperanza. La Esperanza partnered with Flora to become a production unit specialized in producing natural dye fabric for La Comunidad K'em Ajachel. Antonia, a strong, disciplined, and cheerful woman, is responsible for distributing raw materials to weavers in the group, assuring quality control and timely delivery of the products Flora orders from them.

I wanted to help Flora, and her partner artisans like Antonia, learn how to export to Global Girlfriend. They had developed a local market selling to the community and tourists, but they wanted to increase their sales by exporting to America. I wanted the same. Still, Flora and many of the weavers and jewelers she partnered with had been mistreated by Western businesses in the past, and they wanted to be assured that our partnership would be a fair and equal one. We explained that we would honor their prices and even help them to be sure they were considering all of their costs and labor in what they charged. We would pay a 50 percent deposit at the time of our order, cover all shipping costs, and wire a final payment when the goods were ready to ship. We would be equal partners as producers and marketers of their crafts. Flora, Mary-Mike, Jorge, and I spent several hours on the nitty-gritty details of shipping, export documentation, packaging, country-of-origin labeling, and all of the things we knew we needed La Comunidad K'em Ajachel to do to help us bring their products into the United States.

The rest of the week was spent boating from dock to dock visiting several of the villages around Lake Atitlán and the homes of more women making products for La Comunidad K'em Ajachel. Women in San Juan La Laguna gave us a natural dyeing demonstration. They used only flowers, barks, and plants to get the colors that dyed the thread they used for their weavings. Each natural colorant was boiled with bamboo, which was used to set the dye. This process created soft pastel shades of sky blue, warm gold, sage green, mocha brown, and soft pink.

In Santa Catarina we visited a very successful weaver who ran a shop in town filled with *huipils*. Then we walked through the narrow passageways in the hillside above the store to meet Rosa, a weaver who lived in a two-room house with her mother and her two children. On our way to Rosa's we stopped in a small bodega (grocery store) a woman had set up in the front room of her house. We bought a bag of rice, a pint of cooking oil, and two bars of soap to take to Rosa as a gift for opening her home to us. Kids followed us as we curved up and around buildings until we found the cement bridge walkway that lead to Rosa's yard.

As we approached, Rosa came to meet us while her daughter hung back timidly by the small traditional Mayan sweat bath, an outside room the size of a large doghouse attached to the side of the house. The sweat bath is used for cleansing, like we would in a shower, but uses only small amounts of water and is more similar to a sauna. It is also used for healing, and plants are often added to a person's sweat bath to stave off illness. The home was a gray cement-block building with a tin roof and a pink lace curtain that could barely keep out bugs, let alone danger, hanging as the front door. Rosa had a round face with an infectious smile. She was wearing the traditional bright but deep turquoise blue *huipil* that we had seen on every woman we passed in Santa Catarina. After explaining that she makes *huipils* as her main source of family income, Rosa went right to demonstrating the art of backstrap-loom weaving.

Rosa's hands never stopped moving and her face never stopped smiling as she worked on another inch of the intricate blue *huipil* she was finishing for market. Each *huipil* took Rosa two to three months to create. In order to get more for her weaving, she would travel a slow and winding couple of hours on public transportation to Antigua for the weekend to sell to tourists and collectors. Rosa's mother watched the children while Rosa and a few other women from the villages around Lake Atitlán shared one room in a local Antigua boardinghouse. Her goal was to try to sell one *huipil* a month and to supplement her income with small beaded jewelry pieces she, her mother, and her daughter made when they were not weaving. Because of her skill level, each of her *huipils* could sell in Antigua for over $200 U.S. Still not that much if you consider the time invested in each piece, but much more than the local market would bear. As a master weaver, highly skilled at the centuries-old Mayan tradition of intricate weaving, Rosa had elevated her creations to works of art. She was teaching her daughter in the ancient traditions, hoping to preserve the craft of backstrap-loom weaving for future generations.

Hungry from a long day of visiting with women, Dakota and Robert pulled Nestlé Crunch bars from their backpacks to enjoy as an afternoon treat as we left Rosa's house. The chocolate bars were like kid magnets. First two little girls appeared, looking up at the boys and their candy. When they gave each girl a hunk of the bar, a few more kids came, seemingly out of nowhere. Dakota and Robert shared a few more pieces of their candy, until soon the kids were plentiful and the bars were gone.

"Boys, aren't those the best candy bars you never ate?" Connie asked, smiling.

The boys agreed that they were.

We were all charmed by the Guatemalan people. So often on trips to visit our artisans I go with the goal of helping them progress, helping them learn new things. I often spent much of my time working with our artisans on how to run more efficient small businesses, helping them analyze their cost structure, source materials, and take advantage of trade agreements that favor products made by less developed countries. I also spent a lot of time working with women on market trends. In Guatemala I was so mesmerized by the traditions of their art, my drive to repurpose their art to more Western products was almost forgotten. While we had come to help the Mayan women of La Comunidad K'em Ajachel find a larger Western market for their products, they had taught us much more about tradition and family, and that ancient ways are sometimes the best ways.

In our busy, high-tech lives we often forget about the importance of tradition, thinking newer is always better. But there is something to be said for relishing family and community, and the traditions that bond the two together. Mayan women had held on to a strong sense of community through their weaving, and were passing that culture of community on to their children. Mary-Mike and I felt compelled to help preserve the art that had come to be synonymous with Mayan women—backstrap-loom weaving. We hoped providing a market would help to keep this art and tradition alive.

Once we had gone with Flora to visit several of her artisans around the lake, we had to figure out what they could make for Global Girlfriend, how much each artisan could produce, and what it would cost. Our first day of ordering and pricing went long past dinnertime, late into the evening. I sketched and reviewed photos of items we had seen on the trip around the lake. We worked on designs, trying to streamline the women's beautiful weaving into products that would fit our American market. I did not know anyone, except Connie on special occasions, who wore a *huipil* back at home (although I bought two to hang on my walls). But I did know that the quality and craftsmanship of the weaving would warrant attention and orders if we could just apply them to the right item. Handbags seemed the key for weaving, and bracelets the winner for the women's beautiful beadwork. We went over each color for the jewelry in painstaking detail to be sure it was right. *"Claro,"* I repeated again and again, wanting to be sure we got beads that had a clear, shiny finish instead of the solid-colored beads that looked more like what we had from Gertrude in Africa.

On our final evening, Flora prepared a home-cooked Guatemalan meal for us in the kitchen under the Friendship Bridge office. She made wonderfully seasoned rice and baked local small squash to accompany fresh black fish from the lake. I worried as I saw the plates of fish coming toward the boys with heads and tails still intact, eyes looking up at them. Dakota and Robert just smiled at me and then got to eating as Flora showed them how to bone the fish. My plate had a large fresh halved avocado where the fish should have been. Flora made sure to feed me as well as the others, despite my vegetarian diet. Our dinner together was, for me, a celebration of the new partnership we were forging. Microcredit borrowers and fair-trade companies did make good mates.

I admired the small business Flora had built with the help of loans through Friendship Bridge. I admired the way Mari had parlayed her position of borrower into the role of a respected loan officer with Friendship Bridge—a career woman in every respect. Dr. Yunus had been right in his assumption that poor women were both credit-worthy and capable; they only needed to have the opportunity and they could provide their own success. I appreciated that like Grameen Bank, Friendship Bridge was willing to stretch beyond its perceived boundaries as a lender and go one step further to connect capital to markets. Friendship Bridge was also on the forefront of pairing educational programming with microlending. The organization was teaching women that they were worthy of credit, and that as women, they had rights to their own future, to their hard-earned money, and to their dreams for building a better life through small investments in those dreams. Dr. Yunus and John Hatch were my idols in this field, but I had become an even greater fan of the Mayan women of Guatemala. They had taught me that tradition and progress were not in opposition. Building on Mayan traditions would, in fact, be the vehicle the women of La Comunidad K'em Ajachel used to bring sustainable livelihoods to their community.

Flora, Mary-Mike, Connie, Jorge, Jim, the boys, and I raised a toast with bottles of cold Coca-Cola to celebrate a successful start to our new partnership.

# 10

# HAITI

We are each other's harvest; we are each other's business;
we are each other's magnitude and bond.
—GWENDOLYN BROOKS

I traveled with Druce to Haiti in January 2009, exactly one year before the horrific earthquakes of 2010 devastated the island nation, which up until the tragedy had been largely ignored by the rest of the world. I think it is critical to say here that I am not an expert on Haiti. As with all countries I've traveled to for Global Girlfriend, I've been a visitor, an observer, a business-woman, and a friend wanting to make a difference for women in poverty. I have only visited Haiti once, and as of this writing I have not been back. I am proud to be part of a company that is actively involved in ongoing fund-raising for Haiti's recovery efforts, and even more proud to be buying products from Haitian artisans to help rebuild their economy. But the real backbone of the recovery in Haiti is the Haitian people, supported by some of the most amazing, efficient, and effective nonprofits I have encountered, including Partners In Health and the Global Orphan Project. Responsibility also lies squarely with the world community to act in partnership with Haiti for the long term to rebuild Haiti stronger and better than it was before. This chapter is simply a recollection of my trip to Haiti and our attempts at Global Girlfriend to invest in Haitian women.

Druce had worked with Aid to Artisans to arrange a buying trip for us. Tim had encouraged both Druce and me to go on the trip because he wanted Global Girlfriend and the Greater-Good sites to invest more heavily in Haitian artisans and their products. The Hunger Site had carried a spattering of products from Haiti over the years, but no GreaterGood buyer had ever visited the country to work with artisans firsthand. Global Girlfriend had no Haitian-made products at all. Our trip was an effort to change that.

Most businesses in the world strive to work in places that provide opportunities to be more efficient, or get more cost-effective labor, or save on transportation and material costs. American companies importing goods from foreign nations look for locations that make doing business easy or that are at least laden with trade incentives that make working there attractive. Haiti traditionally has not been an easy place to do business. In 2006 the U.S. Department of Commerce issued a Country Commercial Guide to doing business in or with Haiti. The guide pointed out a list of challenges to commercial export with Haiti, including few government subsidies, political insecurity that threatened both capital investments and productivity, the highest port fees in the Caribbean, and a limited and deteriorating transportation infrastructure. Rather than deter Global Girlfriend and GreaterGood from working in Haiti, these were issues that drew us there. It is only through employment opportunities that countries with obstacles can improve economically. Our entire team felt that we had a moral and social obligation to work in the places people and economies needed the most help.

As my colleague at GreaterGood Michelle Schectman had proven to us through her two trips to Afghanistan to work with artisans (most of them women), the investment in the hardest places on earth could have not only the largest social impact but also an economic payout for both the artisans and the business. In the year after Michelle's first trip, our company sold over $150,000 in products made by Afghan artisans. The sales of these products (which continue to grow today) employ over a hundred Afghan artisans, which in turn improves the lives of their families and their communities.

The first leg of our Haitian journey would be spent visiting a women's group in rural Cerca-la-Source organized near one of Paul Farmer's globally acclaimed Partners In Health (PIH) hospitals. A PIH doctor had introduced Druce and me to this group, whose members were hoping to develop a product and a market for their product outside of their very rural community. Partners In Health has been working in Haiti for over twenty years, providing world-class medical care to underserved Haitians and raising a new generation of Haitian doctors and nurses. GreaterGood has been partnering with PIH since 2007. Through our Gifts That Give More program, our customers help to support PIH with donations that provide clean child-birth kits to mothers, free school lunches to children, and bed nets to protect families from malaria. From this partnership I knew about the good work PIH was doing, but it was not until I read Tracy Kidder's book *Mountains Beyond Mountains: The Quest of Dr. Paul Farmer, a Man Who Would Cure the World* on my plane ride home from the 2008 World Conservation Congress in Barcelona that I was truly moved to make sure Haitian women were represented through Global Girlfriend. The issues discussed at the World Conservation Congress—including the impacts water management, deforestation, health, and human dignity had on communities—were spelled out on every page of Kidder's book. Reading Dr. Farmer's story, I felt a serious sense of guilt that Global Girlfriend had not yet reached out to work with women in Haiti. Like Tim, I felt that needed to change.

A warm tropical breeze met us on the tarmac as we walked off the plane and into the Toussaint Louverture International Airport on the outskirts of Port-au-Prince. The flight from Miami had been packed with Haitian travelers and overflowing carry-on bags. I was glad to have checked my luggage, since the overhead compartments had not a square inch to spare. I also didn't think I would be able to get past U.S. security with five brass hammers in my carry-on.

Two weeks before our trip to Haiti, I had started to panic. My anxiety stemmed from the fact that I didn't have a handle on a specific craft the women we were going to work with could make. The women's group in Cerca-la-Source had been given training in jewelry making by volunteers from the United States, but they had limited access to beads or materials other than what had been donated to them by their trainers. Researching Haitian crafts online, I learned that Haiti seemed to produce very few traditional women's crafts for sale in the United States. Some paintings and oil-drum art were popular, but most often men made these. Global Girlfriend typically worked to design products from the traditional skills the women brought to us, but in rural Haiti we would actually be bringing a craft to the women. In this instance Druce and I would be conducting a different kind of training than I had ever done before— one for which we were supposed to possess a crafting skill. I had done many business training sessions for women. Global Girlfriend had given me great insights into costing, production time studies, trade agreements, consumer safety issues, fashion and color trends, import specifications, shipping, and marketing. These were topics I felt confident talking about with our women partners in developing countries. I also felt confident in directing our artisans in tweaking their traditional crafts, suggesting new colors or shapes for what they were already making to help their products have a more universal appeal for women consumers in America. But making something myself was a completely different story. Thankfully, Druce, unlike me, was a true designer. She would be an enormous asset both to me and to the women we were hoping to help.

We agreed to go to Haiti with some crafting ideas and resources in hand. The goal of the trip was to find a marketable product, whether it was one discovered while in Haiti or one we brought with us to teach the women. Ideally, the craft would be something the women were already doing, but we did not want to arrive empty-handed. While Druce collected jewelry-making books and focused on designing some glass-bead bracelets and necklaces for the women to copy, I turned to my craftier staff to help me with the ideas I was charged with bringing to Haiti. Mary-Mike, Alison, Sheri, and Alyssa got to work immediately, scouring Web sites and local boutiques for a skill we might teach the women that wouldn't be too hard to learn or too heavy to ship. Alyssa found metal stamping. All I would have to get to Haiti would be a first round of brass hammers, steal pounding plates, and pendants. Then the shipping of the lightweight finished pendants would not be difficult. They could even ride down and back with volunteers traveling back and forth from Haiti until we figured out how to help the women find reliable shipping methods. I ordered around $1,000 worth of supplies two days before my trip, had the goods sent overnight to my office, and hoped for the best.

Flights to Haiti left from Florida only in the morning. Since I had no way to fly early enough from Colorado to arrive in Florida to make a morning flight to Haiti, I had to spend one night in a Miami hotel. It was a good thing—I needed time to teach myself the art of metal stamping. After a quick dinner alone with John Grogan's book *The Longest Trip Home,* I headed to my room to get learning. I paid for the Beaducation .com online introductory metal-stamping course and set up my tools. As the instructor taught from the screen of my MacBook, I pounded, colored, buffed, punched, and added a jump ring to my first sloppy Haiti pendant for hope. As I practiced on a few more samples, I realized it was approaching midnight and my hotel neighbors might start wondering about the loud hammering I thought might pass as construction clamor earlier in the evening. I packed my hammer, block, letters, and markers carefully back into my suitcase, where they'd sit until they met their new owners.

After a long wait at baggage claim in Haiti, my bag showed up, but only one of Druce's two suitcases arrived. Her clothes made it, but the bag she'd filled with her jewelry designs and some additional craft ideas, samples, and supplies was lost. With her half of the ideas missing, my midnight metal stamping grew ever more important. Going to visit the women with just one idea for a product they could make made me nervous. What if they didn't like the craft, or worse, what if they did like it and we were inept teachers?

Outside the Port-au-Prince airport we were greeted by Anne Pressoir, our hostess from Aid to Artisans, and a white Mitsubishi four-wheel drive ready to take us out of the city. The palm trees and UN security forces vehicles that lined the front of the airport quickly gave way to cement-block buildings, potholes, street vendors, *tap-tap* buses, and city crowds. Morning life in

Port-au-Prince chugged along under the tropical sun and amid its ramshackle buildings, water pouch (like kids' juice pouches but filled with clean water) and fruit vendors, and endless stalls of used clothing. Haitian people seemed impeccably well put together. Although I knew they were clothed in almost 90 percent used apparel from Goodwill and Salvation Army clothing bales shipped in on cargo barges from the United States, I could not help but notice how white their whites were and how crisply pressed their pants and dresses appeared.

Before the 2010 earthquake, over 80 percent of the estimated 9 million people living in Haiti lived beneath the poverty line. Fifty-four percent suffered in abject poverty, known as the poverty that kills. In pre-earthquake statistics, Haiti ranked 149th of 182 countries rated on the United Nations Human Development Index, a tool aimed at measuring human development and the opportunities people have in their country for access to education, employment, health care, and other basic human needs. Haiti is the only country in the Western Hemisphere on the United Nations list of Least Developed Countries. The 2010 earthquake—in which the Haitian government estimates that over 230,000 people died and 1.2 million Haitians lost their homes—only magnified Haiti's challenges.

The government estimates that about half the population is unemployed, although no one is idle. There may not be enough "official" employment, but most Haitians are very busy working in the informal sector. In addition, organizations like Aid to Artisans and a new nonprofit formed in 2009 (the same year as our trip), called 1,000 Jobs, are working to increase employment in Haiti through business training, marketing, and recruiting foreign investment in Haitian industry. As is true of any island community, Haiti must rely on other countries for resources that are not native to the island, such as fuel. With a scarcity of alternative fuels, the country has been forced to turn largely to charcoal, but overreliance on charcoal has lead to deforestation across the central plateau. The widespread deforestation in turn makes for harsh living conditions, and the lives of Haitian women are especially difficult.

A major problem average Haitians face (and did prior to the earthquake), in addition to lack of income and scarce fuel sources, is the lack of clean water. Sourcing water is a daily struggle for many Haitians living in rural and urban areas. The Haitian government estimates that 60 percent of people in the country do not have access to safe drinking water. For some, the daily walk to water may be miles. In urban areas, the government has provided spigot taps on fountains for public use, but no matter where the poor get their water, it is rarely safe to drink. In the slums of Port-au-Prince, housing is erected with little planning, and even when there is a clean water source nearby, it often becomes contaminated by runoff from human waste. People are advised to add bleach to the water or at least boil it to kill the wide variety of parasites that haunt Haitian water supplies. The problem is that when mothers have no money for bleach to treat with or charcoal to boil with, water remains a basic daily need. So they take the risk and let their children drink anyway. Consuming unsafe water leads to dysentery, internal parasites, typhoid fever, severe diarrhea, and, ironically, dehydration. According to USAID, one in eight Haitian children dies by age five, typically from preventable causes like diarrhea from unsafe water, starvation, or malaria. Additionally, one third are chronically malnourished.

But for every obstacle Haiti faces, the country has something positive working in its favor. First and foremost are the Haitian people. Kind, smart, hardworking, and with strong resolve, tenacious and adaptable Haitians keep their country moving forward. Second, committed Haitians, in partnership with organizations like ours and 1,000 Jobs, are working on developing industry. And third, in my estimation, is the presence of Partners In Health. From a small idea that people everywhere deserve to be healthy—and especially deserve protection against preventable diseases and access to care no matter their economic status—Partners In Health has grown a hospital, clinic, and health-care presence in Haiti that is unparalleled in the rest of the developing world (and rivals the best care in the United States if looked at on a dollar-per-dollar basis). In the aftermath of the earthquakes, PIH has instituted mobile health clinics to conduct health-care outreach to displaced Haitians. Most important, PIH's world-class HIV/AIDS programs are run almost entirely by Haitians. PIH not only provides care but also enables Haitians to care for themselves, building a generation of new Haitian medical professionals. PIH cares for whole human beings, not just sick people. If their patients don't have access to food, or clean water, or shelter, and that is the root of their illness, PIH works to treat not only the current symptoms but also the disease called poverty.

I had been nervous about the road to the town of Cange, home of PIH's first hospital, Zami Lasante, because it had been such a focal point in *Mountains Beyond Mountains*, which I had finished reading before my trip. I was pleasantly surprised to find that the first leg of our journey, while still bumpy in spots, had been paved. As we rolled away from the banks of Lake Péligre and past Cange, the road from Cange to Hinche deteriorated quickly. Instead of feeling like a country gravel road outside my hometown of Hinckley, the roads seemed to be made of lumpy river rocks camouflaging deep potholes. Sitting behind the driver's seat by the door, I soon felt the sting of a raw rug burn on my elbow. My arm was raw from scuffing and bumping along the plastic armrest as we were jostled in the backseat. Druce tried not to hit me as we knocked into each other's shoulders and then into the doors like two pinballs between bumpers. The white road dust of daylight quickly turned to a faint fog as night set in. Despite the darkness, people walked everywhere along the roadside. Across the distant hills we could see lines of fire burning vertically out of the rural darkness. The subtle scent of campfire hung in the air as I watched a mountain burning, deepening the deforestation plaguing Haiti, all for the production of charcoal. With few other energy sources on the island, a steady stream of charcoal was in constant demand.

I was growing ever more tired from our daylong drive when, just as we were traversing what seemed to be a path of boulders, a cloud of dust suddenly fogged the front window. The vehicle in front of us came to a stop, and there seemed to be chaos in the crowd ahead. Neither Druce nor I said a word. We just waited in silence, not sure what to think, not knowing what was happening. The silence made me fearful. When a car finally rolled up going the opposite direction, our driver rolled down his window and asked in Creole, "How many?"

The driver of the other car answered, *"Deux."*

Just two cars ahead of us two people had died when their overloaded *tap-tap* bus hadn't been able to stay upright. A *tap-tap* was the most common form of group transportation, the Haitian public bus. Mango and vegetable farmers often ride on top of the *tap-taps* with bulging bags of fruits or veggies. Two of these travelers would not reach their destination tonight. As the road turned from rocks to boulders, the top-heavy bus had simply fallen over; its wheels were still spinning when we passed.

Shocked by the reality of the deaths just ahead of us, we rolled past the *tap-tap* in somber and mournful silence. I whispered a prayer for the victims and longed for our arrival in

Hinche, the largest city in the central plateau. While there were no distinct welcome signs, it was clear that we'd reached a hub as people and buildings broke the silence of the countryside. Hinche was lively, with roadside fires and music, but the hospital where we would be spending the next couple of nights was quiet. We knew that wasn't typical. In the morning we could expect to see two hundred to five hundred patients waiting in line to see eleven doctors.

After a meal of fried plantains and the local delicacy, guinea fowl (not for me but for the meat eaters in the group), we went to bed. The buzzing mosquitoes that circled overhead did not seem to faze Druce. I pulled the covers over my face, despite the heat, and tried to sleep. Tomorrow was an important day, and Cerca was still a few hours away.

Cerca-la-Source was near nothing, by my best estimation. In the morning we drove and drove for about three hours before we realized we were lost. Getting lost is not hard. Not that there are so many road choices or turnoffs, but at the few junctions there are, most roads are unmarked. Whenever we would see a gathering of people or a small trading center, our driver would ask simply, "Cerca-la-Source?" The question was most often met with a blank stare. When we finally reached the wide, shallow, clean river at the border crossing of the Dominican Republic, we knew we'd gone too far.

We watched what might be considered a commercial convoy of donkeys cross into Haiti with oversized bags of rice or possibly maize flour. The tranquil tree-lined river looked just like one back at home in Colorado, and I smiled to myself thinking of my husband, Brad, an avid fly fisherman, on the bank looking for trout in the river with his special polarized "fish-ray glasses," as I like to call them. Our driver did his best to turn the SUV around in what was no more than a one-lane road lined with food vendors who seemed to have carved out a niche feeding people at the crossing. Meanwhile, I was concerned about the time. The ladies in Cerca had been waiting for us since early morning.

As we finally approached the village, the dusty, dry emptiness of the central plateau began to green up like nowhere we'd passed since we left Cange. It was the dry season, and the plateau was covered in white dust and brown brush, and dotted with the occasional cluster of shacks, some made of wood and scrap metal, some of mud with thatched roofs, and others with rocks or a combination of all three. During our mid-January visit, food was very scarce. But soon it would be mango season. Mango trees dotted the landscape, and we could see the flowers that would soon turn to fruit starting to bloom. "In mango season, everyone eats," our driver said with a smile.

On the outskirts of Cerca-la-Source, people were tending fields and small plot gardens. Obviously, this community's proximity to a water source gave it a vitality unseen in places farther from the river. We could hear singing as we approached the community church where the women were waiting for us, and I felt a surge of excitement to have finally arrived. I stopped worrying about what we might talk about with the women, or how our jewelry-making training might turn out. I was just eager to meet them and get started. Druce felt the same. Cerca-la-Source means "near the source." I could tell we were now near the source of hope.

Inside the church the women were lined up in front of the bench-style church pews singing in lovely unison. We filed into the sanctuary and sat in white molded-plastic lawn chairs near tables set at the front of the sanctuary. There were not many smiles in the crowd of about forty women, though I did notice two women grin when I made eye contact with them. Before beginning introductions, the women sang a few more songs I thought I recognized as Creole versions of hymns I knew. The group had given themselves the name Club Mama, the mothers' club, since they had come together as mothers to try to build a school for their children. Our hosts were eager to start on our training, but they promised to show us the public school next door at the end of the day. The Haitian government does provide public schools, but they are completely inadequate, underfunded, and understaffed and require a uniform and supplies fee of about $15 per year per student, far more than many families can afford to pay.

Druce and I introduced ourselves. I explained what Global Girlfriend did to partner with women like them all around the world. I passed out copies of our holiday catalog so they could see photos of some of our products and the profiles of some of the women we work with. I wanted them to have a sense of being a part of something larger outside of their rural community, part of a sisterhood with women worldwide. In the past when I have shared the catalog with women in other parts of the world, they have been curious about the other women we work with. I liked sharing with women that they were not alone in their struggles and that by working with Global Girlfriend, they were working collectively with other women all over the world.

I also wanted a deeper understanding of how this group had come together. I asked each woman to introduce herself and share what she was interested in contributing to the crafts cooperative. One by one, smart and articulate women rose to state their names and the organizations they represented. I came to realize that these women were only forty of over two hundred women in Club Mama. Club Mama was made up of other smaller groups of women—some taught health to their communities, some had started small fisheries, some worked on improving local agriculture, some cooked, and others did crafts—all working together as mothers to make improvements in their community and for their children's futures. In addition, all of them wanted to learn a craft and earn an income. I was most impressed by a woman named Jacqueline, who spoke from the back of the room. Jacqueline loudly described her group's activities, but she also brought with her a book of embroidery patterns and crafts she had made herself. I had thought I would see more craft samples from the other women in the room, but Jacqueline's were the only ones.

Because the women had little access to materials and no market for things other than agricultural products and fish, there appeared not to be a strong craft tradition. Catholic nuns and missionaries had taught hand embroidery throughout Haiti, but fabric and embroidery floss were dear commodities that were not plentiful in the area. With limited personal income, there was rarely extra money for making art even for private enjoyment. As a result, the women did not have a good sense of how to cost out their labor or materials, or what the market in Port-au-Prince or abroad would bear. It was also clear that they would need help in supply-chain management. While Jacqueline's embroidery was lovely, the thread and fabric were outrageously expensive for her to buy locally. The fabric was also very low-quality polyester, something that is less than desirable to women customers in the United States. I asked about embroidering on cotton, but polyester seemed to be the only fabric around. We investigated getting fabric from Port-au-Prince, but again, the price of transport to and from rural Haiti made the finished-piece price too prohibitive. The necklace stamping would be the simplest craft to transport.

The late morning buzzed by with a flurry of questions and discussions. Before a lunch of rice and beans was served, it was clear to all of us that the women were ready for a little less talk and a lot more action. Five stations, based on the number of brass hammers I had, were set up on the tables across the front of the room. Each station had all the tools needed to complete a pendant: one hammer, one steel pounding block, an alphabet set of letter stamps, a Sharpie marker, a cleaning cloth, a metal punch, jump rings, a jewelry tool, and pendants. As I explained the craft I was about to demonstrate, I paused. "I have brought these tools for you so we have a place to start," I told them. "These things are yours to keep, and I will get you more if you need them. But these are not your husbands' hammers—these are women's hammers!" This got the very first laugh of the day. "These tools are yours. Don't let anyone take them from you."

We went to work and spent the rest of the afternoon crafting. There were clear leaders among the women of Club Mama. One of the women who had excelled in the jewelry training given by volunteers a few months earlier took over jump rings, a woman dressed in an International Women's Day T-shirt showed others how to make sure the letters stamped evenly, and another was the obvious choice to head up quality control as she inspected each pendant the others made and gave them feedback. I had planned that the pendants would spell out the word *hope*. "*Espwa* is the Creole word for hope," one of our interpreters mentioned in a sort of verbal nudge. Good idea. The artisans wanted to use the word *hope* too; but they wanted it to mean something to them. We started with *espwa* pendants.

As evening drew near, the women took us out to see the school. I had seen rustic schools before, but this one was caving in on itself on one side. The school was comprised of two rooms. The first room was a six-by-ten-foot cement-block box with a blackboard at the head of the class but no windows or seats. I did not see chalk or any other resources or materials, just an empty room. The second room was slightly larger, with the only light coming through the back wall that was falling in on itself. Two strands of twine crossed in the center of the room and divided the space into quarters. Shards of worn and ripped black plastic sheeting hung down from the twine to make four classrooms. Again, there were no books, papers, pencils, maps, or resources of any kind. Two hundred kids used this school, and those were only the ones lucky enough to afford the fees. These kids needed some *espwa*. I thought about my own children's school, full of colorful art, books, resources, technology, and teachers, the kind of learning environment kids the world over deserve. I understood why the women of Club Mama would want nothing less for their own children than I wanted for mine.

The women of Cerca impressed me deeply. Not only were they committed to starting something, but I knew they would continue to build on their skills and generate new ideas if only a market would open to them. They were already experimenting with the stamps and practice pieces we brought. They were arranging strings of beads and talking through possibilities. Before we left the church to head back to the hospital in Hinche for the night, the women asked to share one last song. I recognized it instantly—"How Great Thou Art." They sang in Creole, and I sang softly in English. Moved by the song, I asked our translator to share my good-bye. "I believe we are each 'blessed to be a blessing.' You are a blessing to your children, your community, and one another. I feel very blessed to know you."

Anne Pressoir met us again as we checked into our beautiful hotel in Port-au-Prince. On our first drive through the city days before, I had not seen any nice areas, but the homes and hotels behind the large brick walls and iron gates of Pétionville were lovely. Aid to Artisans had an office in the hotel for Anne, though she preferred being out working in the field with the groups. The Aid to Artisans project in Haiti had been closed down for a while and had just reopened the month of our trip. We were the project's first visitors since the reopening and wanted desperately to make an impact for the artisans by placing orders while we were in the country. Anne took us to the three artisan shops around Port-au-Prince, one with mostly metal crafts; a second with more of an art theme, with paintings and voodoo art, which was owned and operated by an American expat named Ira; and finally to meet with Simone at Kay Artisan.

Inside Kay Artisan there was a host of beautiful Haitian crafts—from painted papier-mâché and metal crafts to sequined bottles, jewelry, embroidery, and appliqué. There were definitely more crafts being made in the Port-au-Prince area than we had found in rural Haiti, primarily due to access to resources. We learned, though, that men made most of the crafts. These crafts would be perfect for Druce and The Hunger Site, but I struggled to find a women-made craft that would work for Global Girlfriend. The appliqué and embroidery were made by women, but I noticed that most of the embroidery was done on the same polyester cloth Jacqueline had been working with in Cerca. I also noticed that every table in Simone's restaurant (a small café adjacent to the craft shop) was covered in brightly colored tablecloths made from this same 1970s flashback fabric. When I asked Simone gently about the polyester, quizzing her about access to cotton, she answered, "But that is the nicest fabric in Haiti. It's Haitian cashmere. It has the best colors and does not get wrinkles." I feared I would have trouble convincing Global Girlfriend customers to buy polyester.

When I told Anne that we did very well with soaps, she

took me to meet entrepreneur Marlène Alerte, who was working on turning her small soap-making hobby into a company
that could provide opportunities for women. Anne drove past
the entrance to Marlène's shop twice, and once we finally arrived I understood why. We entered a narrow pathway lined
with broken, dust-covered televisions and stereos and into the
basement of a dark building. I was sure Anne still had the
wrong location. The tunnel opened into a basement electronics
repair shop with no windows; only hanging exposed lightbulbs
illuminated the area above the service counter. "Marlène?"
Anne asked.

"Yes," answered one of the two women from behind the
counter as she walked out to greet us. Marlène was pristine in
a crisp white cotton dress, a wide black belt, and a slim black
cardigan. After introductions she escorted us through the TV
graveyard to a back room. The space looked like a summer day.
Marlène had taken over a very small room at the back of the
fix-it shop, painted the walls a pale but showy yellow, and
added shelves and a small display table. The room was filled
with her sweet-scented handmade soaps. Marlène had been inspired to start making soaps by her love for plants and garden-
ing, which she learned from her grandmother as a young girl.
"I want to expand this business so that I can teach and employ
more women who need help, but it is hard to find buyers." I
placed an order for fifty bars each of six varieties to start. I
would have bought more, but Marlène felt three hundred bars
would be a lot for them to handle and wanted to be realistic.

Next we were back in Pétionville at the gate of a U.S. embassy staffer home; not exactly where I would have expected to
find a small sewing cooperative working out of the basement.
Kevin Lynn McCarthy, a young blond woman in her early
twenties with a slight limp, met us at Anne's car. Kevin's mother

worked at the embassy. Kevin's parents had always been in Foreign Service, so she had spent much of her growing-up years in developing countries. She had attended college, of all places, at my husband's alma mater, Colorado State University, where she studied fine art with a specialty in weaving. Living now with her parents in Haiti, she had combined her craft with compassion, convincing her parents to let her run a women's cooperative in the downstairs of their large estate. Kevin, also deeply concerned with the environment, had created a new handbag and accessory line that was made from 100 percent recycled materials. The women cut chip and cookie wrappers into long, thin strips and then wove them together. Once the wrappers were woven, a bottom lining layer of recycled scrap fabric was added to the back and a strong protective layer of plastic fruit bundling mesh (like the red mesh bags your apples and oranges come in at the grocery store) held it all together and gave texture to the front. Brilliantly original.

As Kevin limped down the cement stairs toward the workroom, she shared with us that she was still recovering from an accident that had happened six months before. She had been walking along the jagged sidewalk in Port-au-Prince when she fell into a hole. Her leg was badly broken. After having the break set in Haiti, she soon developed an infection and had to be taken to the United States for surgery and IV antibiotic therapy. "I'm doing a lot better now," Kevin assured us.

Kevin guided us through the small production room, showing off the cutting table, sewing machines, and wrapper collection bin. Three women buzzed around the industrious hive working on an order of bags for Ira's local artisan store. Then we went to the sample table she had laid out for us. Here were her Rara bags, named after the colorful Haitian Rara bands that roam the streets during Carnival, playing handmade instruments from found materials. Her repurposing of materials, generating life-altering employment opportunities for women, was innovative and very marketable. Again, I placed an order.

On my last day in Haiti, we went to visit a cooperative of card-making ladies in the slums. Our driver took us into ever-tightening streets that eventually could accommodate only one car, if that, at a time. As we turned off the main road that led back to the airport, I noticed the DHL facility located right across the road from this particular slum. I thought that might make shipping from this group easy. Anne pointed out that the crafts-producing factory she had owned once stood on the corner. When Anne would not give in to extortion threats from a local gang, they burned the factory and her livelihood to the ground. She never rebuilt the factory, but she resiliently reconstructed her daily life in Haiti.

The card girls' cooperative was named Cherche La Vie. When our car could not wiggle us any closer to our destination, Sylvana Paul, one of the card makers, came to lead us through the twisting buildings to the group's rented room. Grain sacks, used bits of everything, and charcoal seemed to be the main commodities available from the slum market vendors we passed. I took photos of at least five charcoal stands and a darling boy and his father leaving one after buying just a small coffee can full to take home. Despite my feelings about human destruction through deforestation, I felt an even stronger pull toward these two human beings who needed this necessary evil to get by. People in poverty are especially limited as to the resources easily available to them. There is great opportunity to bring simple solar and biofuel technologies to Haiti's poor to improve their lives and their environment.

Sylvana lead us up a slim alley, where we stepped around

some boys playing with rocks and a couple of girls doing their wash in a shallow bucket. A man reeking of liquor begged for money, touching my arm and standing shoulder to shoulder with me. Anne shooed him away just as we turned into the card ladies' stall. It was sparsely furnished, with plastic school chairs and a plywood table. Women holding tiny squares of embroidery gathered in the small room to show us their work. Sylvana emptied a bag of worn rubber stamps and an ink pad onto the table to show me the wide variety of designs they could embroider, while someone's gamecock crowed just outside our door. The women took each small, embroidered piece of fabric (the ever-present polyester) and mounted it into a tiny frame on the front of a blank greeting card. I wasn't sure how much I liked the cards, but I was impressed with the women and what they had developed as a grassroots group of girlfriends in a slum. I usually tried to make decisions based on product marketability. In this case I wasn't sure if the cards were our best investment, but I wanted to invest in Sylvana and her friends. I felt it was okay to make an exception and lead with my heart; I went ahead and bought the cards, polyester and all. Luckily, in the end, the cards sold better than I had anticipated. All of the products and groups I found in Haiti would need some work to find consistent success in the marketplace, but these women were worth the patient investment of time and capital.

With some groups in Haiti we were starting from scratch, building women's employment from the ground up. In the months after the earthquake, many aspects of Haitian life and economic development had to be started again from scratch. But building anything from the ground up gives those doing the building the creative liberty to make the very thing they dreamed of. We can't be afraid to invest in and take risks on people. Now is the time to invest in building the Haiti of Haitians' dreams—one with enough food, clean water, industry, employment, infrastructure, education, clean energy, and connection to the rest of the world to help the country thrive for years to come.

# 11

# AFRICA AT LAST

༄

I've learned from experience that the
greater part of our happiness or misery depends on
our dispositions and not on our circumstances.
—MARTHA WASHINGTON

In April 2009 Tim traveled to Uganda to meet with the women of One Mango Tree and their founder, a twenty-nine-year-old American named Halle Butvin. Tim had met Halle at the Los Angeles Gift Show. The gift show, once a top destination for buyers from boutiques and big-box retailers nationwide, was suffering a severe decline in the midst of the worst worldwide economic downturn since the 1970s. Halle had chosen LA Gift as her first wholesale trade show, hoping to entice buyers with her radiantly colored African wax-cloth handbag line made by women in northern Uganda. With few buyers inquiring about her products, Halle sat in the back corner of her booth updating the Web site for her newborn company, One Mango Tree, and planning her trip back to Uganda. When Tim inquired about her products, telling her about GreaterGood and Global Girlfriend, they became instant friends. Halle was working with a group of talented seamstresses who were sewing her bag designs from a market stall in Gulu. Tim wanted to meet the women artisans, and less than four months after meeting Halle in LA, he went to Uganda to see the project for himself.

In Gulu, the seamstresses' skills, products, and warm welcoming personalities impressed Tim. The women had survived a long and arduous civil war and were now moving on with their lives in a new time of peace for their country. He was impressed by how much they were producing from a small ten-by-ten-foot market stall, but worried that the group's capacity to grow might be capped in the limited space with only three sewing machines. Tim thought Halle had stumbled onto a treasure trove of talent. But with only a small market in the United States for the women's products, Halle did not have the capital to maximize the women's production and earning potential. While the quality of the products was high, due to her presence in Gulu, she did not have a broad customer base to sell them to, tapping primarily expats and aid workers in Uganda and friends and family back in the States. Tim proposed that Halle work with Global Girlfriend to help expose the seamstresses to a wider market.

I had been trying to find women to sew an organic cotton apparel line in Africa for Global Girlfriend. African producers and U.S. importers were benefiting from the African Growth and Opportunity Act (AGOA) trade agreement, which helped importers bring in some African goods duty-free, in turn increasing orders to African companies. One of the qualifying AGOA items was organic cotton apparel. Women's clothing had become Global Girlfriend's best-selling category of merchandise, followed by bags, jewelry, body care, and small gifts, in that order. Our apparel was coming from great groups of women in India and Nepal, but I was determined to find a third source of organic, women-made, fair-trade apparel to increase our overall investment in African products and in the lives of African women. I knew that Uganda was a major source of Africa's organic cotton. It was a relatively easy crop to grow in northern Uganda. There were few pests or diseases in the region that could not be controlled easily by natural methods locally available, and the farmers in the area were already well acquainted with these natural farming methods. And for the famers, there appeared to be no yield differences between cotton made with chemical herbicides and pesticides and organically produced cotton. Because buyers would pay slightly more for organic cotton, there was an incentive for Ugandan famers to choose organic growing methods over conventional cotton farming.

I knew that U2 front man/philanthropist, Bono, and his wife, Ali Hewson, were using both Ugandan organic cotton and fair-trade Ugandan labor to produce their Edun clothing brand, which they founded in 2005 to promote trade with Africa as a way of solving poverty. There had to be potential for Global Girlfriend to work with women in Uganda to make our own fair-trade, organic line. Before Tim's trip I had connected him with various people in various places to scout for me as possible partners for sourcing the organic fabric and sewing the garments. He thought my connection to the Phenix organic fabric mill in Kampala would pair perfectly with the skills of the seamstresses at One Mango Tree in Gulu, if we could only provide the Gulu seamstresses with more space for production. Tim and I bounced several e-mails back and forth, then agreed to take on developing One Mango Tree's apparel production—despite the fact that they had no building and had never sewn with jersey cotton or exported large amounts of any product. Just as in Haiti, where we tried something we had never done before by bringing the women a craft to make, in Uganda we were actually investing in developing a production facility. This was a whole new approach for us, making a deeper commitment to one group. Tim told Halle we would help rent the women a production facility to sew from in Gulu and provide them with more sewing machines for their seventeen seamstresses and that he would send me to Uganda to get the apparel production under way. Halle loved the idea, and I was soon planning my trip to meet the resilient seamstresses behind the One Mango Tree products.

After two days of travel, Brad and I could see the spiderweb of red dirt roads winding between the small huts and farms in the miniature model of African life below our plane. The city's name, Entebbe, spelled out in white stones on the hillside directly adjacent to the runway, announced that we had finally arrived. To my surprise, the world below looked more green and lush than I had imagined. Over the preceding weeks, I had talked with my friend Susan in Nairobi, Kenya, about the devastating drought her artisans were suffering through. With Uganda being just one country away, I expected to find the same drought conditions here. Instead, the area was fertile and alive with tropical greenery, and for me, alive with possibility of amazing new women to meet and products to make.

Before coming to Africa, I knew what most people know about Uganda: it is a small landlocked country sandwiched between some of the most violent conflicts on the continent, with Sudan bordering to the north and the Democratic Republic of Congo to the south. Uganda is famous (or infamous) for its oppressive dictator of the late 1970s, Idi Amin (profiled in the 2006 film *The Last King of Scotland*, starring Forest Whitaker and James McAvoy). Uganda is also famous for its more recent madman and leader of the Lord's Resistance Army (LRA), Joseph Kony, who brought an insurgency and a reign of terror to the northern region—stealing children to use as soldiers, porters, and sex slaves while forcing close to a million Ugandans from their homes. Kony formed the LRA in 1985 in rebellion against the Ugandan government. Believing, and convincing others, that God spoke to him directly, Kony set out to create a new Uganda based on his warped interpretation of the Ten Commandments combined with local Acholi (one of the most prevalent tribes of people in Uganda) traditions. In the process, Kony's LRA wreaked havoc on their neighbors, perpetrating countless human rights violations, all in the name of God. The LRA war is one of Africa's longest-running conflicts.

Uganda is home to all the best in African wildlife—including the big five safari animals (lions, rhinos, leopards, elephants, and buffalo) in the north, hundred-pound Nile perch in the rivers, and jungles of mountain gorillas in the south—yet civil strife had ensured that the tourism industry was kept in its infancy at best, and in most places it seemed nonexistent. Although our flight from London was full, most travelers were on their way to Gulu as post-conflict aid workers, not vacationers.

The majority of the volunteers coming to work with people still living in the internally displaced person (IDP) camps were young. They helped build schools, provided job skills training, worked in orphanages, and dug wells. When I was younger, I had longed to go to Africa. As I stepped down the roll-up staircase that met our plane, I was overcome with emotion and most of all excitement to finally stand on the continent for myself. When the Peace Corps had not worked out for me at twenty-two, I had not been worldly or savvy enough to think of another way to get to Africa. I did not know how to access the vast array of NGOs giving aid or doing development work all across the continent. I never thought maybe I should just sign up on a trip and go myself. But my host, Halle Butvin, had done just that.

Halle, an impressive student, had struggled with what to be when she grew up. At the University of Ohio she majored in Spanish literature as an undergrad and then in urban planning in graduate school. She was recruited and interviewed to work for the Central Intelligence Agency, but after going through an extensive vetting process, she could not see herself in the CIA and withdrew her candidacy. In searching for work in D.C. she found an ad in the classified section of the paper for an executive assistant at a nonprofit education agency and got the job. It didn't take long for her colleagues to realize she was a bit overqualified for her position, and she was quickly promoted to the contracts department, where she settled into becoming a paperwork expert in the NGO world. At her desk job, learning about the education needs of children around the world, Halle began to long for Africa. The agency she was with was doing a lot of work on the African continent. As she read about and documented projects for them, she found herself wanting to be on the ground in Africa, not just filing someone else's reports.

Unsatisfied with paper pushing, Halle started looking into working in international development. Similar to my Peace Corps experience, she found that no one wanted her without development experience, and she knew she'd never get experience without first getting a development job. So she settled for a volunteer vacation and went on a trip to Uganda organized by Global Youth Partnership for Africa. Halle spent three weeks in Gulu and in Uganda's capital of Kampala with the goal of learning more about the conflict in northern Uganda. Passionate about her experience, she was invited by Global Youth Partnership for Africa to lead a group back to Uganda. On a subsequent trip in July 2007, Halle had the good fortune to meet Auma Lucy (Lucy for short) in the Gulu marketplace.

Lucy, a highly talented seamstress with a successful market-stall sewing business, was a smart and enterprising Ugandan businesswoman. She had to be. Lucy's life, like that of most people in Gulu, had been forever changed by the LRA war. In addition, Lucy's husband had left her and their two children early on in their marriage. Then one of her brothers was killed in the war and a second brother died of AIDS shortly after. Lucy took on the task of raising both brothers' children, her family suddenly swelling from two kids to thirteen. And just like the sandwich generation we talk about here in the United States where people are balancing caring for their children with caring for their aging parents, Lucy also had to take on the care of her father, who had polio, and her mother, who suffered a debilitating stroke. The weight of her family's world rested on Lucy's shoulders, and she was only forty years old. When Halle met Lucy in the market and asked her to sew some bags, Lucy appreciated having Halle as a new customer. But when Halle came back with more and more orders for bags, and then ordered a few boxes of bags to send back home to the States, Lucy recognized that Halle was the start of a golden opportunity to broaden her market beyond Gulu.

I had come to Uganda to help Lucy, Halle, and the rest of the Gulu seamstresses expand what Halle had started into a larger and truly sustainable business. Global Girlfriend was now doing well over $1 million in sales of women-made, fair-trade goods annually, and Lucy's bags would be a unique and desirable addition to our line. We had already helped Halle rent a large gated home on the outskirts of Gulu that the women could use as a sewing center. We had provided sewing machines for all of the women, and would soon be introducing organic cotton apparel to their offerings. But first we had to make the six-hour journey from Entebbe to Gulu. Entebbe sits on the shore of Lake Victoria, Africa's largest lake, spreading out across over twenty-six thousand square miles and touching Uganda, Kenya, and Tanzania. The White Nile River flows out from this massive lake, churning north toward Sudan and leading a path to Gulu.

Brad had never gone with me on a trip to visit the women I work to support. He didn't long to travel the way I did, and was supportive of me and content to be our family's anchor while I was away. The one trip he had promised to join me on, if I ever went, was to Africa.

Brad and I paid $50 each to enter the country, and we laughed as we checked our visa stamps to be sure we were in Uganda. Barclays Bank was obviously pushing to be the leader in Ugandan banking; the entire airport was covered with signs and banners that read Barclays. If you didn't know where you had landed, it would be easy to mistake Entebbe Airport for the country of Barclays. Halle was easy to find waiting for us just outside of customs. It was not that Halle was the only Caucasian person waiting at arrivals (there were others). She was easy to spot because I had seen her photo on Facebook, and she looked like my best friend, Ann. She had Ann's wildly welcoming personality as well.

Tall, thin, blond, and beautiful, Halle knew how to command an audience, and she dove right into telling me how she ended up in Uganda, and about her business, her yoga practice, and the new place in Gulu that Global Girlfriend and the Greater-Good Network had rented for her seamstresses. Her long legs led the way out of the airport to the parking lot. "I just bought a used car, but I hired my friend Medi to pick you at the airport and drive us up to Gulu so we could talk the whole way," Halle said as she looked for Medi in the crowd.

I giggled slightly at the term "pick you," which Halle apologized for, saying that in Uganda no one says they are picking you *up* for dinner or from the airport, simply that they'll pick you. I was glad to be picked.

Medi flagged us over to Halle's used white Mitsubishi Pajero, a Jeep-like car we'd see often during our time in Africa. Medi was warm and friendly as he helped us with our luggage. His English was good, and he looked as American as we did, wearing a Boston Red Sox T-shirt, jeans, and a baseball cap. His smile revealed some missing teeth. Medi and Brad jumped into the front, and Halle and I took the back so we could use our long drive time to chat and plot strategy. Brad almost hopped into the driver's seat, not used to cars with the wheel on the right-hand side of the car. The first forty-five minutes from Entebbe to the capital of Kampala were pleasant, but then we hit smoggy Kampala traffic. Buses, large aid trucks, cars, and crazy *boda-boda* motorcycle taxis competed to merge from multiple unmarked lanes of traffic into two tidy lanes. The rule of the road was simply the fastest or the biggest wins. Brad was a little shocked. He kept asking me if this was what traffic was like in Indian cities, or Guatemala City. I had complained about the driving in both places. "India's worse," I answered, unfazed by what I had now come to accept as developing-world city traffic and pollution.

Halle barely noticed the slowdown as she shared her vision for her company, One Mango Tree, and explained all the services provided for the women with whom she worked. In addition to economic empowerment through employment opportunities, Halle had promised each of the seventeen seamstresses that she would pay their children's school fees, give the women bicycles to get to our new facility just outside of town, and provide lunch each day they came to work. She wanted to work with

Global Girlfriend's Gifts That Give More program to help pay for these things. I agreed that we would like to do that but worried that she had not set herself up as a nonprofit in Uganda yet, though she had plans to do so. I was also worried about overpromising services to the women before we had built enough work and made enough sales to move her business toward sustainability. As I had learned early on with Global Girlfriend, promises to provide assistance other than jobs had to be balanced with the company's income—even (or especially) for a fair-trade company. I understood that Halle wanted to serve these women, and she wanted the best for them and their families. But I had come to realize several years ago that, as my friend Anita from Conserve India had accurately pointed out, I couldn't solve all of the women's problems. But if I could provide them with an economic and market opportunity, they could then choose to prioritize how they spent that income.

I had to admit, though, that the social worker in me loved that Halle had built more than just work for the women in her program. She had looked at helping to meet some of their most essential daily needs for food, transportation, and an education for their children. I admired Halle's ideas about what One Mango Tree should become. Her heart was in the right place, but her finances had not yet caught up to her dreams. Global Girlfriend's partnership was more crucial to the sustainability of this women's cooperative than I had first imagined. Halle's sales were sporadic, and the product demand was not enough to keep the seamstresses working full-time. One Mango Tree would need a steady stream of orders to fulfill Halle's promises to the women.

I knew orders could not grow to the women's full production potential until we solved the group's fabric-sourcing problem. The first order Global Girlfriend placed with One Mango

Tree was the largest they had gotten, but the women could not find enough fabric in the patterns I had chosen to complete the order. Sourcing enough materials to complete a large order was an issue. Reordering a well-selling bag in a winning fabric pattern once the item sold out on our Web site also seemed to be impossible. When I started working with One Mango Tree I wrongly assumed that the cloth the group was using for the bags was authentically African, made in Uganda or at least in Africa, but it was not. It was made in China. China has not only done an amazing job of filtering low-cost goods into every level of product offerings in the United States, they have also figured out how to sell into even remote areas of Africa. Chinese reproductions of handmade African wax-print cloth are all that can be found in the marketplace both in Kampala and in Gulu. While there is still some Tanzanian batik fabric ferried across Lake Victoria into Uganda, it is sparse and expensive compared to the plentiful Chinese knockoff prints flooding the market. You would think that this would actually help, not hinder, the amount of bulk fabric available to Halle's seamstresses, but it does not. Chinese exporters learned that their African shoppers wanted variety in their colors and patterns and delivered just that. Traditional African women buy their fabric in four-by-four-foot squares, and so Chinese exporters ship specially cut squares in packs with several different patterns to a pack. The problem for us was that we wanted a few hundred pieces made all in the same color and pattern, and this was a real challenge with the current Chinese supply chain.

I had planned to help Halle find a reliable fabric source for the group's wax-cloth bags as well as an organic cotton jersey source for the new line of custom Global Girlfriend apparel I planned to get the women in Gulu sewing. But my second problem with Halle's first shipment to us had been the shipping cost. As with any landlocked country without good road and transportation infrastructure to a port city, we knew we would have to have the Gulu goods sent to the United States by airfreight. Airfreight is always more expensive than ocean freight, but I had been okay with that since Halle assured us that her bags fell under the AGOA and would be duty-free (duty is the customs fees charged by the U.S. government when goods are imported into the United States). We found out after her first shipment, which she sent through DHL (which is much more expensive than our preferred method of commercial air or sea freight), that the bags did *not* qualify for AGOA. Shipping and customs duties charges came to over 25 percent of the total order on the first shipment. We strive for far less. Our goal is to keep shipping below 7 percent of the cost of the order.

As we rolled along the surprisingly well-paved (at least for a developing country) highway that cut a straight path from Kampala to Gulu, I was impressed by the entrepreneurs that lined the highway every so many miles. The informal stands selling everything from water bottles to vegetables to goat on a stick were inspiring. Trade meant two things to me: first, that the country had good natural resources to grow and support agriculture, and second, that at least some local citizens had enough income to make selling on the roadside a profitable venture. My favorite sight along the drive were the gigantic mushrooms the size of my head that women held out like huge white wedding bouquets to the passing cars. I did, however, worry for the safety of the roadside salespeople. The road was slim and shared by walkers, bikers, sellers, livestock, buses, cars, *boda-bodas,* and trucks, each of which seemed to feel they owned the road. Pedestrians made sure they were not in the way of vehicles, but they always seemed to be too close for my comfort as we sped by. About halfway to Gulu we stopped for water at a trading center that mimicked the Merc or the Board of Trade in Chicago. Each trader wore a colored jacket with a large number printed on the back and front. Buyers in cars and on foot gestured to different traders for the goods they desired. Then the traders would run to the buyer with their merchandise and barter for a fair price. Clearly this was a highly evolved system, though none of us in the car could figure out how it worked. I was grateful for a fresh cool bottled water to wash away the dry aftertaste of dust and carbon monoxide we had seemingly bathed in on the highway in Kampala.

The rest of the ride was sort of like playing the Atari game Frogger, except we were the car and not the frog. In the video game of my childhood, a little green frog tried to cross a highway without being squished by cars and trucks. Here, we tried not to squish the many obstacles crossing our path. We avoided people walking, people on bikes, a goat, a calf, and even a wild turkey that wandered out in front of our car from the roadside brush. Brad, who had been very quiet in the front seat, became excited when we saw our first family of baboons just on the edge of the Nile River crossing, at the only bridge between the capitals of Juba in southern Sudan and Kampala in Uganda. He reached for his camera to photograph the beautiful falls and rolling rapids of the lush green Nile, but Halle quickly alerted him to the armed soldiers on all sides of the bridge and the signs that clearly said no photos may be taken.

About twenty miles outside of Gulu we reached Bobi, one of the largest IDP camps in the area. One Mango Tree had trained and recruited seamstresses from the Bobi and Unyama IDP camps in Gulu District. Most people living in the IDP camps were from the Acholi tribe, and the camps were comprised of traditional Acholi round mud huts clustered closely together. This simple and traditional structure had lulled many foreign aid agencies into believing that these camps for the internally displaced were not as bad as some tent camps constructed in other war-torn countries. But the fact is, a typical Acholi family usually had several huts on their land just for their family. Historically the Acholi tribe had practiced polygamy, with the family sharing one hut for cooking and each wife having her own hut that she shared with her children. While families were moving away from polygamy as more and more Acholi families converted to Christian religions like Catholicism, they still typically had large families and lived in more than one hut on their land. The IDP camps housed large Acholi families in one small hut. Driven from their lands, they could no longer farm, thereby losing their main source of income and becoming dependent on aid to survive. As in so many refugee camps, there were water and sewage problems, and, worse, sexual and interpersonal violence occurred far too frequently, leaving women and children in the camps very vulnerable to harm. Five of One Mango Tree's seamstresses from the more remote Bobi location were sharing a room in Gulu during the week to be closer to work. They rode their bicycles several miles at the beginning of the week, and then came back to the camp on the weekends. I admired them for seizing the opportunity for a job but worried about their children while they were away at work.

It was easy to recognize when we had finally reached the city of Gulu because of all the NGO signs lining the streets to town. I saw the CARE offices and the UN World Food Programme distribution center, alongside headquarters of a host of other aid agencies big and small working in northern Uganda. We twirled around the city's central roundabout, passing the "cheap shops," as they were called, where merchandise like toilet paper, candles, kerosene, plastic dishes, and other necessities could be purchased. We passed Café Larem, the town's only coffee shop. Café Larem was started by an American couple, Rita and Justin Garson, who had come to Gulu as volunteers but felt the best way to benefit the community was to start a small business. The coffee shop employed local Ugandan people and donated a portion of its proceeds to St. Jude's orphanage in Gulu to provide the children with medical care. We passed the market stalls of used Salvation Army and Goodwill clothing sent to Africa in bales just as it was sent to Haiti. Finally, just outside of town, we pulled off the road to face a brick wall with a metal gate secured by a flimsy chain and padlock: the new sewing compound. The suite of two buildings—one sprawling as if it had had several additions over the years, and the other just a simple rectangle with two bedrooms out back— shown bright in the afternoon sun in ever-so-girly shades of bright pink paint. This color was not unusual for the area, and I thought it was perfect for an all-women's sewing center. We had painted the Global Girlfriend office raspberry pink, so I felt a kinship to the women's color choice. The compound was tucked back and off the road between the ACDI/VOCA (Agricultural Cooperative Development International and Volunteers in Overseas Cooperative Assistance) food security program office on the left and a bombed-out building that used to be a mess hall for Amin's soldiers on the right.

If the outside was bright and cheery, the inside was aglow with hope. The front door off the large open veranda led to the main production room (it had probably been a living room when this was a wealthy family's home), in which twelve of the seventeen women had arranged their black treadle Singer sewing machines in a semicircle. There was no electric power needed to sew, since these machines were the old-fashioned kind that the women worked by pumping the treadle foot pedal. Most of them preferred to sew barefoot to have the most control over the speed of the machine. To the left of the door was a large cutting table where each bag would be cut from the raw cloth and then taken to a sewing machine to be hand-crafted by one of the women. Above the cutting table was a classroom-size blackboard with the directions for cutting and sewing aprons, the project of the day. The women greeted us with smiles and excitement but each stayed at her machine, showing how committed she was to her work at hand. I no-ticed one small face peeking out at me from behind her mother's skirt. It was a tiny girl around two years old with watery eyes who looked feverish. "She has malaria," a new voice said from behind me.

Hilary Dell, an extremely talented design intern from Kent University in Ohio, and Sejal Shah, an adventurous seventeen-year-old interning for three weeks in Gulu, came in from the guesthouse rooms behind the sewing production room. "I guess the malaria problem was really bad here this spring," Hilary continued, "but it has died down some, except for this poor little one."

I had exchanged several e-mails with Hilary; she had been assigned to work on designing, pattern making, and training the women to make the new line of Global Girlfriend organic cotton clothing we hoped to start. Hilary had arrived in June and would be staying in Gulu until the week before she had to fly back to start her senior year in college at the end of August. After finishing our brief tour and dropping our bags in one of the three rooms in the main guesthouse, we were introduced to Mili, the cook who made lunch every day for the seamstresses and the staff. Mili handed Halle, Brad, and me each a large bowl of rice, cabbage, and beans, and we sat down over purse and clothing samples to eat. I could feel the magic of commu-nity in this place, now in use for about three weeks. These women had been sewing in a crammed market stall, and now they had not only a production facility but a safe haven—a place to find friendship, training, a meal, an income, and a renewed sense of hope and dignity.

Visiting with the seamstresses, I found their personal stories touching and triumphant. Shipping, sourcing fabric, and providing for services seemed like small obstacles compared to the enormous potential of the women and their work. The LRA had stolen, raped, abused, and enslaved countless young women during their reign of terror in the region. Like so many young Ugandan women, Akello Pamela was subjected to extremely cruel treatment by the LRA. She once wrote that she had been "uprooted and forgotten." A bright young woman, Akello Pamela also had to interrupt her schooling when she became pregnant. Working with One Mango Tree was giving her a new opportunity to learn about sewing, business, savings, and even how to use a computer. Another seamstress, Aber Grace, was the sole supporter of her seven children. She had been forced to live in the Bobi IDP camp for five years. She was able to move from the crowded camp to Gulu after receiving the tailoring training that Lucy provided at One Mango Tree. She had started working full-time at the new facility just three weeks before my visit. Seamstress Awoto Margret lived for thirteen years at the Unyama IDP camp. The Unyama camp was crowded with over twenty thousand inhabitants competing for scarce resources. Sanitation was the biggest concern at the camp, followed by infectious disease, domestic violence, and alcoholism. Diseases such as yellow fever, diarrhea, malaria, and HIV/AIDS were everyday battles people of the camp faced. Oftentimes there was little to no medical care available. Forty-four-year-old Awoto Margret, her husband, John, and their four children had finally been able to move from the camp, and had built a modest hut in a peaceful clearing about six miles from the town of Gulu. Every day, Awoto Margret happily rode her bike those six miles to work at One Mango Tree, passing the Unyama camp each way.

After spending the bulk of the afternoon with the women and learning about their skills, their histories, and their production, we headed into town to visit the Gulu market, where I would meet the famous Lucy. All of the seamstresses at One Mango Tree had been trained to sew by Lucy. She was the linchpin in rebuilding their lives and livelihoods, and I was anxious to meet her. The marketplace was a labyrinth of small tin sheds in very tight quarters lined with red dirt pathways and puddles. The paths had been known to flood on occasion, one time with a sewage leak that made the market horribly smelly and dangerous. The market was the hub of activity in Gulu and the place you could buy everything you needed, from clothing to dishes to food. Most merchandise was packed into small cement-block stalls or even less elaborate stick and tarp structures in the outer areas. The food market was a series of open-air shelters with tin roofs and wooden tables in the center, surrounded by women on blankets on the ground and small umbrellas for shading themselves and their produce. The fresh vegetables rivaled the vegetable stands of the Rue Mouffetard in Paris; the extensive dried fish section of the market incited my gag reflex, and I could hardly make it through without lifting my shirt to cover my nose and mouth.

Lucy was just where Halle had found her two Julys earlier, sewing and chatting in her small market stall. She was not the only seamstress in town. In early efforts to aid people affected by the LRA war, NGOs had trained at least a hundred local women in sewing and tailoring. Now, my rough guess estimated, over half of the at least twenty-five non-food market stalls were occupied by seamstresses—steep competition in a very slow market with little demand. In addition to competing with one another, the seamstresses had to compete against the flood of used clothing shipped into the country that lined the streets in Gulu. Lucy, however, seemed to have plenty of work. Halle had commissioned her to make all of the bedcovers and curtains for the new complex as well as hired her to be the head trainer for the women. Halle wanted Lucy to give up her place in the market and work at the complex full-time, but Lucy was both proud and possessive of the small but thriving business she had built from her stall and wanted to keep working with Halle but also for herself. I totally understood her need for continued independence as a businesswoman in her own right.

Africa has been saddled with many obstacles to larger market success. For instance, Uganda is a landlocked country with no ports. In order to get orders to a port city like Mombasa, Kenya, shipments must cross international borders and pay exorbitant trucking fees, and even then truckers must tackle the poor infrastructure and road systems to get the goods to port. Shipments can be flown out by airfreight shipment, but the cost to put cargo on an airplane is almost ten times as high as it is to put it on a ship. These issues make goods very expensive and make it hard to compete with countries like China and India that have abundant access to raw materials, low-cost labor, and ports galore.

Halle also had her own challenges. She needed to be in Uganda in order to help the women get the cooperative off the ground, but if she was in Uganda building the group, she was not in the United States selling their products. Sales needed to happen in the States in order to create more work for the women in Gulu. That is where Global Girlfriend fit in. Still, I always worried when we became any group's main source of income. Before I merged with GreaterGood, my biggest concern was what would happen if I were hit by a car the next day. Who would pick up working with the women, especially those groups I had started or for whom I was their biggest client? As part of a larger organization, I was no longer the linchpin—the women would continue to have a market with or without me. Being an American who didn't plan to live in Uganda forever, just for a few years, Halle needed to be sure the business she'd created for the women through One Mango Tree would go on without her. She had started the export business by tapping Lucy's talents, and I hoped to see her empower her Acholi women partners so that this business could last for years to come, no matter where Halle ended up in the future.

After a restless night's sleep under a mosquito net to the sounds of distant drums and music, Brad and I met Halle, Hilary, and Sejal on the veranda and headed into Gulu City. Our first stop of the day was the coffee shop Café Larem. While the space was small, the Internet connection made it a hot spot for aid workers. Gihan De Silva, a sales rep with Phenix Organics in Kampala, drove up for the weekend to work with us on fabric sourcing and to meet the sewing group. Phenix was supplying all of the Ugandan organic cotton for Edun, Bono and Ali Hewson's clothing line. Like Global Girlfriend, Edun was a for-profit company aimed at providing dignity and opportunities through employment. Edun was another example of how business could invest in people and places hit hardest by poverty, provide jobs that increased incomes, create an outside market, and deliver a product to consumers that met the highest fashion trends while achieving broader social goals. While the brand had grown to include trade relationships with low-income producers in places outside of Africa like Peru and India, trade with Africa lay at the heart of the Edun brand. Edun's mission was based on what they call the four respects: respect for the people who make their products, respect for the community where the product is made, respect for the materials used and the effects of those materials on the environment, and respect for the consumer who wears Edun. My research on Edun had lead me to Gihan and Phenix as a source for certified organic cotton that was grown and milled in Africa, and with the help of our women's group in Gulu, it would be sewn in Africa.

We ordered up lattes, chapati (a flat bread similar to a pita or a thick tortilla) with peanut butter, and yogurt parfaits, and then dug into our pricing and plans. Pricing a brand-new product was a first for One Mango Tree. The women had been sewing bags before Halle, and she had added great designs, but the prices for One Mango Tree bags were drawn from the pricing structure of the work the seamstresses were doing before they met Halle. Apparel was new. We needed to factor in the transportation costs of the Phenix fabric up to Gulu and of the finished product back to Entebbe, materials, airfreight, export visas, the new training involved with switching materials from woven cotton to jersey knit, and most important, the labor of the women, assuring them a living wage for their work. Thirty-one-year-old Gihan, who had helped set up a full sewing production factory for the Sri Lankan company Tri-Star at the young age of twenty-six, shared with us his deep well of knowledge in how to construct a fair but cost-effective pricing structure for our new endeavor. Brad, having heard enough about women's clothing for one morning, went outside to visit with the kids playing soccer in a dirt field just outside of Café Larem. (I had to excuse myself to get a photo of his new pals edging closer and closer to him as they sat on the cement stoop by the makeshift soccer field.)

Our next stop in Gulu was the storefront of the Wawoto

Kacel Cooperative Society. Wawoto Kacel, which means "walking together" in Acholi, is a crafts cooperative created in 1997 by a group of HIV-positive women with the help of the Ugandan NGO Comboni Samaritans of Gulu and the Italian organization Good Samaritan. The shop showcased many of their products, including seed jewelry, woven place mats, and banana-fiber art greeting cards. We wanted to meet the artisans and not just see their products, so Halle asked the shopkeeper how to get to the Wawoto Kacel production compound. When the directions were too confusing, Halle flagged down a local *boda-boda* driver and had the shopkeeper give the directions to him. Halle jumped on the back of the *boda-boda* and we followed behind in her car.

What the women at Wawoto Kacel had built, with the help of their NGO partners, was impressive. In Gulu District, twenty-two years of war, and the use of rape as a cruel weapon of war, had helped fuel the HIV/AIDS infection rate in the area. The AIDS epidemic in Gulu had reached rates high above the national average for the rest of Uganda. When the founders of Wawoto Kacel were unable to continue their traditional and tiring work in the fields due to their disease, they asked for help from the Comboni Samaritans. The NGOs recognized that illness bred poverty and work brought hope, and they became the women's partners in growing the cooperative. More than ten years later, the cooperative employed over 150 people in six different production units. The three buildings had spacious rooms that all opened to a large yard with a long covered porch and a mature shade tree. When we arrived, all of the women embroidery artisans were sitting on the lawn working while they visited with one another. We took a tour of each craft section, including embroidery, tailoring, tie-dyeing, weaving, beads, and greeting cards.

Brad and I found everyone at Wawoto Kacel, and everyone in Gulu for that matter, to be delightful—friendly, smiling, and seemingly happy most of the time. It was hard to believe that they had lived through the atrocities of the LRA war. The Acholi people had a resiliency that I deeply admired. They were especially kind and welcoming, answering almost every question or greeting with "You are most welcome." On Sunday at Lucy's niece Prisca's home we felt "most welcome" as guests at her family dinner.

Prisca, like Lucy, had also been sewing for One Mango Tree since the beginning. While she was not a fast sewer, she was detail-oriented and smart. Prisca was also a real role model for the other women in the group. Most of the women were single mothers with several children and were struggling to get by. Prisca was married with just three children and was a very reliable worker. She embraced using the savings account One Mango Tree had helped her set up at the local Barclays Bank branch, and was saving for her children's education, for expanding and improving her home, and for her family's future. The other women looked up to her as a leader. She handled herself professionally at all times and tried to teach other women by example. If a new seamstress was struggling with how to make a product, Prisca would not tell her how best to sew it; instead she would sit down beside her colleague and show her until she understood and felt confident in her own ability. Prisca strove to be the best worker, the best mother, the best wife, and the best friend she could be.

Prisca and her husband, Charles, had a nice plot of land along the road that led to one of the Gulu District's largest Catholic churches. The family had started in a simple traditional round Acholi mud hut with a thatched roof, which they still used as Prisca's kitchen hut. As they earned and saved, Charles built a more modern mud home with a tin roof and a generator. This house had two rooms, both of which were painted a pretty shade of green with brown trim at the bottom to resemble a baseboard. Charles had also started a humble but nice brick home on the property. They added bricks as they earned money. Some walls were completed, but some were still in progress, and no windows, doors, or roof had been added. Cornstalks and weeds grew up from the floor of the half-done brick house. They had been working on it for a little over a year and predicted that, if all went well, they would be able to complete the brick house in another year's time.

Prisca welcomed us into the green-walled house and brought in tea and fresh chapati for us to snack on while she started the chicken and vegetables. Her three darling children—Cynthia, eight; Isaac, five; and little Goretti, three—sat on a mat by the door observing the new *mazzungu* (white people) who had come to visit. I pulled out some stickers and pipe cleaners Cali and Ellie had sent in my suitcase for any children I met in Africa. Soon we were bending flowers and animals from the strange new playthings.

When Charles came home from work, all of his children lit up to see him. They hugged their father, and Goretti settled in on his lap in his chair. He lifted her off for a minute while he wiggled the cords of his electric converter box, which was connected to a generator outside, and then turned on his small television. It struck me how similar Charles was to Brad, or other American men, settling in his chair to watch TV at the end of the workday. There were no stations available, but he had many, many videotapes. "You like music?" Charles asked us as he popped in a tape of local Ugandan music videos.

The children began singing along to the songs, most of which were in English, and soon we had a small crowd of neighborhood kids peeking in through the lace curtain that lined the door. Charles invited everyone in. I got out more stickers and pipe cleaners. When the third video on the tape came on, Charles jumped up quickly to fast-forward. "This is too sad for my children," he said.

"'War Child'?" I asked, having seen the name of the song at the bottom right of the screen as the video started to play.

"You know it? You know 'War Child'? It is so, so sad; so true, but so sad." Charles shook his head as he forwarded the tape to the next happy song. "This one is so nice, so good." As he swayed along to the upbeat song, I did not have the heart to tell him I did not actually know the song "War Child" but had known instantly by the name at the bottom of the screen that it was about the children of Gulu.

The kitchen hut was dark, with only one window and the natural color of the earth lining the walls. Inside, Prisca was holding a raw chicken directly over the coals of her floor-level cooking stove, as Sejal helped clean the rocks from the local rice before it was boiled. Halle smiled at me and asked Prisca if she would come outside for a moment.

I had been impressed with Prisca's leadership at work and Halle agreed. We both thought that Prisca could run the sewing center in Gulu when Halle was away in Kampala, where she lived the majority of the time. In analyzing the production process at One Mango Tree, I was very concerned that they did not have a quality control manager. Bags could have a little more variance than clothing could. Once we started sewing the new Global Girlfriend clothing line there, I had to be confident it would be consistent. Whole Foods was our main apparel buyer, and they expected consistency in the products they offered their customers. After I observed Prisca and heard about her leadership abilities, she was my first choice for our quality control manager. Halle was not sure if Prisca would want to stop sewing herself and do quality control and training as her full-time job, but we determined a salary we thought she would appreciate and picked this special dinner as the time to ask. Prisca responded very enthusiastically and accepted the job. Now she might be able to finish her brick house in less than a year.

I could not say that I wasn't nervous about our new joint venture with One Mango Tree. Investing directly in a group's building and equipment, and promising a certain level of annual support, was new to Global Girlfriend—and even to Tim and GreaterGood. It was jumping from a marketing role into a manufacturing role. While we always remained committed to all of the artisans we supported, product orders were determined by the sales of each artisan group's products. We never made promises as to the size of the orders. Here, we assured Halle and the seamstresses that we would purchase no less than $50,000 worth of product annually; that we would provide the new, more technical over-lock sewing machines necessary for sewing our cotton jersey fabric; and that we would do our best to get One Mango Tree products into the stores of all our best retail partners like Whole Foods. But making a deeper commitment to the women in Gulu felt like the right thing to do. For the seventeen seamstresses at One Mango Tree, their childhood had been about witnessing and surviving a brutal war. I hoped their adulthood could be about rising above and realizing their potential as women, as workers, and as precious human beings. I was appreciative of Halle for daring to partner with us and forge ahead in this commitment together. I was even more grateful to Lucy and Prisca for leading the way as career women for their Ugandan sisters.

Prisca served the chicken that she had roasted, then boiled and fried for a special flavor. Brad, who ate a lot of chicken in

Africa, claimed it was the best meal of the trip. We dined on macaroni, rice, chicken, omelet, and a green vegetable called *bock* that was similar to spinach but was not the Asian bok choy. After our meal we had to say good-bye to Prisca and Charles, and also to Gulu. As Brad and I posed for a photo with their family, I thought how similar they were to our family—a working mother and father, three kids (two girls and one boy), and a dream for a better life with more opportunities for their family. They wanted for their lives and for their children's lives what Brad and I dreamed for our lives and for our children—peace, prosperity, and the bond of a close-knit family.

# 12

# FARTHER AFIELD

The future belongs to those who believe
in the beauty of their dreams.
—ELEANOR ROOSEVELT

Leaving Uganda on a plane bound for Nairobi, Kenya, I felt we were venturing into the heart of the Africa I had imagined. When Africa comes to mind, I think most people envision the people and the wildlife of Kenya. I had loved Uganda, especially spending time with the seamstresses and at Prisca's home, but as sad as I was to leave the women of Uganda, I was excited to meet the women of Kenya.

As our taxi driver, Francis, pulled away from the Jomo Kenyatta International Airport, Brad noticed a lone giraffe amid the wide-open expanse of brush lands. "I think he's a tourist plant," Brad teased. "They probably have him on a chain and feed him." Wild or not, he was a fine ambassador, greeting guests like us on their first visit to his country. Once we hit the Nairobi city limits, the traffic started. I passed the time looking up at the huge storks nesting in the acacia trees that lined the highway. Brad and I noticed the large number of young professionals who seemed to be leaving the office for the day. We observed how much less chaotic their afternoon walk seemed because there were sidewalks or at least dirt walkways, unlike in Kampala, where everyone was walking along the roadside. Nairobi seemed more well thought out.

Drivers all around us turned off their engines as traffic came to a standstill. When Francis joined them in their gas-saving efforts, I could hardly take our snail's pace any longer. "Francis, is the traffic in Nairobi always this bad?" I asked him.

Frustrated, Francis grumbled back, "It's your Mrs. Clinton." He went on to complain that the Kenyan government had shut down whole city blocks and closed some of the main roads through town for U.S. Secretary of State Hillary Clinton's arrival in Nairobi for the eighth annual AGOA conference. African leaders and world leaders alike would be discussing how to continue trade growth in the poorest African nations.

AGOA, the African Growth and Opportunity Act, was signed into law on May 18, 2000, under former president Bill Clinton as part of the U.S. Trade and Development Act of 2000. Since its inception, the act has seen several amendments, additions, and extensions to its provisions, but the overall mission—to help sub-Saharan countries gain wider access to the U.S. markets—remains unchanged. The major goal of AGOA was to encourage substantial new investments in Africa, encouraging more trade and therefore more job creation across the continent. The biggest perk for importers wanting to trade with Africa was that AGOA made over six thousand different item classifications duty-free. This made African companies much more attractive as commercial partners for U.S. companies. Just as I had gone to Uganda specifically to help One Mango Tree produce apparel for Global Girlfriend so we all could capitalize on the trade preference system AGOA provided, I hoped to find products and artisans in Kenya who might also benefit from the AGOA trade agreement.

While experts, importers, and African companies have complained that AGOA has not lived up to its growth promises, AGOA has brought both increased trade and investment to Africa. One example of successful growth had been in Kenya's clothing exports to the United States. For example, in 2000 Kenya exported about $30 million in apparel to the States annually, but that number soared to $258 million in 2005 with the help of AGOA. According to the U.S. Department of Commerce in 2008, U.S. imports under AGOA were $66.3 billion, up 29.8 percent over the previous year. Like anywhere in the world, more jobs equaled more prosperity.

When I asked Francis his thoughts on AGOA, he responded positively, before amending his thoughts to chastise me about my country's unfair farm subsidies for large U.S. growers. He was angry at how subsidies to huge corporate farmers, largely secured by the powerful U.S. corn lobbyists, hurt global prices, keeping them artificially low. Cheap grain hurt small U.S. farmers too, but artificially low prices that only multinational agribusiness firms could produce competitively especially hurt small African farmers. He also thought using U.S. corn for African food aid was unfair. He felt the government and aid organizations should not be importing U.S. corn to use as food aid in Africa, when that corn could be grown and purchased from African famers directly. I appreciated his candor. As I would soon learn, there were few Kenyans who did not have strong opinions on matters of politics, whether local or global, and they were often eager to discuss those opinions.

When we reached the hotel, I was surprised by how nice

it was. It had come recommended by my friend Robin at Adventures Within Reach in Boulder and had not been too expensive. I assumed it would be nice, but the Fairview Hotel was breathtaking. Built in the 1920s, it was like an old-world oasis in the crowded city, constructed of stone and teak wood, with golden yellow walls, rattan dining sets, leather sofas, maps of the country's game reserves, and antique photos of the hotel in early days. Brad and I settled in at an open table in the outdoor restaurant and sipped wine in the garden by the pool as we talked about the logistics of delivering the four hundred pounds of maize flour I had planned for tomorrow's visit.

I had been working with Susan at Craft Link Kenya since early spring. She had found Global Girlfriend online and sent me photos of her group's sisal baskets. As far as accessories went, I had not carried many traditional crafts like baskets, opting usually for the shiny bauble or anything recycled. This was because our customers preferred items that resembled current fashion trends, and we had had little success with items that looked more ethnic or culturally authentic. But Susan's baskets were well made, and the group had adapted traditional shapes and styles with modern color combinations. Each was made from sisal twine, which was woven together in a tight round pattern. The sisal was strong but flexible. The baskets could be folded flat without being damaged, which made them more appealing than some other baskets for importing. While the baskets were not originally intended for handbags, the women could fashion them with handles of either woven sisal or nicely finished leather. They were experimenting with making oval-bottomed bags instead of the traditional wide-bottomed round basket used for storage or hauling. One of the bags was brightly

striped in pink, yellow, purple, white, and green with thin purple leather handles. It was not too big or too small and looked
like the perfect summer casual purse. I had taken a chance on
them, ordering three styles. I liked these styles better than any
more traditional decorative basket styles I had seen from Africa,
and more important, Susan and the women of Craft Link
Kenya were women I wanted to work with. I had taken a
chance on the salability of their bags because I felt the women
were worth the risk. They were capable and talented, and work
was scarce in their drought-ridden area. I thought their products would make great additions to our summer line. But summer was going by quickly with no delivery in sight. Just a
couple of weeks before my trip, Susan sent me an e-mail about
the women's progress:

*Dear Stacey,*

*I hope your plans for the travel to Kenya are going on well. Just a
quick update on the baskets—we are very near completion now and
should let you know when we will be ready to ship.*

*I have to really apologize for the delay in delivery but we really
are having challenges with production because of the famine in the
country. The women are having to walk far (sometimes for days) in
search of food and especially water. This has really affected their
production. They are actually calling me all the time to explain the
difficulties they are having in completing the order. We hope things
improve and really praying that we get some rains.*

*I truly hope that you will understand the circumstances we are in
causing the delay in delivery of the order.*

*Kind regards,*
*Susan*

I reassured Susan that the women's well-being was my deepest concern and that they needed to take care of themselves and their families first and foremost. We would accept the baskets whenever they were completed. Actually, I told Susan, it was better this way—I could buy lots of samples of new styles for our future orders during my visit, and the samples could be included in the shipment of the current products they were finishing. I realize that this is a much different approach than that of a regular corporation. A traditional business might have canceled the order when the vendor could not deliver on time, but we had to be able to bend our expectations to adapt to the needs of the women we were supporting. We would never cancel an order for a delay, or for any reason I can imagine. While we worked with the women on how to deliver on time, to check for quality, and to strive to produce to market trends, sometimes that all went out the window and we just had to help them navigate their circumstances at hand. The purpose of my business was helping women first, and my vehicle for helping was sales. Sometimes sales had to wait. This was one of the benefits of having products from diversified groups in a number of different countries. Sales of products made by women in Nepal could help to finance deposits on products made by women in Guatemala, and sales of products made by women in Cambodia could fill in the product offerings gap while we waited for delayed products made by Susan's group of women in Kenya. Our artisans were a global network of girlfriends whose work helped the others in times of need.

I knew nothing I could do would change the drought, but I asked if I could make a gesture of friendship and concern for their health by bringing the women lunch when I met them. A few days later Susan sent a second e-mail with more bad news.

*Hi Stacey,*

*Thanks so much for your understanding. I agree that we ship the order after your visit to include the samples you'll have collated.*

*Thanks also for your offer to buy the women lunch—they however actually prefer to have something to take home with them to share with their families. I could purchase maize meal flour for them (they use this to make porridge etc.). 1 kilogram is approximately USD $1.50. There are about 150 women so if we could buy approximately 150 kilograms of the flour each woman could have one. This will not be much, but it is a great gesture, and they will be able to share with their families.*

*It would also help if you have any leads or contacts to organizations here in Kenya that can actually fund food for the women. I know there are people out there wanting to help the situation, but sometimes getting to them is very difficult. Just for your information, there is a lady here who passed away two days after giving birth to twins because she had not eaten for days, and her babies were demanding to be breastfed. This made all of us cry. The famine situation is just so sad.*

*All in all, I look forward to your visit.*

*Thanks for everything Stacey.*

*Kind regards*
*Susan*

My heart broke for the women. Susan's organization, Craft Link Kenya, was a fair-trade company supporting over two thousand women producers in the marketing of handmade products. The group of women we had ordered from were sisal basket weavers from a semiarid region about three hours' drive from Nairobi. These hundred and fifty women weavers were members of the Akamba tribe (also known as the Kamba) who lived in a rural area commonly called the Ukambani region. Approximately 1.3 million Akamba settled in the Kitui, Machakos, Makueni, and Mwingi districts in southeastern Kenya. The increased population in the Ukambani region had strained the local water supply. The area does not have sufficient reserves of groundwater to drill for in times of drought when lakes and rivers run low or dry. This made women's daily task of fetching water a daunting one. Women and girls from Susan's group walked fifteen miles each way to collect water from the only river still producing enough flowing water to source from. It seemed the tribe should move closer to the city of Machakos, but few people were willing to leave their tribal land, even when water and other resources were scarce, for fear the land would be claimed in their absence.

In precolonial times, the Akamba were traders and hunters. Today most are farmers and craftspeople. The men are skilled at wood carving and the women at basketry, both crafts that they use to barter for other goods. While in good times, the Akamba around Machakos grow their staple crop of maize (corn), as well as beans, peas, cassava, yams, and pumpkins, a three-year drought had left their fields fallow. Poverty levels had been growing steadily, largely due to the increased frequency of prolonged droughts, low livestock production, environmental degradation, poor infrastructure, high illiteracy levels, and gender inequality. Women face particularly acute levels of poverty, as they do not have the right to own property such as land and livestock.

I asked Susan how many kilograms of maize flour she thought we could fit in her car. When she said about ten 20-kilogram bags would fit if she rented a small SUV for the day, I had our accountant, John, at GreaterGood wire her the money to buy the flour and rent the vehicle. The rental SUV would allow us to bring approximately 440 pounds of maize as a gift to the women and their families.

Susan pulled up at the Fairview with her husband, Edward, in the driver's seat. The couple had two young children, a seven-year-old son named Nick and a one-and-a-half-year-old daughter named Nicci. Both Susan and Edward were impressive. He had run a call center in Nairobi until the worldwide recession hit and the call center was closed. Susan had worked in marketing for an NGO but grew frustrated with the bureaucracy and struck out on her own to found Craft Link Kenya. She said she felt that what people needed above all else was an income, and even though giving up the NGO paycheck hurt hers, she wanted nothing more than to help the less fortunate women in her country. With Edward temporarily out of work, he was helping Susan with the business. Brad and I were both glad he was along for the day. It was fun to spend time with a young couple, similar to us in many ways but living halfway around the globe.

We stopped briefly at the small second-floor office Susan rented. The room was about eight feet wide and ten feet deep with a display table, shelves, her desk, and a computer. Most of her office was filled with sisal baskets from the women we would be visiting shortly, but she also showed me samples of items we wouldn't be seeing, like beaded jewelry and woven fabric place mats. She wanted to print me a price list she had forgotten to get from her computer, but the power was out, so we piled back into the SUV and headed out of Nairobi.

When I commented that the road out of town was not too bad, Edward said that decent roads were a recent phenomenon. "For as long as I have been driving, the roads have always been terrible, but now the Chinese are working on them and they are getting more done than the Kenyan government ever did." He continued, "The Chinese bring their prisoners over, and the prisoners build the roads." Although I appreciated the road, it seemed like a waste to me that the Kenyans were not benefiting from the jobs created by the road construction. In a country where the unemployment rate is 40 percent, and 50 percent of the population live below the country's poverty line, it didn't seem right that tax money to build the roads did not also bring Kenyan employment.

As we passed the outskirts of Nairobi National Park, we saw zebras and antelope close to the road and to businesses. Edward commented, "The animals used to be able to roam very far, but human encroachment has taken up so much of their habitat."

"What do you think is the biggest problem in Kenya?" I asked.

"Human beings," Edward replied. "Human beings are the most dangerous animals on the planet. They devour everything in their path." He paused as he turned off in the direction of Machakos, our next stop.

"Second in Kenya is corruption," he continued. "Although I guess that's human beings too."

Kenya got its independence from British colonialists on December 12, 1963, when Jomo Kenyatta of the Kenya African National Union (KANU) became Kenya's first president. The KANU was one of two opposing tribal political groups vying for power in the newly formed republic. The KANU was made up primarily of members of Kenya's largest tribes, the Kikuyu and the Luo, who together comprise about 35 percent of the Kenyan population. The Kenya African Democratic Union (KADU) was founded to defend the interests of Kenya's smaller tribes like the Kalenjin, Maasai, Samburu, and Turkana. While the names of the political parties had changed and evolved over the years, the deep tribal divisions had not.

Kenya has forty-two tribes, and tribal loyalties often produce political gridlock. Kenyans did not align themselves by conservative or liberal values, but instead by tribal affiliation. While Kenya had not had a tribal civil war like their neighboring East African countries of Rwanda, Uganda, and Sudan, just two years earlier the world witnessed the worst flare-up of Kenya's tribal feuds in recent memory when violence broke out countrywide following their widely disputed presidential election in 2007, leaving over 300 people dead and 250,000 more displaced. It also brought Kenya's tourism industry to a standstill. Tribal divisions had cost land and lives, political unrest, rioting, intertribal violence, and gridlock for much-needed economic development.

When Susan and Edward first met, neither of their parents wanted them to be together because they came from different tribes. Now that Susan and Edward had been married for ten years and had two children, their parents had softened and accepted their union. "Our kids don't really know what their tribe is, which is okay with us," Susan shared. "We want the next generation to see themselves not as individual tribes but as Kenyans." She added, "That doesn't mean people have to lose their traditions, just that they might lose the senseless infighting that comes from not liking each other simply because they are from different tribal heritages."

Edward chimed in, "Just like you've done in America with your new president. We could hardly believe it when you elected a black man."

If there was one thing about America that Kenyans loved, it was the election of President Barack Obama. He is, after all, half Kenyan. You could find beaded bracelets sporting the Kenyan and American flags together with the name Obama at almost any gift shop in Nairobi. President Obama's Kenyan father had lived near Kisumu on Lake Victoria. Anyone we met from that region reminded us that they just might be his distant cousin. Women even had President Obama's face imprinted on the backs of their long brightly colored wrapped skirts. Kenyans were, however, wondering when he was coming to Kenya as president. We tried to assure everyone we met that he was very busy in his new job, but cared about Kenya and the rest of the world. (I only hoped he wouldn't mind me speaking on his behalf.)

Not quite two hours outside of Nairobi we reached the town of Machakos. Machakos is a metropolitan hub for the surrounding rural villages. A small city of roughly 140,000 citizens, it is a good place for local trade, with its large open-air produce market and used clothing market. We pulled into a parking spot that lined a row of storefronts including a restaurant, a butcher shop, and what looked like an old-fashioned dime store. Soon a woman dressed in full traditional regalia made from brightly printed African cloth approached us and was welcomed warmly by both Susan and Edward. Her name was Jacinta.

Jacinta joined us in the car, and we headed out of Machackos toward the basket weavers' village. From our earlier conversation, I knew Susan and Jacinta were from the same tribe, so it surprised me that Jacinta was dressed so traditionally, while Susan was dressed like a U.S. businesswoman in a two-piece brown suit. I stared at Jacinta. "Jacinta, you look just like a beautiful American actress named Jennifer Hudson," I explained. "Did you ever see the movie *Dreamgirls*?" She had not, but it didn't seem a stretch to ask. On our trip, we had discussed with Edward and Susan several American movies and documentaries they had seen. At one point, Edward had asked, "What about the Amish?"

"What about them?" Brad replied, sort of shocked. "How do you know about the Amish?"

"We saw a documentary," Susan answered.

Brad and I had watched several documentaries on Africa. On wildlife, culture, wars, and history. It was funny to think of Susan and Edward at home watching documentaries on American culture—like the Amish. We really were a lot alike.

About fifteen miles outside of Machakos we turned off the paved road onto a red dirt road, pitted and unmaintained. Our car bottomed out driving over potholes from the weight of the maize flour in our trunk. "That is not us girls dragging down your back end," I joked as our rental car clunked hard on stones in the road.

The fields on both sides were completely barren, with only some scrubby brown bushes to line the roadside. Little goats running wild in the fields picked at the bushes, willing to eat anything. A few chickens also pecked around the dried-up shrubs, and we passed an occasional emaciated cow chewing up mouthfuls of dust. "The cows will all die eating the dirt," Edward told us. "With no grass, they get the dirt in their empty stomachs and then get colic and die." It seemed not much life had a chance in this brown empty expanse.

After a long stretch of nothing we came upon a school yard full of kids. We had hardly seen a person along the road, yet here was a whole schoolful of children in bright green and yellow uniforms playing soccer with what appeared to be a dried ball of mud and sticks. Brad said for the second time in our African travels how he wished he had brought a bag full of deflated soccer balls and a pump with him. "There would be nothing more fun than throwing those kids out a real ball."

Susan explained that in Kenya, public education is free, so everyone sends their children as long as they can afford the uniform. Most people figure out how to afford it, since the schools also serve a free lunch, and many times it is the only meal some kids get for the day. Although free education was a great step toward universal education in Kenya, the school system still has tremendous problems. When new students flooded into the open system, classes suddenly swelled from twenty-five students to eighty. The Kenyan government didn't fund any additional teachers to staff the now fuller schools. The students need more resources, especially teachers, to really make the education system work.

As we moved on down the road I noticed that there was a saying painted on the side of the school: "The sky is the limit." I wondered how long each of those students would attend school and what they might grow up to be if they had just one more teacher to nurture them or a few more books to read. Today the sky hung low above us. The clouds were gray and looming like they were threatening rain, but the rain never came. There seemed to be nothing but limitless sky in the distance ahead.

As we rounded a curve, we saw a few buildings and one lady with a very sparsely stocked vegetable stand. In the back of one of the small huts we saw a gathering of women sitting in a circle. I started to get excited, thinking these had to be our ladies. "Is that them?" I asked.

"No," Susan answered. "That must be some sort of church meeting."

Sure enough, as we came a bit closer we saw a pastor standing up front reading to the women from an open Bible. I started to feel a little nauseous from the mixture of heat and motion as we knocked along what seemed like a road to nowhere. Around another curve on our right-hand side we saw what looked like a huge black depression in the earth lined by a rock desert. "I call this the moon," Edward joked. But it was really no laughing matter. This used to be a small lake where the local villagers would come for water for their families and to irrigate their crops. But according to Edward, it had not had water in at least two years.

Just beyond the moon I saw a huge leafless tree in the distance. Bursts of color, like tiny fireworks exploding, bounced beneath the tree until suddenly the tight bundle stretched out into a mixed-up rainbow of women dancing exuberantly toward our car. Despite their initial distance, they moved so quickly straight at us that Edward stopped the car and said, "Go ahead and get out and I'll bring the car up." He started laughing. "Hope you're ready to dance!"

Rhythmic sounds of percussion, referee whistles, stomping feet, clapping hands, and women's voices filled the void left by the dry landscape. Only two steps from the car door I was encircled by women gyrating their hips and shoulders toward me, jumping and clapping, all while shaking my hand and pulling me deeper into the nucleus of their dancing cell. A former pom-pom girl and a fairly good sport, I joined right in, mimicking their moves and laughing when I messed up, which ignited even more energy from the group, raising the pitch of the whistles and the clank of the ankle shakers. The colorful women of the Akamba tribe danced me far down the road, around a collection of three or four mud shacks, until we reached the makeshift canopy that would serve as the stage of our natural amphitheater.

It was hard to tell in all the commotion just how many women had come out for our meeting, but it seemed somewhere around 150 if not more. Jacinta introduced me to the group's leader, Mary-Regina, who directed me to my seat among the plastic lawn chairs under the shade structure constructed of soiled tent canvas and tree limbs. Then the dance show really got started. Our freestyle street dance was only a warm-up for the women, who had been rehearsing daily, from what Jacinta told me, to put on this show. They lined up in three long lines, and three leaders faced them to lead the dance. The first whistle blew, "Toot, toot . . . toot, toot . . . toot, toot, toot, toot," and then everyone joined in a unison dance that was absolutely magical. In early times there was a strong belief among the Akamba people that evil spirits attacked only women, and that the spirits could be driven away with intense drumming and dancing. Dancing among Akamba women had evolved from a tool to drive away evil into a jubilant activity the women practiced and performed regularly. During their spectacular performance, the women showed agility and perfect unison as the three long lines of dancers jumped in sync. They shimmied their shoulders to the beat of their whistles and the gravel-filled tins strapped to their ankles. The dancers leaned forward, pumping their arms as they hopped in a pattern backward, then stood upright to stride forward together, arms in the air. I was mesmerized by their creativity and ability, and most of all by the joy that seemed to overflow from their bodies as they moved together in time. I worried that they were exerting so much physical energy for me when I knew food was so scarce that many of them were not even getting one full daily meal, but the dance seemed to feed their souls.

As the performance continued, women slowly filled up the empty space between our seats and the dancers by placing the sisal baskets they had woven at my feet. Two, then ten, then twenty baskets appeared, until there were at least as many baskets as women, each basket as colorful and unique as its creator. When the dancing ended, Susan, Jacinta, and Mary-Regina joined me at the front of the group and the women moved in close, sitting on the ground in front of us. In her sweet and gentle voice, Jacinta introduced us in Swahili and thanked the women for their wonderful dance and the bounty of their crafts in front of us. Next Mary-Regina spoke as the leader of the group, welcoming us. While I did not know exactly what she was saying, her welcome was warmly felt through her facial expressions. Jacinta tried to translate for me all that the women had to say, but they were speaking very quickly, and she was trying not to talk over them. Finally, Susan stood and told the group about Global Girlfriend. I heard the word for woman, *mamas*, used over and over, and the women nodded, smiled, and sighed as she shared my mission and desire to embrace them into our group of global women artisans.

I spoke briefly, with Jacinta as my translator, thanking them for blessing me with the gift of their dance and their friendship. Then I asked them to share any questions or concerns they had. Immediately the discussion started. The women wanted me to know that their lives over the last few years had been very, very hard. The rains had not come to their fields for three straight years. Every year, they spent their money to buy seeds, spent their energy tilling and planting, but for three years there had been no crop. Now they did not even have the money to buy seeds in hopes the rain would come the next season. They were desperate, and all that was left was the sisal that grew freely no matter how dry the land.

Sisal looks like an oversized version of the little aloe plant my mom used to keep in her bay window. I remember her snapping off an end of the aloe when my brother or I got a burn on our finger or a sunburn on our nose. The aloe juice was her magic natural salve. Now the aloe's larger, look-alike cousin seemed to be coming to the aid of the Akamba women. In the Ukambani region of Kenya, women earn their living mostly by weaving baskets, using sisal as a raw material. Sisal is a natural fiber (its scientific name is *Agave sisalana*) that grows wild in the region. The sisal leaves, which regrow quickly, are plucked and crushed to render the sisal fiber, which is then turned to twine using traditional skills.

Mary-Regina brought a long pointy leaf of sisal to the front, along with a dark iron machete. She demonstrated how the plant was sliced and then peeled into fibers, which another woman took in hand and wound quickly on her bare knee, spinning the strands into sisal fiber yarn. I reached out to touch the excess fibers in Mary-Regina's hand and the whole crowd gasped. Jacinta touched my hand and said, "The wet sisal will make your skin itch badly if you are not used to it. They can touch it because they have gotten used to it."

Next, three women came to the front to demonstrate different steps of the basket making, from starting a basket to weaving in colors and forming intricate patterns. One of the women was forty-eight-year-old Mercy. Mercy was married with four children, three girls and one boy. Mercy had been weaving baskets ever since she was a young girl, using the traditional weaving skills taught to her by her mother. Mercy only went to school through the sixth grade, then she had to drop out because her parents could not afford to pay for her to attend. With her lack of formal education, Mercy learned to rely heavily on her skill as a weaver. She wove very quickly, and was able to produce one basket in an eight-hour workday. But on a normal day, Mercy combines her basket weaving with other household chores that include cooking, taking care of her goats, and making a two-hour trip to fetch water from the river. She receives payments for each completed basket, so while she would like to make more, her time is divided. But the income derived from the sale of her baskets is crucial to her family for buying food and clothes, and also for paying for her children's education.

Then came the hardest part of the day: selecting the samples. The women moved back a bit and began working on baskets they were starting or had in progress. They acted uninterested but kept an eye on the front to see if I chose one of their creations. Susan had explained that no matter which samples I chose today, I would be placing a large order they all could work on, which they understood, having just completed my first 150 basket bags the week before. At the same time, they needed the money, and it was very rare that a buyer came to them with cash in hand. After hesitating and exchanging worried glances with Brad and Susan, I decided that since it was impossible to buy every basket that day, I would just pick the ones I thought would be good options to order in the future. We had brought only about 7,000 Kenyan shillings, close to $100, with us that day, so when I had filled up the small table by my seat, I stopped. Mary-Regina and three other women brought out the ledger book to record the prices of the items I'd picked and the name of their makers. Each woman had hung a small cardboard tag on the top of the basket with her name. All told, we had spent about half of our money on hand, so I let Brad pick his favorites until we had doubled our haul.

Edward pulled the car up to present the maize meal, and I remembered that I had pipe cleaners with me that I had brought for the women's children. With only three children in the crowd, I went to each one and bent them a flower. The women's eyes lit up. One motioned that she'd like to try for herself; then another, and another. I went back to the car for my last five packages, and Brad and I hurried around, trying to make sure that every woman who wanted a fuzzy bright wire got one of her own. I plopped on the ground in the middle of them, which drew a giggle, and we bent our own twelve-inch sculptures like kids in kindergarten art class. Each woman took her turn hovering over me to show off her masterpiece.

Brad, Edward, and one of the male village leaders unloaded eight large bags of maize meal, which were stacked like a bunker in front of the group. The man presented Brad with a large wooden crocodile he had carved himself. I passed out the hundred toothbrushes my kids' dentist, Dr. James Urbaniak, had donated, and after a couple of quick photos it was time to leave. The whistles blew to start our procession back to the car. This time even Brad stepped to the beat as we all moved toward good-bye. At the car, the music flared louder than before and I was passed around, dancing feverishly with each woman. It was like Simon Says, with each lady directing the move and me following her lead. We thrust and jumped and shook in a sweaty and sometimes sexy swirl until I finally found my hand on the door handle. After about three attempts to get in the car and say good-bye, the fourth attempt was successful. The women danced on as our car sped away, kicking up a cloud of red dust behind us. Along with the whistles, the words of one of the women during our discussion rang on in my head: "Please don't forget us."

Impossible.

I woke up staring at the white ceiling of the Fairview longing to be sitting back in the red dust of the Akamba tribal lands. I felt a deep ache inside to do more than breeze in for a day of dancing and basket buying. Oftentimes my visits to the women we support felt too much like drive-bys. I was essentially a tourist taking a snapshot of the women's lives. The social worker in me, and the friend, longed to spend more time. To sleep and eat and live with the women, to really experience their lives on a regular day, not on a holiday my visit created. Everyone dropping their daily tasks to be with me was flattering, but in the wake of one woman's death from starvation, I knew that life was not as pretty as the women's colorful skirts and their jubilant dancing. Life in rural Kenya was a daily challenge to meet their basic needs. Their problems were huge and life-threatening. My basket order wouldn't change that. My visit wouldn't change their reality. I struggled with the depression that comes with not being able to do enough.

I confessed these insecurities to Brad, and he tried to reassure me. "Just trying is enough. It's far better than the alternative of doing nothing." He reminded me, "Yesterday's flour will be this week's meals for their whole community, and it wouldn't have arrived, maybe just in time for someone, if you hadn't come. The basket order deposit may help feed them the week after, and into next month. So now sell some baskets, and order again, and again, and that will help the month after that and next year and the year after."

His support reminded me that I couldn't fix everything, but I could do small things that could have a big impact on individual women's lives. Global Girlfriend customers could do these same small things. Buy one basket, one Gifts That Give More item. One woman's life will undoubtedly be impacted. And the sum of Global Girlfriend customers' purchases could impact thousands of women's lives—small acts equal big impacts. The fog of my doubts cleared and I was reenergized to visit the groups we would be meeting in the Nairobi slums.

We were soon back in Susan's car, circling the roundabouts of Nairobi on our way to visit a women's sewing cooperative. I had asked Susan if she knew of any sewing groups we could work with, as we were always in need of a new style of wrap skirt or tote. She had arranged for us to meet with a group she knew well and whose work she was very fond of—Maridadi Fabrics. *Maridadi* means "beautiful" in Swahili. Their location was not as beautiful, in an industrial part of town near an auto body shop and across from a used plastic water jug vendor. Inside, Donna, the production coordinator, and Irene, the project's director, greeted us. The shelves of Irene's office were filled with bolts of spectacular hand-printed cotton fabric in a wide variety of colors and designs. I had only expected seamstresses and had no idea the group was screen printing their own material to sew from.

Donna took us on a tour of their large facility. I was flabbergasted at the volume of screens they had for printing. A library of over two hundred designs lined two walls around their printing tables. Most were dusty and underutilized, and I wondered if the women had ever even used all of the pattern choices they had. Donna and another woman put on overcoats that looked like medical lab jackets and demonstrated the printing process. A long piece of fabric was laid flat on the print table and clipped in place, then the screen was set on top carefully and filled with ink. A spreading tool was passed across the screen, with one woman starting it on her side and then handing it to the other woman until the tool passed evenly from one side of the screen's wooden frame to the other. They slid the tool eight times, and then lifted the screen and moved it to the next section of the fabric. Once the printing was complete, the fabric was sent to a setting machine, then rinsed in a rinsing machine, and finally hung on large racks above the printing room to dry.

Upstairs, a team of three was sewing simple church vestments. There were currently only five women working at Maridadi because that was all the staff they needed for the orders they had. At one time, the Anglican Church, which had set up the project, had trained over a hundred women to print and sew. The Church had also provided the space and the equipment. What they had not provided was a market.

I was almost drooling over this unique find. I purchased ten yards of fabric samples, which I planned to have Susan ship for me, and left Donna with two wrap skirt samples I wanted her to use as patterns. I promised Donna that Susan would be in touch soon, as she would be helping me coordinate all of my Nairobi orders. Another amazing day, with more talented women simply needing a chance. This feeling, the feeling of opening a door where one was not open before, is what fuels me. I am driven by the chance to create opportunities for women, to open markets, and to encourage growth that has the potential to create change in women's lives, in their children's lives, and in their communities. The products were just an added bonus; this small but mighty group of tenacious sisters was the real prize, like a buried treasure, ripe to be unearthed. I would not have met the women of Maridadi if I had not ventured to Kenya. No number of e-mails could have explained our mission to Susan the way a few days together could. I knew our customers appreciated new products that were fresh and different. I appreciated their support and embraced the opportunity to welcome new artisan partners to the Global Girlfriend family.

Brad and I bid a final good-bye to Susan at the hotel and headed to Wilson Airport for Brad's part of the trip, a three-day safari in the Maasai Mara National Reserve. Suffice it to say that a Kenyan safari during the great wildebeest migration might be one of the most spectacular sights left on earth. And sitting steps from wild lions, elephants, giraffes, cheetahs, zebras, and hippos made us feel pretty small as we watched the circle of life unfold on the Mara. Surrounded by hundreds of thousands of wildebeests, I could not help but wonder if this was what Nebraska looked like back when the great buffalo herds roamed my home country. Of course I snuck in a morning excursion to a local Maasai tribal village to visit some women jewelry makers doing traditional Maasai beadwork. Brad laughed as the Maasai men in red-checked tribal dress, leaning on long beaded herding sticks, stood around inspecting the Global Girlfriend catalog I brought to show the women. He found it funny the way they combed over the details of each photo and compared the beading skills of their wives to those of the Nepali and Indian women whose jewelry was featured on the pages. Three men marched me over to their wives, showing off each woman's beautiful beaded creations. I picked out styles that seemed a possible fit for our collection, and one of the men wrote down an e-mail address, then handed it to his wife to give to me. It was an address at the safari camp, an example of how the camp and the Maasai tribe were sharing the best of their traditions and technology. The women serenaded us and pulled me into their semicircle, decorating me with a beautiful beaded collar.

Back at Wilson Airport, I was anxious for our driver to arrive. We had one more group, the one closest to my heart, left to visit before we headed home. Our trip had gone so smoothly, I never expected that for the final leg, our ride would not show up. The one piece of advice clearly repeated by every guidebook was to never, ever get into a cab in Nairobi that had not been prearranged by a reputable company. There was a line of available cars outside the airport, but none of them was ours. Luckily, a staff member from & Beyond—the group we had gone on safari with—was there to greet all of their safarigoers. Our friend Moses had a checklist in hand of the passengers who had just returned from Kitchwa Camp and was checking them off as they connected with their ground transportation. He saw my panic after we had been waiting almost forty minutes and our ride hadn't come.

"Let me call the office and see if one of our drivers can come," Moses said in a reassuring tone. He returned with car keys in hand. "It is your lucky day; he's already here." Brad and I probably looked a little confused as Moses loaded our bags into the back of a very upscale & Beyond SUV and jumped into the driver's seat.

"Moses, this is so nice, but I am going to meet a women's group I work with, and I don't think it's in the best area of town," I said apologetically.

He asked for the address, but I had no idea. I only had a phone number to call once we arrived back from the Mara. "Here is the number I'm supposed to call to get the directions," I said, handing a slip of paper to Moses. "The woman's name is Josephine."

Josephine Karimi of Jorova Crafts was the woman who had written to me early on when Global Girlfriend was new. Her first letter to me hung next to my desk as a constant reminder of why we do this work. When the work seems more about sales, or about spreadsheets, or about pleasing corporate partners than about the women, it is Josephine's envelope on my magnet board that refocuses my energy back to where it should be—on the women we strive to champion. She and her friends had persevered without my help, but had worked hard to keep their group and their product offerings moving forward.

When Josephine contacted me a second time, a few years after her first letter arrived in a brown paper envelope, I marveled at her group's progress and placed an order. Josephine was overjoyed to get Moses's call. When I was late, she worried I might not be coming. After a short conversation about how to find her, Moses seemed confident he could get us to Jorova. "You are right," Moses said, then laughed. "No one on our trips ever asks to go there."

We drove for what seemed like a long time, past shanty homes and garbage dumps, until we pulled into a gas station. I thought maybe Moses was lost or needed fuel, but as soon as we pulled over, a woman opened my car door, smiling widely. It was Josephine.

She and Jorova's secretary, Mary, had been waiting patiently in the gas station parking lot looking for the white car Moses had described for them over the phone. After a long embrace, Josephine turned and led the way toward the market stall where her group of women had been waiting patiently. She was dressed in a beautiful green Kenyan traditional blouse and matching print skirt. We wound our way past carpenters painting and crafting furniture along the roadside until we turned down an alleyway that led to their market stalls. The first stall was a ten-by-ten-foot space filled with a semicircle of plastic chairs and twelve smiling women. I wondered where the product was, but I did not mention it. I greeted each woman, shaking her hand and asking her name, and then Josephine explained that each woman represented a larger group of women from the slum where she lived. Josephine welcomed us warmly as their first guests.

Once we finished with names and greetings, I asked Josephine to share with me the story of how they got started, beginning with their name, Jorova. She explained that Jorova was started by three girlfriends in the slums, Josephine (her), Rosemary, and Eva—Jo Ro Va. The women loved making crafts and wanted to find a way to earn the extra money they badly needed for their families and children through a crafts business, but they did not have the money to buy the materials they needed to start. Instead, the three women and some of their friends started a cleaning business; they cleaned houses and offices around Nairobi and pooled their earnings to save toward their dream. When they had cleaned enough houses, the women were able to buy one sewing machine, and Jorova Crafts was born.

They set up a small market stall in the Dandora slums, in which they shared the sewing machine and gathered to make crafts. Josephine went out to local hotel gift shops and convinced shop owners to carry their products, though usually on consignment. Slowly products sold and more orders came in. This was about the time Josephine first wrote to me. While I did not become a customer, the women were finding local sales and sharing those local profits. A small amount of every order was reinvested in the business to help it grow, but the women often used that money instead to help one another when money was tight. If one of the women could not afford school uniforms for her children or pencils and exam books, Jorova would help her pay for what she could not. Then came the post-election violence of 2007.

As rioting swept over Dandora, panic set in. Gunshots rang out, violence erupted, and fires burned homes and buildings in a place where people could barely afford the little they had. Jorova's market stall with the women's sewing machine—a machine bought on bended knee, toilet by toilet, dusted and mopped into existence—burned as the plague of unrest swept down on the city. All that the women had saved for and built, their tools and their crafts years in the making, were gone in an instant. Even more tragic, one of the craftswomen was shot and killed running from the terror.

But Josephine and her girlfriends had created something much larger than any market stall could hold. While they thought they were busy building a business, they were really building a community; one cemented by a sisterhood of survival and faith in one another. They cleaned again. They saved again. And they succeeded again.

I was almost breathless sitting in the shadow of their courage.

Josephine crossed the walkway and swung open the heavy blue steel doors directly opposite where we had been sitting. I wiped my tears on the bottom of my T-shirt and looked up just in time to see how Jorova Crafts had taken wing. Their market stall was filled with gorgeous products. Beads and jewelry, bags and pouches, cards and candleholders. The group's range was so much wider than any photos Josephine had sent. A line of little angel ornaments, each wearing a tiny green dress, floated on a string across the back wall, and I couldn't help but notice how much they resembled Josephine in her green dress—an angel to her girlfriends who had believed in her dreams for them.

I carefully inspected each product on display, trying not to miss any hidden gems hanging from every inch of available space in their small booth. I could tell who made each product by the delight in the faces of the women when I picked up an item they had crafted. I pulled out what was left of the gifts I had brought with me to Kenya from my backpack. I passed out the last of my fuzzy pipe cleaners and a few packs of pencils I had saved for Josephine's group. They diplomatically opened the boxes of pencils and passed out two to each

woman present. It was clear that these simple, seemingly inadequate gifts were both valuable and meaningful to them. I then
purchased as many items as I still had room for in my luggage.
After some photos with the group, Brad and Moses motioned
to me that it was time for us to go. We needed to get to the
airport for our flight to London and then back home to Colorado. Mary reached into a bag under the table and presented
me with a small gift. It was a beaded bracelet one of the
women had made especially for me with the Kenyan flag next
to the American flag and my name, Stacey, spelled out on the
back—just like the Obama bracelets in all of the tourist shops.
I was very moved.

I said my good-byes to each of the women, but when I
looked for Josephine, she was nowhere to be found. Mary hurried over. "Please wait; Josephine will be right back. Please,
please wait."

As Brad started to grow a little worried, knowing we had to
make our flight back home to our own children, we all saw Josephine scurry quickly around the corner, clutching something
under her left arm.

"Thank you. I'm so sorry. Thank you for waiting," she said
as she peeled the plastic film from the burgundy notebook in
her hands. She cleared away a few items from her display to
make room for the book, then centered it squarely on the table
in front of her. I had no idea where she would have gone to get
such a nice book. It didn't look like the sort of thing being sold
by the street vendors nearby. Handing me a pen, she backed
away. "Please be the first to sign our guest book," Josephine
invited. "Your coming here gives us hope for the future. We
hope that where you have come, many more will follow."

I was both honored and moved to put my name first in

what I hoped would be a long list of honored guests. "I am so proud of what you have built all on your own," I wrote, with tears now welling back up in my eyes. "I am proud to call you my friends, and I will miss you all until I come back again."

# AFFTERSHOCKS

Life is not so much about beginnings and endings
as it is about going on and on and on.
—ANNA QUINDLEN

The problem with writing a book about life is that life goes on.
In the three months after I stopped tapping the Global Girlfriend story out on my keyboard and triumphantly turned my
pages in to my amazing editor, Nichole Argyres, my world and
the world around me changed dramatically in ways I could not
have foreseen.

One week before Christmas, on a cold Thursday evening,
my staff and I met up for our annual holiday dinner. The economy of 2009 had been challenging for retailers, yet Global
Girlfriend had fared well and even grown in the trying global
recession. We had kept our women artisan partners working
and earning. We had given women at home a way to spend
frugally but still support a cause they believed in, helping their
sisters around the world rise out of poverty. We had a lot to
toast to, and even more to plan for in the year ahead. As our
waitress at Little Holly's delivered heaping plates of Chinese

delights served family style, my cell phone began to ring. I fumbled with my purse to check the number. It was Tim.

Tim is known to call at whatever time best suits him, which is often outside regular business hours of nine to five. But I answered the phone, planning to respectfully insist he call me tomorrow and not pull me away from our year-end celebration.

"Do you have a minute?" Tim asked.

"Actually, I'm here at dinner with everyone. Mary-Mike, Alison, Sheri, and Alyssa all say hi. Are you calling to join our office party?" I joked.

"Well, say hello," Tim said. "I guess this isn't the most private time to talk, but I need an answer."

"Okay," I replied, wondering what was so pressing that he needed me at 8:30 P.M. while I was out to eat.

"Priya just called," he said, then paused. "World of Good's wholesale business is for sale, and she offered it to you and me first."

"Holy shit!" I screamed into the packed restaurant. "What? What exactly did she say?" I felt my heart race with a mix of excitement and nerves. World of Good had followed Global Girlfriend into the fair-trade arena with a very similar mission and ideas and goals. Both companies had focused on designing beautiful items that women customers would want to buy, even before the customer knew about our cause of helping women escape poverty. Both companies felt it was important to support many groups, from multiple countries. Helping women succeed was at the heart of both companies' core. World of Good had formed two years after Global Girlfriend but had been capitalized earlier through venture funding, which gave them faster market penetration. Priya Haji was an excellent saleswoman, and had taken the crusade into over fifteen hundred retail stores nationwide.

Now her crusade was up for sale, and the opportunities World of Good had created for artisans globally were at risk of disappearing if we didn't act on her offer. I took my phone to the corner of the restaurant by the bathrooms, knowing my voice was ringing out to diners who very probably neither appreciated my exuberance (and bad language) nor cared what I was raving about. "Be on the phone with Priya tomorrow morning at eight thirty before she calls Whole Foods corporate and the deal is a go," Tim directed. "And truly, happy, happy holidays. Hope this gives you something to really celebrate tonight."

Celebrate we did, as we contemplated expanding Global Girlfriend into all the places we knew World of Good to be, more Whole Foods, Wegmans stores, Target.com, and even Hallmark and Disney stores. It was a great night, dreaming of expansion and toasting to an incredible 2010 for our artisan partners.

In July 2009 we had purchased a smaller fair-trade company, Gecko Traders, which had given us the confidence that as a team we were primed for what another merger would entail. Kim Person had run Gecko Traders for ten years, importing from women and disabled artisans in Cambodia, and had been delightful to deal with. Kim was a constant advisor in the process and helped tremendously in integrating her brand into ours almost seamlessly.

World of Good would be a very different sort of acquisition. Instead of a one-person company, small and nimble like Gecko, World of Good had grown into a company with forty-three employees and very segmented duties. Global Girlfriend, on the other hand, had five employees, and while we did have support from our colleagues in Seattle, we operated fairly autonomously in Colorado. With a small team and a lot to do, we ran an all-hands-on-deck operation. My role as company president comprised duties that people might find glamorous, like buying and travel, but was also loaded with the mundane, including spreadsheets and conference calls, to the less than glamorous toilet scrubbing and Dumpster runs. We soon learned that acquiring World of Good was a case of the minnow swallowing the whale. Or as our warehouse director, Mike Aultman, so eloquently put it, "I'm not sure how you're gonna get that pig in the python!" At lease in his scenario, we were the python instead of the minnow I had made us out to be.

Weekends, sleep, feeding my family dinner I actually cooked, and carpooling duties gave way to learning all things World of Good and just trying to hang on. World of Good had based their business on a kiosk model. Each store that bought a World of Good kiosk received a fully loaded fair-trade store within a store. This was a great way to pack a powerful fair-trade punch in a small but meaningful footprint inside a larger retailer. In the beginning, each kiosk was serviced by a merchandiser (an employee of World of Good) who kept it looking fresh and cycled slow-moving inventory back to the World of Good warehouse. After a while, both the merchandisers and the trade-outs were a financial hardship on a company running on low fair-trade margins. They were heavy in inventory, which had been a fatal flaw in the World of Good business model. But even knowing the challenges, we couldn't refuse the chance to pick up where World of Good was leaving off, and widen the opportunities for our women artisans. World of Good had great customers, a great sales staff that was coming on with us, and an identical fair-trade mission. Better yet, Global Girlfriend was welcomed warmly by their customer base, and national companies like our trusty partners at Whole Foods were both supportive and patient during the transition. Once we pulled the old

signs down at stores around the country and introduced the
newly branded kiosks, Global Girlfriend suddenly appeared
in places we had never been. The cheer from artisans around
the world when we ordered up items by the thousands instead of by the hundreds was almost audible through my
e-mail in-box.

I didn't mind the five pounds I gained from eating poorly,
the bags under my eyes from sleeping minimally, or the split
ends I grew from not having my hair trimmed for three months—
the mission came first. Which is why on January 12, 2010, I
stood at my kitchen counter writing out a birthday card to my
younger brother Adam in Illinois. January 12 was Adam's actual birthday, and while I was thinking of him enough to buy
the card along with a precooked chicken for my family to eat
for dinner, the card would be late like everything else in my
personal life since the fateful Chinese dinner call.

Laughing with my kids as they signed Uncle Adam's "Ma-
cho Man" singing Hallmark card, I glanced up at breaking
news on CNN to find that a catastrophic earthquake had devastated Haiti. The breath was suddenly sucked from my chest.
My e-mail in-box started chiming almost instantaneously. Druce
was asking if I had heard from any of our friends in Haiti. I
asked her the same. We had been in Haiti together this exact
week in January a year earlier—a thought not lost on my husband and children. Alden Smith, executive director at Aid to
Artisans, rallied quickly, e-mailing everyone with connections
to the Haitian artisan community, creating an information flow
on the well-being of artisans in Haiti. I sat numb, staring at
CNN with tears rolling down my face. Not Haiti. Not in the
face of so many challenges. Not now. Then I did the only thing
I knew could help absolutely and immediately—I donated
money to the one organization that I knew had the vast presence,

resolve, and wherewithal to bring fast action into the crisis: Partners In Health. I sent a mass e-mail to my entire address book asking friends to donate too. They did. And we all waited for news.

I was never as proud to be part of our larger company, GreaterGood, than on this night. Within hours, Jennifer Fermon, GreaterGood's senior projects director, and her team had created a disaster relief Gifts That Give More donation on all of our Web sites for Partners In Health. As always, 100 percent of the donations went directly to the charity our customers chose. In less than two weeks, Global Girlfriend customers and customers throughout the GreaterGood network of stores helped raise over $250,000 to support Partners In Health's relief efforts in Haiti.

Global Girlfriend customers had always impressed me with their deep concern for the women of the world, but I had never been so inspired by our customers' generosity than in the face of the Haitian tragedy.

When the earthquake hit, I was worried most for my friend Marlène Alerte. Her small soap-making business was still located in the dark basement of the old three-story building in Port-au-Prince that we had visited. As news slowly came in about each of our artisan partners, I had no word from or about Marlène. I e-mailed several times with no response. Finally, on January 29, Marlène e-mailed, "My family and I are okay. Thank you for your concern and kind words. Haiti and all of us need your prayers." Just two weeks later, Marlène let me know that she and the women were ready to make their soap again. She wrote, "We are glad to announce we are back to work. Our soap production is available. We thank you for your help and support." Hope and tenacity prevail over the coldest of circumstances. The news of the January 12 earthquake was devastating, but we found hope every time we received an e-mail or a call informing us that some of our friends and artisans were safe.

As news reporters left and the world went on to worry about the next big story, Haiti got back to work. While the aftershocks kept coming, the women we work with simply went on with life—just as all of our tenacious women do every day, making a living, and making a life with joy and triumph over circumstance and poverty. And we got back to work helping to create a market for their creations, with new kiosks to stock.

# AFTERWORD:
# AND BEYOND

*One woman can change anything,
but many women can change everything.*
—CHRISTINE KARUMBA

In Kenya, Brad and I had treated ourselves to what was deemed by many travel companies to be the "trip of a lifetime," a tent safari in the Masaai Mara. The company we chose was called & Beyond. This trip was all we imagined and more, but so was the outfitter. They impressed me with their commitment to the wildlife, to the environment, and to their customers; but first and foremost I was moved by the company's commitment to their employees. In the aftermath of the Kenyan post-election violence, when tourism in Kenya ground to a halt for almost two months, & Beyond lost all of their clients for that time. No one came on safari at what was typically the busiest time of the year. The company did not lay off a single employee.

Commitment to one another, even in the hardest of times, is a goal we should all strive for. No effort to help a person in need is too small or inconsequential. My favorite Mother Teresa quote is, "We can do no great things, only small things with great love." I believe this is true, and it is what I strive for personally and through Global Girlfriend. Others have done more than I have—maybe you are one of them. People have traveled farther, and more often, dedicating years of their lives to countries and people living in poverty. They are my heroes. But so are the girlfriends who stood out in the rain with me peddling women-made goods at street fairs, who brought me coffee while I wrote this book, or drove my kids to endless sporting practices, or who have seen me through the joys and pains of growing my family and my business simultaneously. Girlfriends, you especially have something to give; do not ever doubt that your contributions matter. Big or small, our unique efforts on behalf of one another when pooled together can change the world.

In computer programming, there is a growing movement called "open source" software. Programmers develop software for public use and input, giving free access to their programs' tools and knowledge. Just the opposite of a traditional copyright (the coveted trademark symbol that gives exclusive rights to an invention or intelligence), "copy left" means simply "take my ideas, use them, improve on them, and share them with someone else." If you are inspired to start a social business or to get involved in the journey to help women around the world rise out of poverty, I hope something I have said in the preceding pages has inspired you to take action. Consider this book an open source. Copy whatever you want. If we are going to end extreme poverty and solve our environmental crisis, we must share and replicate the best ideas for people and the planet.

If you are moved to make a difference but do not know where to start, I suggest you first take a good inventory of your life and all that you are already doing to touch the lives of others every day. Maybe you volunteer at your child's school, at church, or in your community. Maybe you give blood, or cook for a sick neighbor, or organize a food drive at your office, or

hammer nails for Habitat for Humanity. Maybe you've dedicated your life to raising great kids, or growing an organic
garden, or becoming a foster parent, or running to raise money
for cancer research. Appreciate those things—they count. Then,
challenge yourself to stretch beyond what you think you can
do, to what I know you can offer the world. Take the leap into
doing more. I suggest five steps to start you on your own
Global Girlfriend journey.

## 1. LEARN

Today, more than at any other time in history, we have a world
of knowledge at our fingertips. The Internet was my gateway to
connecting with my girlfriends worldwide. It is a place to dig
into the problems facing women in our world and also where
to find the organizations working toward solutions. Here are
just a few jumping-off points for learning more about the issues facing women in poverty:

Acumen Fund—www.acumenfund.org

AfricAid—www.africaid.com

Aid to Artisans—www.aidtoartisans.org

The Business Council for Peace—www.bpeace.org

Camfed (Campaign for Female Education)—www.camfed.org

CARE—www.care.org

Central Asia Institute—www.ikat.org

The Emancipation Network—www.emancipationnetwork.org

FINCA—www.villagebanking.org

Friendship Bridge—www.friendshipbridge.org

The Global Fund for Women—www.globalfundforwomen.org

Grameen Bank—www.grameen-info.org

Half the Sky Movement—www.halftheskymovement.org

Kiva—www.kiva.org

Mercy Corps—www.mercycorps.org

Millennium Challenge Corporation—www.mcc.gov

Mothers Acting Up—www.mothersactingup.org

Partners In Health—www.pih.org

Peace X Peace—www.peacexpeace.org

Pro Mujer—www.promujer.org

Run For Congo Women—www.runforcongowomen.org

10,000 Women—www.10000women.org

United Nations Development Fund for Women—
www.unifem.org

The Urgent Action Fund for Women's Human Rights—
www.urgentactionfund.org

Women for Women International—www.womenforwomen.org

Women Thrive—www.womenthrive.org

Women's Foundation of Colorado—www.wfco.org

Women's Funding Network—www.womensfundingnetwork.org

World Pulse Magazine—www.worldpulse.com

You can also visit my Web page, www.staceyedgar.com, for an updated list of links.

## 2. STOP LEARNING AND JUST DO IT!

Now that you've researched and read all about helping women in poverty, or fostering literacy, or rescuing shelter animals, or whatever cause ignites your passion, stop learning and get doing. You don't need to know everything there is to know about a topic to make a difference. It's important to not get bogged down in learning the whole of a problem—you need to get out there and work. You'll gain new insights, and with fresh eyes on whatever the problem may be, you might just see an answer no one has thought of before. No matter the cause, many hands make lighter work. You don't have to solve the problem yourself; all you need to do is take part in the collective solution. Trust me, while you are busy reading, the world is waiting for what you have to offer. Jump in!

### 3. START LOCAL

Women in your town or community need your support. Whether you volunteer your time at a local women's shelter, give your old clothing to a Dress for Success–type program, teach an adult literacy class, or just head up a committee on your own PTA, your efforts will make positive waves of change right where you are.

You can also change the way you shop, choosing gifts and goods that make a difference for the people who make them. Shop fair trade whenever possible. Start by changing your clothes. At Global Girlfriend we make it possible to dress in fairly traded clothing right down to your underwear with our line of trade apparel and undergarments made by women in India, Uganda, and Nepal. Or resolve that all of the gifts you buy for one year will be fair trade. You'll be making an impact on both the person who receives your gift and the woman who made it. Switch to buying only fair-trade coffee and you'll be making a difference with your daily morning cup. Of course I suggest shopping the selection at Global Girlfriend (www.globalgirlfriend.com) or shopping locally at one of the over five hundred stores we partner with around the country, like Whole Foods. But I also suggest you shop our competition, because there are many great fair-trade items and talented artisans to be found once you start looking for them. Green America (www.greenamericatoday.org) is a great place to start.

Take care of the people around you, making the extra effort for the simple things. Don't forget to also take care of yourself; it is an important way you can change a life—your own. And teach your children well. They will be the ones we count on to change the future for the better.

## 4. GO GLOBAL

Get that passport and go. There is nothing holding you back, and so much world to see. We can learn an enormous amount about one another and about the world just by visiting and appreciating other lands and cultures. If there is somewhere you long to travel, make it happen. Get out and meet your Global Girlfriends for yourself. Maybe not tomorrow or next week, but with some planning, connecting, and saving, nothing is outside your grasp. If you have kids, take them along.

I suggest you consider a volunteer vacation. Volunteer vacations give you the chance to be both a tourist and a contributor to the community you visit. As a volunteer, you have the chance to serve others in many ways. You can help to build a school, dig a clean water well, care for orphans, teach computer classes, or provide basic health services. The possibilities to serve are as vast as your personal interests. If you think a volunteer vacation might be right for you or your family, you can find information about opportunities and organizations that arrange volunteer vacations online at Web sites including www.united-planet.org, www.gviusa.com, www.globeaware.org, and www

.globalvolunteernetwork.org. Need more ideas? Pick up a copy of Pam Grout's book *100 Best Volunteer Vacations to Enrich Your Life* for a wide array of suggested projects and destinations. Some of these vacations are even tax-deductible. You never know how helping in another country might change the course of your life back home.

## 5. BE YOU

Finally, no one but you can bring your unique gifts to the world. No matter what your talents, let them shine in ways that brighten the lives of those around you. As a social worker, I never imagined myself running a retail business of fair-trade fashion and accessories. But I came to a point where I could not imagine not trying to do something more to help women less fortunate than I am. As a mom, I was passionate about making the world a better place for other moms living and raising their children in places where poverty and war were rampant. I didn't want to ask my husband and children to move to another country so I could pursue my passion, but I was not satisfied with only giving money to organizations doing the work I thought was important either (though I do believe deeply in philanthropic giving as a change agent). I wanted to do more and make helping women in poverty part of my daily life. Starting a fair-trade business was my tool. I was not an expert on fair trade, on women's fashion, on importing, or even on women in poverty, but I was willing to jump in despite what I didn't know. I challenge you to find your own passion and take the leap. It does not matter so much what you are interested in, just that you are willing to get involved. You are what the world needs now. Together we can make a difference—with a little help from our girlfriends, of course.

# ACKNOWLEDGMENTS

An old African proverb claims "It takes a village to raise a child," and as a mom I know this to be true. But this proverb has also been true of growing Global Girlfriend and of writing this book. It has taken the support of many villages around the world to raise Global Girlfriend from a personal dream into an economic tool impacting thousands of women's lives. It is an honor for me to have the chance to thank everyone who has helped me on this journey.

First and foremost, thank you to my entire family, especially to my husband, Brad, for being my business consultant and my best friend. To my kids, Dakota, Cali Ann, and Ellie, thanks for supporting me, for loving me, and for allowing me to start and grow Global Girlfriend even when that sometimes meant I had to be half a world away. To my parents, Steve and Diane Nehring, for teaching me to believe anything is possible. Mom, thanks too for being a great travel mate! Thanks to my grandfather Clark Nehring for teaching me to be entrepreneurial (and maybe a little tough like you), and to my grandma Irene Nehring for making me feel special my entire life. Thank you to my in-laws, Governor Jim and Brenda Edgar, for welcoming me warmly into your family and for being outstanding examples of how to live a life in service to others and to God.

My love, admiration, and gratitude goes out to all of my Global Girlfriend artisan partners the world over who live boldly in the face of challenges many of us could not imagine. Your commitment to overcoming poverty for yourselves, your children, and your communities inspires me daily. My deepest appreciation to all the women artisans who have ever woven, beaded, sewn, done metalwork, knitted, crocheted, embroidered, painted, poured, molded, mixed, boxed, tagged, or made a product for Global Girlfriend. A special thanks goes out to all those who have shared the stories of their lives with me for this book, and especially to my friends Josephine Karimi, Anita and Shalabh Ahuja, the entire Khadgi family, Nawangsarie Harryadi, Halle Butvin, Gihan De Silva, Kelly Weinberger, Gertrude Protis Kita, Flora Can Queche, Jorge Salem, Susan and Edward, Prisca and Charles, and all of our cooperative partners.

My heartfelt thanks to my own local "village" of girlfriends who helped make Global Girlfriend a reality. To Courtney O'Shea for starting us off with a great logo and for the many projects that came after. To Robin George for your friendship and fantastic photography on my grassroots budget (and for that first catalog where I forced you to be both model and photographer!). To all of my go-to girlfriends who have worked countless events, stuffed boxes, mailed postcards, cared for my children, and purchased more women-made, fair-trade accessories than any woman could possibly need, including Stephanie Salter, Amy Klefeker, Dottie Mann, Laurie Wexler, Jill Anderson, Lisa Cleary, Libby Stone, Carol Carlson, Carey Bohan,

Cheryl Jameson, Debbie Ahern, Lisa Kantor, Dana Hess, Terri Lowe, Madi Fisher, Laura Martin, Logan Payne, Pam Payne, Marianne Walthier, Janet McMahon, Kim Rogers, Traci Takaki, Sue Ochu, Lauren Mirable, Amy Kahn, Lisa Graver, Ellen Cook, Masami Covey, Anna Bahr, Helen Gair, Kim Crawford, Heather Lurie, and my sisters-in-law Elizabeth Lowe and Andrea Nehring. Also, special thanks to the many moms and teachers from St. Philip PreSchool, Bradford, Mullen, St. Andrews Methodist Church, the Denver Junior League, the Women's Foundation of Colorado, and the Ken Caryl Valley. Thanks to all the women who opened their homes early on for the home parties that turned Global Girlfriend into a grassroots movement, including Candice Reed, Erica Shafroth, Jill Redlinger, Michelle Thayer, Barb Harwell, Betty Aga, Whitney Mackintosh, and many more. To our volunteer catalog models, Sabryna Liddle, Audrey Nelson, Hannah Nelson, Crystal Hinton, Brittany Ure, Prarthana Shahi, Nikki Crouse, Stephanie Schneiter, Jill Peterson, Carolyn Winterbottom, and Meridith Mansfield, who let us pay them in purses. Thanks to Kim Malueg for our first Web site. To Betsy Martin for great PR representation. To Ruthanne Neville for being a volunteer model, and the first to champion Global Girlfriend outside of Colorado. To my dearest friend from high school, Dana Inman, and my best friend from college, Ann Gobel, for thick-and-thin friendship and a lot of good laughs—that *In Style* placement was pretty nice too!

Thank you to the many stores, large and small, who carry Global Girlfriend products, with a special thanks to Whole Foods Market for helping us learn how to sell to stores in the first place. Special thanks to Allison Trembly for discovering us, and to Kathy Oglebay for taking a chance on us. And to everyone at Camfed, Women for Women International, Friendship

Bridge, Kim Person, Ming Tan, the Como Foundation, and the Armani Exchange technical fit team.

Thanks to my friend and colleague Tim Kunin, who saw something special in the work we were doing for women in poverty and invited us to be a part of the GreaterGood Network. It has been an honor to work with you and with the entire team at GreaterGood/Charity USA who are committed to changing the world. Thanks to my colleagues in Seattle, with whom I work closely, including (but not limited to) Lisa Halstead, Greg Hesterberg, Michelle Schectman, Druce Biggerstaff, Mariel Ramos, Sheila Clark, Sara Hall, Suzanne Aoki, Julia Christophersen, Laura Reynolds, Julissa Hafen, Erika Vanvick, Abby Lisk, Annie Chang, Kristen Wagner-Patterson, Phil Armstrong, Nathan Crowder, Tim Collins, Tom Gwilym, Jennifer Fermon, Catherine Warren, Timmy Ting Liu, Rian Cool, Brian Smith, Doug Moore, Scott Thorson, Jemimah Okantey, John Ghert, Nikki Burns, and the entire customer service team. A special thanks to Mike Aultman and his team at our warehouse (especially Sean, Sam, and Todd); not much happens without you! To all of the women's organizations, churches, and individuals who've hosted or partnered with us over the years; to the media who have shared the Global Girlfriend story (with a special thanks to Donna Owens and O, The Oprah Magazine); and especially to our Global Girlfriend customers. There is no way possible to list in these short pages the countless supporters who have shopped, volunteered, and spread the word about our mission, but please know that you are the ones who make the real difference—and trust me, I know who you are. I have the list.

I want to thank my friends from that little "village" called New York City for believing in my story enough to make it a book. Thanks to my literary agent, Laurie Abkemeier, a great cheerleader, advocate, business consultant, saleswoman, counselor, and friend. Thank you for believing in this book and the women it is meant to champion. To my kind and skillful editor, Nichole Argyres, for helping to shape the essence of this story to shine the brightest spotlight on the individual women we work with. Your time, attention, and thoughtful edits were crucial and appreciated. It has been an honor and a delight working with you. Special thanks to Editorial Assistant Laura Chasen, Associate Publisher Matt Baldacci, VP of Special Markets Jaime Ariza, Associate Marketing Manager Monica Katz, Senior Publicist Katy Hershberger, Special Markets National Director Alice Baker, and the entire incredible team at St. Martin's Press, who have gone the extra mile in forming and promoting *Global Girlfriends*.

Finally, to all of my staff, past and present—thanks is hardly enough. Your hearts for the women we work with are full, your commitment strong, and your tolerance for me and my controlling need for perfection at work much appreciated. To former and temporary staff members Cathy Maiocco, Jeanine Smith, Amy Bleakney, Susan Kubilus, Logan Payne, Mack Golden, Brett Hasse, Lauren Bratshun, Soemoe Aung, and Jagadha Sivan, thanks for helping build something special. To my dedicated team in the office, Sheri Hasse, Alyssa Boettcher, Keely Bannon, and Hilary Dell, as well as our tireless sales team in the field, Juli Bittner, Sharon Glasser, Rachael McKee, Tracy Hantman, Jody Todd, Laura Crawford, Elizabeth Argen, and the REWCO team, I appreciate you all beyond measure. To Alison Evans, thanks for being my left hand; I am lucky to have recruited such a talented and dedicated friend to help carry the load. And to my right hand, Mary-Michael Simpson, thanks for being a sister on this journey. From the basement, to Barcelona, to the shores of Lake Atitlán, and back to our messy desks you have been with me, and the women we do this for, every step of the way. A "sister from another mother" and a true Global Girlfriend—I'm exceptionally blessed to call you my friend.

# ABOUT THE AUTHOR

A passionate advocate for women and children, Stacey Edgar started Global Girlfriend in 2003 as a way to provide economic security for women in need by creating a sustainable market for their products. She used her ten years in social work practice with women and children as a springboard to her role as a social entrepreneur. She has traveled extensively to visit the women with whom Global Girlfriend works.

Stacey has been honored by the Microsoft Corporation as a recipient of one of the company's Start Something Amazing awards and by the *Denver Business Journal* as a "40 Under 40" Business Leader, and has been featured in *O, The Oprah Magazine*, in *Multichannel Merchant* magazine as a "Maven of Merchandise," and in *Organic Style* as one of the magazine's Women With Organic Style. She holds a master of social work degree from the University of Illinois and a bachelor of social work from Western Illinois University. Stacey is the mother of three children, Dakota, Cali Ann, and Ellie, and is married to her best friend, Brad. They make their home in the beautiful Colorado foothills.